Contributions to Management Science

The series *Contributions to Management Science* contains research publications in all fields of business and management science. These publications are primarily monographs and multiple author works containing new research results, and also feature selected conference-based publications are also considered. The focus of the series lies in presenting the development of latest theoretical and empirical research across different viewpoints.

This book series is indexed in Scopus.

Niccolò Persiani · Ilaria Elisa Vannini ·
Anna Romiti · Anastasios Karasavvoglou ·
Persefoni Polychronidou
Editors

Challenges of Healthcare Systems in the Era of COVID-19

Management Practices, Services Innovation and Reforms

Springer

Editors
Niccolò Persiani
University of Florence
Florence, Italy

Ilaria Elisa Vannini
University of Florence
Florence, Italy

Anna Romiti
University of Florence
Florence, Italy

Anastasios Karasavvoglou
Department of Accounting and Finance
International Hellenic University
Kavala, Greece

Persefoni Polychronidou
Department of Economic Sciences
International Hellenic University
Serres, Greece

ISSN 1431-1941 ISSN 2197-716X (electronic)
Contributions to Management Science
ISBN 978-3-031-43113-5 ISBN 978-3-031-43114-2 (eBook)
https://doi.org/10.1007/978-3-031-43114-2

This Springer imprint is published by the registered company Springer Nature Switzerland AG
The registered company address is: Gewerbestrasse 11, 6330 Cham, Switzerland

Paper in this product is recyclable.

Introduction

The organizations operating in the healthcare sector have experienced two dramatic years since the end of February 2020. They have been the main of every possible response to the pandemic. Never before the functioning of these organizations has been so crucial for the lives of individuals and society as a whole, consequently they have had to endure an unprecedented level of operating pressure and stakeholder expectations.

The Covid-19 public health crisis has raised questions about many of the established models of governance, management and organization, highlighting their limits and contradictions.

At the same time, however, the crisis has also been the driving force behind the development of new services and the rethinking of management models.

In this perspective we can expect a future of significant reforms and organizational and managerial change.

Strengthening health and welfare systems is consequently a shared challenge for all the European countries, but particularly for the Balkans and Eastern ones, where the pandemic has accelerated the transformation process.

It makes valuable to compare the choices made by different European countries, starting with Italy, which was the first to face the COVID-19 pandemic, in order to learn from the best experiences and practices.

The common goal of Countries is indeed a more efficient and responsive healthcare system to better address future pandemics as other ongoing issues.

For this reason, the reconfiguration of European, Balkan and Eastern European healthcare systems is being supported, in some cases, by the significant resources, made available by the EU for the post-pandemic development. It is undoubtedly an opportunity to fill the existing gaps in the infrastructures devoted to the provision of the health services and to take advantage of healthcare reforms for the development of systems and organizations.

This special issue includes papers relating to the role that Economics and Management can play in supporting healthcare reforms with particular reference to the Central and South Eastern European countries.

From this perspective, this special issue of the EBEEC Conference allows us to deepen and discuss, on the one hand, the important impact that the pandemic has had on healthcare organizations and on the other hand, the lessons that can be learned from this crisis in terms of managerial practice.

The 14th International conference "Economies of the Balkan and Eastern European Countries (Ebeec)", held in Florence in May 2022, has been organized jointly in Florence, by the Experimental and Clinical Medicine Department of the University of Florence (Italy) and the Finance and Accounting Department of the International Hellenic University, Kavala (Greece).

The conference brought together more than 130 manuscripts and by more 150 authors from 20 countries from Europe and all over the world.

A broad range of issues have been discussed at the conference and in the resulting published books.

Aim of the conference was to gather scholarship and practitioners who presented academic papers and to exchange theoretical and empirical results, on issue in economics and management on healthcare with a specific focus on the future reforms due to COVID 19 pandemics.

The papers presented draw, upon the experiences of Central and Western Europe, particularly of Italy, among the countries where the pandemic was first detected, and provides a specific focus on Central and Southeastern European.

This volume, as one of the publications resulting from the 14th International conference "Economies of the Balkan and Eastern European Countries (EBEEC)"—Florence, Italy, May 2022, aims to present original research paper in the specific field of Healthcare Economics and Management.

The entire manuscript selection process was managed by the Board of Editors in compliance with the highest standards and best practice guidelines on publishing ethics, paying special attention to issues regarding plagiarism, peer-review, objectivity, funding, privacy, and conflict of interest. All selected manuscripts have gone through a blind peer-review process. Selected papers are independent and do not constitute joint research.

The volume includes 17 selected manuscripts presented at the aforementioned Conference. The book consists of three parts. Part focuses on *Policies, Governance and Strategies*, part is dedicated to *Financing and Performance* and part is relative to *Operations.*

Part—Policies, Governance and Strategies

The first part of the volume opens with a paper written by *Anna Romiti, Mario Del Vecchio (University of Florence, Italy) Caterina Cavicchi* and *Emidia Vagnoni (University of Ferrara, Italy).* The study aims to investigate how CEOs of Italian healthcare organizations shaped the communication strategies toward internal and external stakeholders to keep fulfilling the organization mission during the Covid-19 crisis. Data have been collecting interviewing the CEOs of Italian NHS organizations.

The findings of the study are twofold. First, it allows to identify the extent to which the organizations have adopted new technologies to support their communication processes. Second, the study shows the important role of CEOs as communication hub of healthcare organizations during the crisis and in particular the type of communication strategies they adopted towards different stakeholders. More precisely CEOs often used a personalized communication with key internal stakeholder, while they mainly adopted a collective communication strategy with external stakeholders.

The manuscript by *Guglielmo Bonaccorsi (University of Florence, Italy)*focuses on the need of rethink healthcare organizations in the era of Covid-19. The COVID-19 pandemic has revealed to citizens, healthcare professionals, management and politicians the many problems faced by public health care systems. The manuscript highlights the importance of investing in public health infrastructure, engaging communities in addressing public health crises, and using clear and consistent public health messaging. In addition, healthcare organizations should bring people-focused solutions to the center of their recovery and lay the foundation for a more agile workforce.

The article co-authored by *Martina Giusti* and *Niccolò Persiani (University of Florence, Italy)* analyses the proposal documents written by the most significant associations of each of the 19 Italian health professions. These documents are intended to provide a contribution to the reorganisation of the public health service in the territory, in the community and in the patient's home to support decision makers in the emergency and post-emergency period. The aim of the article is to evaluate what are the priority interventions to be realized to strengthen and reorganize the care network provided by Italian technical, rehabilitative and preventive health professions in the territorial healthcare. The findings show the awareness, by professional associations, of the need of establishment of multi-professional teams capable of taking on all the needs of the citizen and responding adequately to them, in an integrative way, thanks to the skills of all the professionals and the availability of valid technological support.

The manuscript written by *Cansu Guller (Atatürk University)* and *Cigdem Varol (Gazi University)* aims to investigate the relative importance of different criteria for the location strategies of private healthcare facilities in order to support the policies in terms of urban planning. Data was collected from in-depth interviews with the managers of twelve private hospitals selected on the basis of their location in different districts of Ankara. The findings show that the most effective factors in the location strategies of private hospitals in Ankara concern: competition dynamics, building features and investment costs. Furthermore, site selection of private hospitals depends on the socio-economic characteristics of the districts in Ankara. The paper shows that, in disaster situations like Covid-19, new criteria such as walking distances for differentiated age groups, equal distribution of supporting services and spatial distribution of disease intensity can be added to the models for selection of private hospital locations.

The following paper presented by *Silvia Fissi, Elena Gori (University of Florence, Italy)* and *Alberto Romolini (International Telematic University, Uninettuno, Italy)* shows the impact of Covid-19 emergency on pharmaceutical sectors in terms of corporate disclosures. In particular, the aim of this paper is to investigate whether or not the vaccine producers have changed their disclosures to underline the effects of Covid-19 vaccine production. Using a content analysis, the authors analyse the reports provided by the vaccine producers in the years 2020 and 2021. The results of this study identify the need to opening a discussion about the corporate disclosure of Covid-19 vaccine producers. In particular, the authors underline the need of provide a clear representation of global performance in this sector and how this can contribute to the global dialogue about the pharmaceutical sector based on empirical data and analysis.

The paper by *Lana Kordić* and *Josip Visković (University of Split, Croatia)* focuses on the role of local government in supporting healthcare development in order to improve the quality of health services provided. The study is based on the analysis of the legal and institutional framework in the field of healthcare by in-depth interviews with key stakeholders involved in the provision of health services, in the city of Split in Croatia, during the Covid-19 crisis period. The results of the study show that it is important to shift the focus from local constraints, which primarily regards the direct financing of the health system, to the various ways of supporting the development of healthcare infrastructure. Finally, it stresses the importance of horizontal and vertical integration both within and outside the health system, as well as a multidisciplinary approach that focuses primarily on prevention and the treatment of diseases.

The next paper, by *Monika Urbaniak (University of Poznań, Poland)* and *Michele Sanfilippo* aims to investigate the maintenance of the right to health during the Covid-19. The authors, on the one hand, analyse the Polish legislation on health rights and, on the other hand, the actions of Polish public authorities in order to manage and prevent the spread of the Covid-19 pandemic. The results show the difficulty of keeping in balance the restrictions imposed by the public authorities to protect the health and life of the citizens and the standards for the protection of freedoms and rights. The authors in particular argue that this happened in particular because the actions taken by the Public authorities, focused on fighting with the pandemic, in order to protect public health, have caused limitations in access to medical services and especially prevention services.

The study by *Woźniak Maciej (University of Krakow, Poland), Karafolas Simeon (University of Western Macedonia, Greece) and Krupnik Seweryn (University of Krakow, Poland)* investigates the support that many governments have decided to offer to help enterprises survive in pandemic period, particularly small and medium-sized enterprises (SMEs). The purpose of the article is to compare the different support schemes for SMEs in Greece and Poland during the Covid-19 pandemic. The results underline the differences in aid, both in terms of scale and tools, between countries and their impact on some economic indicators of the two countries (such as: unemployment rate, development of deposits, business demography).

Part—Financing and Performance

The second part of the volume starts with the paper by *Ilaria Elisa Vannini* and *Niccolò Persiani (University of Florence)*. The study promotes a reflection on the pandemic impact and its effects on the financing system, on expenses trends, and on economic data incurred by Italian public healthcare organisations in the year of the pandemic outbreak. Focusing on national data, with a specific focus on data from two Italian regions significantly stressed by the pandemic, the study shows that the Italian healthcare financing system was able to cover those costs incurred by the pandemic. The resources allocated to healthcare organisations were sufficient to cope with the structural modification of the services provided and the changes in national health mobility data.

The paper by *Ermira H. Kalaj* and *Kelt Kalaj* investigates the effect of various macroeconomic factors on healthcare expenditure, using time series data for Albania for the period 2000 to 2020. Findings indicate that health expenditure expressed as a percentage of GDP are negatively affected by deposit interest rate, and positively influenced by population aged 65 and over, life expectancy, mortality rate, and number of physicians for 1,000 people.

In addition, remittance flows positively affect the household out-of-pocket expenditure and external health expenditure and they may contribute to stabilization in the use of health care services by poorer households or those households lacking health care coverage.

The paper by *Milena Vainieri* and *Federico Vola (Sant'Anna School of Advanced Studies, Pisa, Italy)* analyses the evolution of performance evaluation systems in Italy, during the pandemic, in order to provide some general considerations on the role of such systems in emergency times and specific lessons about healthcare performance evaluation in times of Covid-19. Firstly, the results demonstrate that characteristics of any evaluation tool (i.e. timeliness and accuracy) have to comply with informative needs the evolution system intends to satisfy. Secondly, the study shows the importance by leveraging a range of complimentary tool in order to support different managerial activities. Thirdly, systems whose adhesion is voluntary and those that are not directly linked to political or economic implication have a greater degree of flexibility also to cope with emergency time.

The article co-authored by *Besa Ombashi* (*University College Bedër, Albania*), *Denita Cepiku* (*University of Rome, Italy*) and *Niccolò Persiani* (*University of Florence, Italy*) examines the dynamics of the monitoring process of public-private partnership (PPP) in the healthcare sector in Albania. The case study is based on the data collected from the analysis of the contracts signed between the parties, different reports and the documentation collection with regard to the management of this contract. The result shows that during the pandemic period, the implementation of PPP became even more important for a country facing a global emergency regarding healthcare. Findings also show a need to adopt a long-term strategy in the field of healthcare as well as applicable standards for the monitoring of the implementation procedures.

The paper by the author *Elen Paraskevi Paraschi* (*University of Patras, Greece)* aims at evaluating the efficiency of the national healthcare systems (NHS) in a number of Southeastern European Countries for the years before and during the Covid-19 pandemic. To achieve this goal, the author constructed a two-stage data envelopment analysis (DEA) model based on data extracted from a combination of secondary sources. The results of the first step of the study show that Cyprus and Albania have the most efficient NHS, while Serbia and Slovakia have the least and that the efficiency of the Greek NHS has significantly improved since 2015. The results of the second step of the study show three particular findings: the GDP does not have a noteworthy impact on NHS efficiency, the increase of aging ratios puts substantial pressure on the health systems and the EU membership bears important benefits to the NHS.

Part—Operations

The part third of the volume starts with the paper written by *Chiara Barchielli, Milena Vainieri (Sant'Anna School of Advanced Studies, Pisa, Italy) and Paolo Zoppi (USL Toscana Centro, Italia).* The paper focus on a first assessment of effectiveness of the reorganization of the community care model based on evolving needs driven by the pandemic, analysing the cross-setting healthcare model of the USL Toscana Centro, one Local Health Authorities (LHA) in Tuscany. The Hospital-Territory intervention group (GIROT), was firstly established to manage the nursing homes' threat of an influx of patients towards the hospitals during the pandemic peaks. It constitutes a multi-professional team of a family and community-based nursing model (FCN) and a specialist medical doctor, able to reach complex patients at home and/or in nursing home within the LHA territory and within a FCN's geographically area with a share of residents. The results show the replicability and scalability of the model to different territories, not only for urban centres but for peripheral areas as well, aiming at a more resilient and egalitarian health provision, enforcing the community-based delivery of care.

The paper by *Veglianti Eleonora (FGES University Catholique of Lille, Lille, France), Alberto Romolini (International Telematic University Uninettuno, Rome, Italy)* and *Yaya Li* (*University of Jiangsu, Jiangsu, China*) aims to investigate the use of telemedicine during Covid-19 emergency, comparing the experience of different countries, especially the members of the European Union and China. The research provides a review of the recent studies and experiences on this topic, summarizing the most common applications of telemedicine for the management of public health emergencies. The result of the study provides a picture about the different approaches in the use of telemedicine applied during the Covid-19 emergency and can offer a support for health managers to develop telemedicine for facing the current and new health emergencies.

The following paper is written by *Giacomo Carli (University of Bologna, Italy), Stanislav Russo, Lorenzo Michelin (Rizzoli Orthopedic Institute of Bologna, Italy),*

Emanuele Adorno (University of Bologna, Italy), Peter Perger (UMIT Tirol, Austria), Beatrice Ricci (Rizzoli Orthopedic Institute of Bologna, Italy), Erik Boetto (University of Bologna, Italy), Viola Damen, Anselmo Campagna and *Matteo Buccioli (Rizzoli Orthopedic Institute of Bologna, Italy).* The purpose of the research is to investigate whether correct organizational procedures associated with correct operating room planning and scheduling led to fewer cancelled patients and improved operating rooms' performance indicators. Different performance and efficiency metrics monitored are included. The study was conducted analysing the case study of the Orthopedic Institute Rizzoli of Bologna, a specialized hospital for orthopedic surgeries. The results show a positive effect of surgical scheduling completeness on operating rooms' waste time, with reductions of the Turnover Time and Start Time Tardiness. These results underline the relevance of proper surgical programming for hospital managers and the areas with more room for improvement.

The last paper by the author *Vesna Lukovic* (Independent Researcher, Thessaloniki, Greece) looking into the state of digitalization from the perspective of a patient in 2020, the first year of the pandemic, and taking into account the context of the Western Balkans, aims to explore online behavior of people in regard to privacy and security issues related to the online delivery of certain health-related data, such as COVID-19 certificates.

The papers selected in this book can provide an overview on the special topic of Healthcare Systems' Challenges in the era of Covid-19.

In particular, this volume can offer on the one hand, useful insightful in terms of management of the crisis and emergencies and economic issue in healthcare, and on the other hand, an important contribution to the development of economic and managerial study in healthcare sector.

Niccolò Persiani
Anna Romiti
Ilaria Elisa Vannini
Anastasios Karasavvoglou
Persefoni Polychronidou

Contents

Financing and Performance

Operations

Policies, Governance and Strategies

Communication Strategy in Healthcare Organizations During Covid-19 Crisis: Insights from the Italian Context

Anna Romiti, Mario Del Vecchio, Caterina Cavicchi, and Emidia Vagnoni

Abstract This study analyzes how healthcare organizations (HCOs)'s General Directors (GD) shaped the communication strategies toward internal and external stakeholders to keep fulfilling the organization mission during the COVID-19 crisis. Italy has been chosen as the study setting being one of the first Western countries to be heavily affected by the pandemic. Thus, a qualitative study has been designed to get an in-depth understanding of how the HCOs' GDs, the crisis managers, defined and adopted the communication strategies both toward the internal and the external stakeholders. The findings allow to define the type of communication strategies that the crisis managers adopted towards stakeholders, more precisely a personalized communication was often used with workforce as key internal stakeholder, while a collective communication strategy was mainly adopted with external stakeholders.

Keywords Crisis communication · Crisis management · Stakeholders · COVID-19 · Healthcare organization

1 Introduction

The organizations may go through different types of crises, although of varying magnitude; when effectively handled the organizations may benefit from the crisis (Ulmer and Sellnow 2000) and to this regard communication is essential. The communication strategy topic may be considered from different perspectives; linguistics theory has addressed how lexica affect communication; information systems theory

A. Romiti (✉) · M. Del Vecchio
Department of Experimental and Clinical Medicine, University of Florence, 3 Largo Brambilla, 50134 Florence, Italy
e-mail: anna.romiti@unifi.it

M. Del Vecchio
SDA Bocconi School of Management, 10 Via Sarfatti, 20136 Milan, Italy

C. Cavicchi · E. Vagnoni
Department of Economics and Management, University of Ferrara, 11 Via Voltapaletto, 44121 Ferrara, Italy

N. Persiani et al. (eds.), *Challenges of Healthcare Systems in the Era of COVID-19*, Contributions to Management Science, https://doi.org/10.1007/978-3-031-43114-2_1

has considered how technologies' innovation shapes different channels of communication and brings new tools to the landscape. In this paper, we use the organizational perspective, steaming from the idea that in times of crisis, organizations are compelled to adopt processes to communicate strategically with stakeholders (Massey 2001) to manage their legitimacy, their functions and fulfill their mission.

Although single speakers seek to appeal to as large an audience as possible, organizations cannot survive unless they are able to satisfy diverse audiences or stakeholders with distinct interests (Ice 1991; Schultz and Seeger 1991). In crisis situations, the interests and needs of these distinct groups are often contradictory; in this regard, organizations in a crisis are expected to implement crisis communication by collecting, processing, and disseminating crisis information in order to reduce publics' uncertainty and minimize reputational damage to the organization (Coombs 2015; Ulmer et al. 2017) focusing on the "external dimensions" of the communication crisis theory.

It seems that the "internal dimensions" of the crisis communication has been neglected by academia (Kim et al. 2019); consequently, key determinants of the ability of an organization to leverage on flexibility, networks, and relations, to provide a timely response has received little attention. The organization can benefit from the knowledge of its employees, from the relational capital they have developed, from different forms of networking as this contributes to supportive behaviors and may help to cope with stress, fear, uncertainty (Mazzei et al. 2012) influencing how the employees interpret and react to the crisis.

The COVID-19 pandemic represented a major determinant of crisis for most organizations and among them, for the healthcare ones engaged in fulfilling their function to protect the population health, through prevention, diagnosis, therapies, and caring. However, the crisis has challenged the ability of the healthcare organizations (HCOs) to achieve their ordinary objectives and expected outcomes during the pandemic outbreak. For instance, Willan et al. (2020) stressed the workforce and infrastructure challenges in the UK hospitals' reorganization for the delivery of every aspect of care by all clinical and non-clinical departments to fulfill the expectation of COVID-19 patients.

Theory has focused on crisis managers and on their behavioral outcomes, often seen from external publics (Heide and Simonsson 2014), as communication in time of crisis requires dialogues, in various forms and formats between an organization and its stakeholders, regarding the crisis (Fearn-Banks 2017).

Although the crisis communication theory recognizes the key role of considering both internal and external dimensions, the internal dimensions of the communication process, such as that with the employees, deserves further investigation considering different crisis types and contexts (Kim et al. 2019).

In this regard, COVID-19 pandemic could be considered a suitable context of analysis, as it represented an unprecedented and complex crisis characterized by a rapidly changing environment (Christianson and Barton 2020), that required public sector leaders to balance the need for control with their capacity to be responsive toward stakeholders' expectations (Christensen and Lægreid 2020).

Based on the above premises, this paper aims at analyzing how HCOs' General Directors (GDs) shaped the communication strategies toward internal and external stakeholders to keep fulfilling the organization mission during the COVID-19 crisis (Slagle et al. 2021). To this regard, a qualitative study has been designed in the Italian NHS organizations' setting and data have been collected from the General Directors of the HCOs for the purpose of deepening how the pandemic crises has defined the communication from the GDs to both internal and external stakeholders and to identify the extent to which the organizations have adopted new technologies to support their communication processes. By exploring the communication from the GDs to the external stakeholders and to the internal ones, the findings of this study can contribute to the advancement of crisis communication theories and practice.

2 Literature Review

2.1 Crisis Management in HCOs

Crisis can be seen as being part of the organization's life, although the magnitude of the crisis may differ. The recent COVID-19 pandemic has attracted attention of both scholars and practitioners on the implications and reactions of organizations to the crisis, considering different disciplinary approaches: psychological, socio-political, technological, managerial. Organizational crises are believed to be "*a low-probability, high-impact event that threatens the viability of the organization and is characterized by ambiguity of cause, effect, and means of resolution, as well as by a belief that decisions must be made swiftly*" (Pearson and Clair 1998, p. 60); the authors clearly state how the crisis pose a threat to the survival of the organization and of its stakeholders. The ability of the crisis to determine consequences that "*threaten the most fundamental goals of the organization*" (Weick 1988, p. 305) has been previously well focused in literature. Thus, when considering a crisis, the role of management theory is relevant; to this regard the recent experiences have focused more and more on the role of the crisis manager (Denner et al. 2019). While some authors contributed to the perspective according to which crises cannot be preventable although recurrent, others' perspective stems from the idea that it is possible to identify ways "to manage or avert organizational crisis". Pearson and Clair (1998, p. 60) consider being unrealistic to link the effectiveness of crisis management to those efforts that "pull an organization unscathed through such events. Conversely, simply surviving a crisis may not be a sufficiently stringent criterion for success". The authors, thus, consider effective crisis management when the "organizational and external stakeholder losses are minimized" and learning occurs so that lessons are transferred to better manage future crises/events. However, only a few definitions consider both the perspective of the organization and of its stakeholders (Ullmer and Sellnow 2000) when how to manage a crisis is addressed.

HCOs have been hit worldwide by the pandemic. The debate on COVID-19 is mainly informed by a policy perspective, while the response of HCOs to the pandemic is still little explored (Fanelli et al. 2020). HCOs were challenged from the strategic and operational issues caused by the virus outbreak; thus, identifying solutions to redefine the operations to deliver health services and protect the population's health became a major goal.

Donelli et al. (2022) has recently addressed the crisis management in HCOs linking the COVID-19 crisis for HCOs to the key components of crisis: it threatened high priority goals, such as delivering care for all the population; decisions had to be taken in a limited amount of time; it was unexpected and unanticipated by HCOs. As from Ali (2014), speed and untowardness are the two strongest components of the crisis that we can recognize in the recent pandemic.

The crisis caused by the new Coronavirus pandemic has several specifics. It is not only a local matter but a widespread global crisis, which affects the most important human value, health, and therefore it is well perceived by the people. It affects them directly, introduces not only healthcare impacts, including deaths, but also economic, social and mental consequences. Jankelová et al. (2021, p. 562) argued that "*the synergic effect of all of the listed aspects of the current Corona crisis causes the respect of all interested groups and also the need for professional crisis management at all levels, from the supra-national, through national, organizational to the individual level*".

Focusing on the organizational level, through a qualitative case study, Donelli et al. (2022) identify the capabilities which inform the organization resilience in the emergency management; among them the "contextual reinforcement" drives the attention at the role of the stakeholders. Tay (2020) has considered the organizational challenge faced by a hospital in Singapore to redefine the operations, and consequently the manpower allocation, in an effective and flexible way; to this regard, among other variables, the authors highlight the key role of the communication strategy toward the staff members and the technological resources adopted.

The literature clearly highlights how the HCOs had to adopt crisis management, with their leaders called to act as crisis managers and deploy strategies and actions to fulfill the organization's mission. To this regard, the theory focuses on the role of competencies, thus employees, and on the contextual factors as key pillars of effective crisis management.

2.2 Crisis Communication

Theory argued how factors such as management of effective communication (especially internal), use of suitable management style, adequate decision-making ability, definition of an effective crisis team and the sharing of information among them are important factors for an effective crisis management (Vainieri et al. 2017; Heide and Simonsson 2014; Bhaduri 2019). Jin et al. (2018) include the stakeholders' activism among the variables that contribute to an ethical crisis communication, reiterating the need to consider stakeholders when defining the communication strategies. Furthermore, the literature highlights how top management's preparedness, training, and perception of communication, in regular time and crisis situations, determine the initial stance of an organization's crisis communication strategies (Jin et al. 2018).

In times of crisis, organizations reframe their capabilities to respond to the emergency (Ortiz 2022 based on Goodson et al. 2020). In this regard Ortiz (2022, p. 237) argue "*as many organizations reframe their capabilities in previously unimaginable ways, they do so as a call to service, not only in response to community need but also in response to cultural and societal expectations around corporate social responsibility, social impact/public value and social justice. The influence of these forces is compelling organizations to reflect on who they are, what they do and how they do it, and to deliver on their mission in distinctive, deliberate and altruistic ways. Industry experts and crisis communication scholars advocate for organizations to demonstrate identity, purpose and core values during COVID-19 by focusing on need-driven actions that align with mission and values and underscore stability, compassion and trust* (Veil and Husted 2012; Rothschild 2020; Dvorak and Schatz 2020)".

In the healthcare context, likewise in the case of the current pandemic, crises have been determined by different viruses (H1N1, MERS, SARS to mention some); although the magnitude of the crisis may have been different, crisis communication is key in the healthcare organizations; in that context, crisis communication is considered one of the most important areas of crisis management. "*It is expected that effective communication during the crisis reduces uncertainty, which can cause an emotional reaction of the public or the employees; therefore, stringency is one of its important elements*" (Jankelová et al. 2021, p. 563).

Literature related to communication in times of crises in the healthcare sector shows that sometimes the managers have engaged in communicating the sense of control more than the update of the information, or even at communicating reliable explanations of the events. Johansson and Ottestig (2011) found that managers overrate the importance of external compared to internal factors and this is manifested in insufficient communication skills in relation to the employees.

Some authors have identified the key components of communication of leaders in crisis consisting of reliable explanation of what happened, directions to manage the pandemic, emphasizing successful solutions, expressing empathy towards patients and families, healthcare workforce and any other entity affected by the crisis (Boin et al. 2016). Thus, the healthcare leaders are expected to deploy a communication strategy that contributes to leverage the key resources for redefining the operations, achieving the goals, and minimizing the damages both for the organization and its context. In this regard, affective empathy that shows concern, compassion, and sympathy toward the stakeholders has been considered as pivotal to convey effective messages to react to the pandemic (Schoofs et al. 2022; Coombs 2007) by ways of instructing and adjusting information: the first is related to protect stakeholders from physical threats through relevant information, the second is related to psychologically reassure them, providing information of the problems born due to the crisis, on solutions that have been implemented and on preventive actions to avoid a new crisis (Schoofs et al. 2022; Coombs 2007).

Crisis communication thus, should accomplish several goals related to instructing individuals to increase their self-efficacy in managing risks, stimulating active participation to increase the societal understanding of the event, generate co-produced solutions that include not only the organizational response to the emergency, but also the cooperation with stakeholders (Palttala and Vos 2012). When exploring instructing and adjusting information strategies adopted by public sector organizations to face COVID-19 pandemic, Slagle et al. (2021) found that a public university's top management communication to stakeholders was primary focused on showing the choices that have been taken in response of the emergency and how these latter could impact on the future of the university; nevertheless, they fell short to show empathy with individual stakeholders in adjusting the information; the study thus concluded that to be effective crisis communication should focus both on ensuring organizational continuity while caring for the individuals, and set quick responses that are a representative of stakeholders' needs.

Internal and External Communication in Times of Crisis

HCOs need to address the multiple needs of their complex audience during crises to generate benefits for both the organization and its stakeholders. Furthermore, in a crisis, the communication needs of the interested parties are greatly intensified (Ulmer and Sellnow 2000); thus, leaders should be able to determine the groups to prioritize the communication and define a communication strategy. Studying CEOs' communication strategies (although related to the private sector), Conte et al. (2017) found that CEOs tend to act as spokespersons, to disseminate values and corporate vision, and do not delegate communication on activities with a strategic value, when communicating with stakeholders. This suggests that the communication can be delegated or not depending on the content to be disclosed. Furthermore, crisis communication should take into account of audiences "who differ greatly in their support for the organization" (Xu 2020, p. 6). To this regard, scholars outline two dimensions of the communication: the internal and the external communication (Bundy et al. 2017).

Considering the external communication, crisis management encompasses a focus on supporting safety and growth of the communities, thus the communication fulfils the transparency, accountability, resilience, and local entities' needs (Garcia 2017). Then, external communication contributes to legitimize the organization in its context, impacts on the reputation, and may strengthen relations with stakeholders that are key to implementing solutions (Pearson and Clair 1998). Nevertheless, the communication style and the content of the message to be conveyed can affect the recipients' perceptions, determining consequences for the organization's legitimacy. For instance, Garofalo and Rott (2018) found that leaders tend to delegate the communication of bad news to avoid consequences, while receivers are more likely to punish both the decision maker and the spokesperson for unfair allocations communicated by this latter if the spokesperson shows emotional regret and there is room for shifting blame. In real-world situations, recipients would be more likely to accept an unpopular decision, when the leader and its employees "are closely linked and share possible consequences" of bad news' communication (Garofalo and Rott 2018, p. 9). Literature on communication crisis in private sector shows the cases in which a CEO should assume the spokesperson's role and those in which the role can be limited to delegating or coordinating the corporate communication. The authors explain that the different roles of CEOs depend on the phases and object of the crisis in terms of impact on the organization (Lucero et al. 2009).

In this regard, the following research question has been defined (Slagle et al. 2021):

RQ1: Which communication strategy the HCO's General Directors (crisis managers) have defined towards the external stakeholders?

Internal communication is important to encourage the individuals, leading to an adequate reaction (Reynold and Seeger 2005). Based on Mayfield and Mayfield (2002) effective leader communication strategies can increase the employees' motivation and commitment. HCOs' ability to fulfill their mission is highly dependent on the knowledge, abilities, competencies of the employees; thus, during the pandemic, an effective communication process of the organization's leaders with the various component of the workforce contributes to activate strategic patterns such as flexibility, planning, competences' shift, networking, etc. enhancing the proper functioning of the management system (Jakubiec 2019). Jankelová et al. (2021) concluded that there is a dependency between the crisis competences of management and performance of teams, during crisis, mediated by the sharing of information.

Considering the communication as ongoing efforts at coordinating and control of activity and knowledge (Cooren et al. 2011), the choices in terms of flow of communication, information, and recipients' group are important for its effectiveness. Considering the crisis communication choices, theory has focused on the role of personalized communication as having a more favorable impact on the organization's image affecting the recipients' perception as well as on privatized communication (Denner et al. 2019). The latter intended at depicting the organization leader as sharing the common value, attitude, etc. In this regard, Deverell (2021) concluded that regarding inter-organizational collaboration, the closer a communication officer works to the spatial place of the crisis and to the rescue service, the higher the status of the communication officer.

Lacerda (2019) found that during crises, leaders' honest speech and culture of active listening, leaders' proximity through closed informal relationships, and leaders' support to think outside the box to solve the organizational problems can reassure and motivate employees, increase their job satisfaction and improve their performance.

Another way to communicate in crisis is using the collective communication. A study of CEO communication strategy during COVID-19 shows the positive results of this communication strategy based on CEO open letters to giving sense to crisis situations and provide emotional and instrumental support (Liu et al. 2022).

In practice, the crisis managers may adopt different styles and strategies to shape the communication process for internal stakeholders; based on this premise, the following research question has been defined (Slagle et al. 2021):

RQ2: Which communication strategy the HCO's General Directors (crisis managers) have adopted within the organization, considering the internal stakeholders?

The Role of Technologies in Communication

Shaping the communication process towards stakeholders can benefit from different technologies the organization adopts. Among them, social media have become an important communication platform in many organizations and are in constant development.

Tay et al. (2021) argues that the best laid plans in time of crisis will not lead to robust implementation without a comprehensive communication strategy focused on different social media platforms: these latter can improve connectivity among individuals while facilitating the exchange of information and mutual learning to support decision-making. Triantafillidou and Yannas (2020) argue that social media pose great challenges for crisis managers, as they are platforms where crises can be triggered, can escalate, and can influence the agenda-setting process of traditional news media. Furthermore, the use of digital platforms for communication platforms can make difficult to share empathy and concerns to the single individuals; nevertheless, digital communication can compensate this aspect by providing a support for shared and agile decision-making, which is based on continuous stakeholders' feedback, daily digests emailed, and social media that act to instruct and adjust information, favoring a major comprehension of the crisis event and stimulating organizational response (Slagle et al. 2021).

Studies have tried to investigate the effect of ICT mediated communication on decision-making. Daly (1993) investigated group collective inductions comparing face-to-face communication and synchronous computer-mediated communication: her research shows that while both practices can facilitate group collective learning and decision-making, those face-to-face brought less time spent in discussion, major interaction among people and less error in taking decisions compared to the computer-aided communication. Other studies also showed that when the computer-aided communication is asynchronous, a lack of control on on-time participation in the communication process is experienced, as well as a reduction in the timeliness of responses to inquiries, and a delay in the information exchange (Smith and Vanecek 1990). In this regard, costs and benefits of the specific communication channel depend on "the relative importance of the recognition of truth and the rejection of error" (Daly 1993, p. 20). At the same time social media can be used to provide effective crisis communication with positive advantages. For instance, several functions can be covered by the use of social media including educating the public, contrasting fake information, providing an open space for dialogue, collecting information and interacting to find solutions to crises (Veil et al. 2011). Effective communication to stakeholders indeed requires balancing social media interaction with the organization's desire on information control (Veil et al. 2011).

When focusing on government and non-government agencies, the use of social media during crises is still limited; their primary use of social media is for information dissemination to the public; nevertheless, social media are rarely used to listen to the public (Saroj and Pal 2020). Studies have also compared traditional vs new media communication during crises. For instance, social media tend to provide higher interactivity that reduces the perceived crisis responsibility, compared to traditional media; nevertheless, they present issues related to the lack of traditional gatekeeping process, accelerating the diffusion of stakeholders' negative opinions on the organization during a crisis (Xu 2020).

Based on the literature review on the use of different communication channels during crisis, the following research question is defined (Xu 2020):

RQ3: Which are the main technological sources and platforms that supported the crisis managers in their communication strategies?

3 Methodology

Based on the above premise, this paper aims at analyzing how COVID-19 crisis affected the communication strategy toward internal and external stakeholders in the HCOs.

To fulfill the aim of the study, the grounded theory methodology has been used (Corbin and Strauss 1990). The Italian context has been chosen as the study setting considering the accessibility criterion to the field from the researchers' perspective and Italy being the first European country to be deeply affected by the pandemic in the early 2020. Italy's healthcare system is based on the universal coverage principle and uniform healthcare access to citizens is financed by the central government through tax revenues (Nuti et al. 2012). The system is of a decentralized nature, based on a broad autonomy of the 21 regional governments to define the healthcare policies and to enhance the HCOs' innovation and strategic management. As a result, the national government acts as a supervisor to ensure the uniform provision of the essential levels of care defined by law across the regions (Nuti et al. 2012).

In every regional healthcare service, local health organizations have the responsibility to provide healthcare services to the people (a) directly, through their own hospitals (b) contracting with public independent hospitals (such as the university hospitals) or (c) through private hospitals (Romiti et al. 2023).

Concerning the governance structure of the HCOs (both local health authorities and public independent hospitals), General Directors (GDs) play a key role both in terms of the organization's strategy and in terms of managing the relationship with the regional government as a key external stakeholder. They are directly appointed by the Region, with a 5 years' mandate, and are endowed with legal and managerial duties (Romiti et al. 2023).

Given the HCOs' General Directors' role to define the strategies to react to the challenges posed by the pandemic, data have been gathered through semi-structured interviews from a sample of 49 GDs of HCOs related to different Italian regions; in this regard, a theoretical sampling technique has been followed to allow for the heterogeneity of the regional healthcare services involved (Robinson 2014). The selection of the GDs started considering the total population of 200 HCOs with juridical autonomy in Italy in 2020 (Ministry of Health Public Database 2022). The interviews were conducted by two researchers, part of the research team; an online interview method was chosen to maximize the availability of the interviewers to participate and facilitate their time management. The interviews were conducted during the year 2021; thus, online interviews represented the only method of data collection consistent with the feasibility criterion.

The interview protocol was aimed at asking questions related to:

- the role played by the GD in the communication process towards internal and external stakeholders;
- the pressures coming from stakeholders in terms of information needs GDs have to satisfy;
- the communication modalities to address stakeholders' specific information needs: in particular, what was the role of traditional and new media in the communication process;
- the scopes of the communication with reference to the different stakeholders addressed by the communication process.

Overall, about 90 h of interviews were recorded and transcribed. Data has been analyzed through NVivo software package. To conduct the study, grounded theory criteria defined by Corbin and Strauss (1990) have been used; in particular, the coding process involved three steps: (a) open coding was performed to constantly compare data to find similarities and differences and let the main categories to emerge, (b) axial coding to relate categories and subcategories and text the relations against data; (c) selective coding which concerns the identification of the core categories that aims at conceptualize and synthesize the findings of the research. Categories and subcategories are presented in the next sections, and discussed in the light of the relevant theory on crisis communication. The data saturation principle has been adopted while collecting data coherently with the grounded theory approach (Saunders et al. 2018).

4 Findings

Given the objectives of the study, the findings are presented based on the analysis of the communication strategies the HCO's GDs defined towards external and internal stakeholders, then on relation at the technological sources and platforms that supported the communication strategies.

4.1 Communication Strategy Towards the Internal Stakeholders

Considering the internal stakeholders, the focus of the GDs was on the employees, and the trade unions. The analysis (Table 1) shows that the GDs adopted both a personalized communication and a collective type of communication.

The personalized communication was based on a communication strategy that was highly centered on the GD, mainly in terms of behavioral personalization. The GDs were found to be in the field and providing emotional support to the healthcare organizations workforce as this was functional to motivate it. Nevertheless, the data collection provides evidence of adoption of the so-called collective type of communication addressed to the workforce, as the personalized one, and to the trade unions. Trade unions often act as intermediaries between the organization's top governance and the workforce, thus ensuring that healthcare professionals' rights are guaranteed.

In the first typology of communication strategies, we included those GDs who used a communication approach mainly based on emotional levers; sharing feelings, as well as acting as role-models being present on the field, were shown to be emotional levers to support healthcare professionals in the management of COVID-19-related emergency.

Table 1 Communication strategies with internal stakeholders

Type of stakeholder	Type of communication	Type of strategy	Motivations
Internal stakeholders: the healthcare professionals	Personal communication	• Being on field • GD providing emotional support	• Building trust • Show ability in taking decision • Know their problems and find solutions • Make difficult decisions to be accepted • Motivate/encourage people • Valorize their work to ensure continuous support
	Collective communication	• Trade unions' intermediation • Collective communication channels (letter, notes, what's up groups, etc.)	• Resolve health and safety issues • Inform employees on the hospital' strategy • Create a collective sense-making around the crisis • Collective effort to react

This was the case of a GD that argued: "*There were many nights in which I have been on site with them [the healthcare professionals], working side by side, I stripped myself of the role I held, in that situation I was one of them and they perceived me as such. This strategy was very satisfactory, because I understood that I had been able to build a relationship with them, they trusted me*" (*GD 1*).

Entering in the ward with the healthcare professionals was also a way to share feelings and difficulties, and find a joint solution for issues that emerged during the COVID-19 patients' management, for instance when the healthcare professionals were very worried about the contagion risk: "*I spoke to the most worried of those nurses and said let's get dressed together and enter the COVID-19 ward' and at the end the message was if someone like the GD who is a top manager can do that, why can't we [the healthcare professionals] do it too? We went and spent an hour sitting with patients and talking, of course we were masked and dressed so the risk of contagion was zero*" (*GD* 2).

The personal relationship of the GD with his employees plays a pivotal role in the process of organizational transformation: "*The relationship that was created at that moment, which was a moment of emergency, in which we really were terrified, was a relationship that went beyond any formality. In front of a specific need, I used all kind of employees (administrative, Department of Prevention workers, university students graduating in medicine), I give them all the needed support for contact tracing and they offered all the cooperation*" (GD 2).

The personalized relationship with employees is of particular importance in emergency situation because making them more confident in the decision making process: "*I no longer used the usual communications, that is, the periodic board of directors meeting. During the emergency I preferred a more informal approach. We talk, we see each other in call every night or when needed, maybe with the same actors but not in a ritual way; so it seems to me that the way of directing has changed in the frequency of meetings, even in the informality with which we contact. I also changed the way of control that was directed by personally going to the ward to talk to the operators directly affected by the changes we had to make*" (*GD3*).

With reference to the second communication strategy, the role of trade unions as intermediaries between the GD and the healthcare professionals was detected. With reference to the relations with the trade unions a GD argued: "*We had a strong and positive relationship with them [the trade unions], we used to meet almost every week. They were worried about the employees' level of stress. Sometimes, they underwent my decisions, and they dissented, but the pandemic was a war that required fast moving, so all of us perfectly knew that we couldn't afford to lose time on discussing. Trade unions understood the situation and comprehended my role, and that the decisions I took were not aimed at penalizing the workforce*" (*GD 4*).

GDs that counted on collective communications strategy aimed at informing their employees about the organization's strategy and reinforcing the organizational culture, through shared values, as the pandemic required a collective effort to provide a response. "*In that situation I relied much on the health professionals, I relied on our values; through communication I wanted to reconstruct the organizational identity.*

Thus, I sent a letter to all the employees; I was constantly communicating with them even before the COVID-19 pandemic" (*GD* 5).

The relationship with the employees in some organizations has been polarized. The GD established one day a week for the meeting with the unions, in order to give information to all the internal stakeholders: "*The Tuesday of every week was dedicated to meetings with the unions in which all communications were given, a meeting of an hour and a half with the unions of the physicians and an hour and a half with the others. In these meetings, I told what had happened, what was the level of the infected, the patients we had and what we would probably do the following week*" (*GD6*).

As mentioned at the beginning of the section the GDs adopted the personalized and the collective communication strategies, however the data analysis demonstrates that in some cases there had been a clear single choice, while in others both were adopted. This allows at arguing that in the studied setting the strategies were not mutually exclusive.

4.2 Communication Strategy Towards the External Stakeholder

Focusing on the external stakeholders two main strategies were detected: those GDs that adopted a centralized approach to control the flow of information to the stakeholders and establish a direct contact with local players to manage the health care locally, and those GDs who preferred coordinated communication strategies in which professionalism and transparency were highlighted, so that the managerial expertise of the GD was flanked by those of healthcare professionals to provide a "technical" response to stakeholders' information needs (Table 2).

Regarding the centralized communication approach, the centralization of the communication function of the General Director found its rationale in informing the local stakeholders about the contagion rate and finding agreed solutions for healthcare management and infections' monitoring in the local area (for instance, how to manage isolation and quarantine measures). This kind of communication strategy was also adopted to fulfill transparency needs and avoid the dissemination of fake news that could threaten the legitimacy of the GD's managerial strategy; in turn, this would have compromised the GD's legitimation. As stated during the interview by GD 5: "*The communication with Mayors, Prefect, and other stakeholders all revolved around my person. This approach allowed me to reduce the time of decision-making. During the different pandemic waves, it helped to keep the rudder straight enough to react. Also, it avoided the manipulation of information from outside*" (*GD 7*).

Another GD argued: "*I interacted directly with the Mayors, I organized a WhatsApp chat. Every day I told them what action we were implementing, based on data. This supported me a lot when I had to manage multiple issues such as the infection tracing, the vaccination campaign, the conversion of some wards and so on.*

Table 2 Communication strategies with external stakeholders

Type of stakeholder	Type of communication	Type of strategy	Motivations
External stakeholders	Centralization	The GD as the reference point for the stakeholders' information needs	• Coordinating the local territory response to the pandemic • Avoid the misinterpretation of the data, fake news • Give information on specific issues
	Coordination	The GD involve professionals based on these latter's expertise	• Let the healthcare professionals' expertise to emerge • Respond with competence to different information requests • Avoid the misinterpretation of data, fake news

We discussed problems, but we also found solutions. I had the opportunity to say 'I have to make fast decisions, if you do not agree you should let me know now'. This served us as an accelerator of the decision-making process! I have learned that, to avoid fake news, communication has to be based on a trust relationship between the organization and the stakeholders and on credible sources of evidence" (*GD 8*).

The narrative data clearly highlights what supported the choice of a centralized communication approach with the external stakeholders; the need to be accountable and transparent toward the local community and the need to not compromise the GD external legitimization played a key role. The centralized approach to crisis communication meant to avoid the clinicians to be involved: "*They [the clinicians] were not allowed to participate in television programs. I strongly stated 'I'll manage all the communication with the press'*" (*GD 9*).

Nevertheless, some GDs preferred to coordinate communication and involve healthcare professionals when their competence was required to satisfy a specific stakeholder's information need: "*I have always shared with the healthcare professionals this type of decisions, in the sense that if I am invited to express my view about the pandemic course, I decide with them in which cases it is appropriate for me or for them to go. Nobody plays a role alone, including myself. For instance, for technical and clinical aspects I can rely on the Public Health Department Director. Everyone has his/her own competence' area, I don't participate to talk about things I do not know. Everyone has their own space in the communication process*" (*GD 10*).

Among the GDs that adopted the coordination strategy, there were those that prefer to choose a spokesperson based on this latter ability to communicate and position covered in the HCO: "*We involved the Director of the Public Health Department, based on his communicative attitude and representativeness. We shared the communication content, but I trusted him and he became soon my spokesperson*" (*GD 11*).

Another GD argued: "*I trusted my press officer, who supported me in the definition of the communication contents. He gave me the whole picture of the interviews that were asked, and together we decided decide which interviews to grant or deny*" (*GD 5*).

Other GDs instead preferred to give to healthcare professionals the opportunity to communicate the crisis: "*I gave general instructions, but I let them [the healthcare professionals] speak as they were at the forefront of the crisis situation*" (*GD 4*).

Strategies were not mutually exclusive: in this regard, some GDs showed to have adopted the two communication strategies. It was the case of a GD that adopted a centralized approach for communication intended to satisfy institutional actors' information needs, whilst the coordinated approach for the operational and technical information, steaming from citizens' requests that were provided by clinicians.

As a result, the management of external stakeholders' pressures was evident when considering the different information needs the GDs have to satisfy. As argued by a GD that adopted the centralized crisis communication approach: "*I have taken over any kind of communication. I had to manage the stakeholders' anxiety: the daily calls with the Health City Councilor; the relationships with the admin offices of the Regional Authority; the relationship with my colleagues [the GDs of the other HCOs of the Region]; the local press request, and the interviews that were asked to the professionals. For instance, to the Mayors I started to give precise communication of patients that were hospitalized. Putting a privacy issue in a situation that could cause the crash of the hospital was like an elephant entering the glassware shop and dancing the samba, foolishness!!*" (*GD 12*).

4.3 Technological Sources and Platforms that Supported the Crisis Managers' Communication

As the communication strategies needed ad-hoc sources, empowering conventional channels and establishing new/unconventional channels were the main means through which to manage the information requirements from the plurality of stakeholders the HCOs had to bridge (Table 3).

During the pandemic, the GDs enhanced the use of phone calls, press releases, participation in television programs and the intranet.

Concerning traditional and new media usage, the first scope of the communication was to provide real time information (avoiding misinformation and fake news) and reassure the external stakeholders. With reference to traditional media usage, a GD reported: "*We had a press conference every Friday with updates until now. This is because the press asks a lot of info, thus we said: 'let's put a fixed moment in which we*

Table 3 The GDs' communication channels

Communication channel	Communication means	Communication functions
Use of conventional channels to communicate	Calls, participation in television programs, press release, intranet, emailing	• To reassure the local territory • Provide real time information • Fast decision-making
Use of unconventional channels to communicate	Social media, videoconference, newsletters	

can talk with the press'. I must say that it has given us good results, in the sense that journalists are cooperating. Then they call every day, but there is great collaboration with the press" (*GD 13*).

Their approach was meant at building a continuous dialogue with the relevant stakeholders, so that real time information could be easily provided. With regard at the sources supporting the internal stakeholders' communication, a GD argued: "*We used the intranet a lot. it worked as a kind of desk for everyone, this allowed us to keep everyone informed daily" (GD 14).*

New communication channels or platforms were adopted to report relevant information to the stakeholders: it was the case of the use of social media (lives, pages, short messages), newsletters and video conferences, all of them allowing at being in direct contact with the citizens and in general, with the local institutions, and providing a real time response to their worries: *"I created a Facebook direct communication that was only accessible by our organization's employees. Trivially, we made a Facebook page in which friendship was given only to the healthcare organization' staff member, so every Tuesday I could make a 40-min talk. Part of that speech aimed at justifying and explaining the strategic decisions undertaken. Initially, it was just a way to spread the information, but after a while I started to ask for healthcare professionals to intervene and suggest ideas and discussion's topics. They did not ask so many questions; nevertheless, they thanked me as they felt involved" (GD 15).*

Someone else commented about the use of specific apps: "*We had chats in WhatsApp for everything, a chat with Majors, a chat with the Prefecture, and so on, producing from 500 to 700 messages per day. Managing those sources was demanding, but at the same time this helped each other, to keep calm, share problems and solutions*" (*GD 16*).

Data collected witness the spread of the use of the digital communication, due to lockdown measures, and allowed the GDs to provide information on a daily/week basis depending on the stakeholders' needs and expectations; thus, objectives such as the transparency of actions, the pandemic management, reassuring the community about the ability of the HCO to provide a response to the crisis were fulfilled. Social media were mostly used to communicate with the employees when collective communication was preferred. Whereas WhatsApp groups and remote interacting were used specially to coordinate actions with the local institutions' actors and the dialogue with the Regional Health Service.

5 Discussion

In line with the crisis' communication literature, GDs were found to use behavioral communication to convey a message of closeness to healthcare professionals' emotions and feelings, as a motivational lever to react to the challenges the pandemic posed (Coombs 2007; Schoofs et al., 2022; Denner et al. 2019). Nevertheless, collective communication has been also enacted by the GDs to share information on the HCO's strategy; reconstruct the organizational identity while conveying a message of stability and empathy; leveraging the role of organizational values and mission, that was aimed at motivating the healthcare professionals' response (Ortiz 2022). Thus, given the studied setting, providing timely information, seek employees' feedback and increasing employees' awareness on the need to undertake organizational change, while emphasizing the need to react quickly, are key features to adopt effective communication strategies that reduce uncertainty and provide effective responses to crises (Li et al. 2021). When the GDs' communication to employees was mediated by the trade unions, a perspective of instructing information (Coombs 2007) was predominant, as the communication was aimed at providing information on the measures to ensure safety to the healthcare workers while managing the pandemic.

The findings have highlighted the importance of managing the communication with external stakeholders during the COVID-19 crisis. Acting as crisis manager, the GDs adopted centralized communication to strengthen the accountability and legitimacy of the HCO in the local area (Garcia 2017), while searching for cooperation and support from relevant stakeholders. In this regard, the predominant role of communication was the one of adjusting information. At the same time when the information to be communicated was mainly based on technical knowledge, the GDs enhanced the involvement of healthcare professionals to deal with different audiences.

The matrix as follows (Table 4) can provide evidence of the different communication strategies adopted by the GDs with reference to internal and external stakeholders, based on Coombs (2007).

The matrix provides evidence of the predominant strategies of instructing and adjusting information in relation to different stakeholders' needs. Although distinctive strategies have been developed by the GDs to communicate information during

Table 4 Crisis communication strategies adopted by the GDs

	Internal stakeholders	External stakeholders
Instructing information	Trade unions acting as intermediaries for information related to health and safety	Coordination to enact competent communication
Adjusting information	Personal communication based on emotional levers to motivate Collective communication based on organizational identity reconstruction to motivate	Centralization to keep the direct contact with relevant stakeholders to co-produce solutions

crises, these strategies were not mutually exclusive, so that some GDs used a combination of approaches to interact with the same stakeholders, because of a complex and challenging situation, and because of the patterns characterizing the organizational complexity.

In addition, the use of digital platforms to communicate the crisis event were functional to support the birth of an organizational response to the crisis, through a continuous interaction with internal and external stakeholders (Slagle et al. 2021). Crisis communication was not only routed towards ensuring organizational continuity but also involved stakeholders to find shared solutions to problems (Slagle et al. 2021). For instance, cooperation with external stakeholders of the local territory aimed at managing the infections, providing healthcare assistance, and organizing the vaccination campaign, benefited from digital communication that enabled fast and shared decision-making.

6 Conclusions

This study analyzes how healthcare organizations (HCOs)'s General Directors shaped the communication strategies toward internal and external stakeholders to keep fulfilling the organization mission during the COVID-19 crisis.

This paper aimed at analyzing communication strategies adopted by the GDs with reference to their stakeholders, specifically the internal ones, during the recent COVID-19 pandemic crisis. Aligned with previous results published in literature the GDs, acting as crisis manager, shaped the communication strategy to keep their legitimacy as the top manager of the organization, as well as to enact cooperation strategies to effectively respond to the pandemic. The paper, thus, contributes to filling the literature's gap in terms of crisis communication to stakeholders in the light of the COVID-19 crisis' characteristics. Furthermore, the paper contributes to the stream of literature about crisis communication from the organizational perspective; beyond the magnitude of the crisis the organizations need to address and the focus of the study on the healthcare context, the paper contributes to the literature providing evidence of the approaches and sources (both conventional and innovative) to build flexibility to manage an organization in times of crisis.

As the study has been designed to collect data from the crisis managers' perspective, not involving stakeholders in data gathering may result in a limitation. Thus, analyzing the stakeholders' perception of the effectiveness of the crisis managers' communication strategies would result in a further research avenue to be developed. Thus, further research is needed to investigate the perceptions of stakeholders that were affected by the instructing and adjusting information' strategies. Cooperation grown during the pandemic in finding solutions for the common good can be considered as a good proxy to understand the extent to which these strategies promoted an active dialogue between the GDs and their stakeholders (Palttala and Vos 2012).

Finally, the paper provides findings and remarks that are relevant to the crisis managers to identify actions and strategies to address their managerial mission during the crisis. Then, considering the current pandemic as a worldwide crisis the paper contributes to raise awareness among policy makers, workforce, and managers, about the key role of communication as a prerequisite for a timely and effective response to the crisis.

Acknowledgements The authors thank FIASO (Federazione Italiana Aziende Sanitarie e Ospedaliere, the Italian association of Local Health Authorities and Independent Hospitals) for the technical and financial support provided to the research project.

References

Ali A (2014) Complacency and crisis management in large organizations. Int J Commer Manag 24(4):274–278

Bhaduri RM (2019) Leveraging culture and leadership in crisis management. Eur J Training Dev 43(5/6):554–569

Boin A, Stern E, Sundelius B (2016) The politics of crisis management: public leadership under pressure. Cambridge University Press, Cambridge, UK

Bundy J, Pfarrer MD, Short CE, Coombs WT (2017) Crises and crisis management: integration, interpretation, and research development. J Manag 43(6):1661–1692

Christensen T, Lægreid P (2020) The coronavirus crisis—crisis communication, meaning-making, and reputation management. Int Public Manag J 23(5):5713–5729

Christianson MK, Barton MA (2020) Sensemaking in the Time of COVID-19. J Manage Stud 58(2):572–576

Conte F, Siano A, Vollero A (2017) CEO communication: engagement, longevity and founder centrality: an exploratory study in Italy. Corp Commun Int J 22(3):273–291

Coombs WT (2007) Protecting organization reputations during a crisis: The development and application of situational crisis communication theory. Corp Reput Rev 10(3):163–176

Coombs WT (2015) The value of communication during a crisis: insights from strategic communication research. Bus Horiz 58(2):141–148

Cooren F, Kuhn T, Cornelissen JP, Clark T (2011) Communication, organizing and organization: an overview and introduction to the special issue. Organ Stud 32(9):1149–1170

Corbin JM, Strauss A (1990) Grounded theory research: procedures, canons, and evaluative criteria. Qual Sociol 13:3–21

Daly BL (1993) The influence of face-to-face versus computer-mediated communication channels on collective induction. Account Manag Inf Technol 3(1):1–22

Denner N, Viererbl B, Koch T (2019) A matter for the boss? How personalized communication affects recipients' perceptions of an organization during a crisis. Int J Commun 13:1–19

Deverell E (2021) Professionalization of crisis management: a case study of local-level crisis communicators in Sweden. J Contingencies Crisis Manag 29(2):131–142

Donelli CC, Fanelli S, Zangrandi A, Elefanti M (2022) Disruptive crisis management: lessons from managing a hospital during the COVID-19 pandemic. Manag Decis 60(13):66–91

Dvorak N, Schatz J (2020) A guiding star during coronavirus: your company values. Gallup Workplace. https://www.gallup.com/workplace/310430/guiding-star-duringcoronavirus-company-values.aspx. Accessed March 2022

Fanelli S, Lanza G, Francesconi A, Zangrandi A (2020) Facing the pandemic: the Italian experience from health management experts' perspective. Am Rev Public Adm 50(6–7):753–761

Fearn-Banks K (2017) Crisis communications: a casebook approach, 5th edn. Routledge, New York, NY

Garcia HF (2017) Strategic choices for managing potential crises. Strategy Leadersh 45(6):34–40

Garofalo O, Rott C (2018) Shifting blame? Experimental evidence of delegating communication. Manage Sci 64(8):3911–3925

Goodson S, Demos A, Dhanaraj C (2020) Shift your organization from panic to purpose. Harvard Bus Rev. https://hbr.org/2020/04/shift-your-organization-frompanic-to-purpose. Accessed March 2022

Heide M, Simonsson C (2014) Developing internal crisis communication: new roles and practices of communication professionals. Corp Commun Int J 19(2):128–146

Ice R (1991) Corporate publics and rhetorical strategies: the case of union carbide's Bhopal crisis. Manag Commun Q 4(3):341–362

Jakubiec M (2019) The importance of internal communication for management of an organisation. Scientific papers of the Silesian university of technology 2019, organisation and management series no. 134, pp 47–62

Jankelová N, Joniaková Z, Blštáková J, Skorková Z, Procházková K (2021) Leading employees through the crises: key competences of crises management in healthcare facilities in coronavirus pandemic. Risk Manage Healthc Policy 14:561–573

Jin Y, Pang A, Smith J (2018) Crisis communication and ethics: the role of public relations. J Bus Strateg 39(1):43–52

Johansson C, Ottestig AT (2011) Communication executives in a changing world: legitimacy beyond organizational borders. J Commun Manag 15(2):144–164

Kim Y, Kang M, Lee E, Yang SU (2019) Exploring crisis communication in the internal context of an organization: Examining moderated and mediated effects of employee-organization relationships on crisis outcomes. Public Relat Rev 45(3):101777

Lacerda TC (2019) Crisis leadership in economic recession: a three-barrier approach to offset external constraints. Bus Horiz 62(2):185–197

Li JY, Sun R, Tao W, Lee Y (2021) Employee coping with organizational change in the face of a pandemic: the role of transparent internal communication. Public Relat Rev 47(1):101984

Liu J, Hong C, Yook B (2022) CEO as "Chief Crisis Officer" under COVID-19: a content analysis of CEO open letters using structural topic modeling. Int J Strateg Commun 16(3):444–468

Lucero M, Kwang ATT, Pang A (2009) Crisis leadership: when should the CEO step up? Corp Commun Int J 14(3):234–248

Massey JE (2001) Managing organizational legitimacy: communication strategies for organizations in crisis. Int J Bus Commun 38(2):153–182

Mayfield J, Mayfield M (2002) Leader communication strategies critical paths to improving employee commitment. Am Bus Rev 20(2):89–94

Mazzei A, Kim JN, Dell'Oro C (2012) Strategic value of employee relationships and communicative actions: overcoming corporate crisis with quality internal crisis communication. Int J Strateg Commun 6(1):31–44

Ministry of Health Public Database (2022) https://www.dati.salute.gov.it/dati/dettaglioDataset.jsp?menu=dati&idPag=68, https://www.dati.salute.gov.it/dati/dettaglioDataset.jsp?menu=dati&idPag=2. Accessed March 2022

Nuti S, Seghieri C, Vainieri M, Zett S (2012) Assessment and improvement of the Italian healthcare system: first evidence from a pilot national performance evaluation system. J Healthc Manag 57(3):182–199

Ortiz L (2022) Leveraging the organizational mission statement to communicate identity, distinctiveness and purpose to primary and secondary stakeholders during COVID-19. J Strateg Manag 15(2):234–255

Palttala P, Vos M (2012) Quality indicators for crisis communication to support emergency management by public authorities. J Contingencies Crisis Manage 20(1):39–51

Pearson CM, Clair JA (1998) Reframing crisis management. Acad Manag Rev 23(1):59–76

Reynolds B, Seeger MW (2005) Crisis and emergency risk communication as an integrative model. J Health Commun 10(1):43–55

Robinson OC (2014) Sampling in interview-based qualitative research: a theoretical and practical guide. Qual Res Psychol 11(1):25–41

Romiti A, Del Vecchio M, Milani C, Sartor G (2023) Italian healthcare organizations facing new dimensions: changes in governance structure. J Manage Governance. https://doi.org/10.1007/s10997-021-09618-1

Rothschild L (2020) How companies showcase their values during COVID-19, chief marketer. Accessed March 2022

Saroj A, Pal S (2020) Use of social media in crisis management: a survey. Int J Disaster Risk Reduct 48:101584

Saunders B, Sim J, Kingstone T, Baker S, Waterfield J, Bartlam B et al (2018) Saturation in qualitative research: exploring its conceptualization and operationalization. Qual Quant 52(4):1893–1907

Schoofs L, Fannes G, Claeys AS (2022) Empathy as a main ingredient of impactful crisis communication: the perspectives of crisis communication practitioners. Public Relat Rev 48(1):102150

Schultz PD, Seeger MW (1991) Corporate centered apologia: Iacocca in defense of Chrysler. Speaker Gavel 28(1–4):50–60

Slagle DR, McIntyre JJ, Chatham-Carpenter A, Reed HA (2021) The perfect storm in the midst of a pandemic: the use of information within an institution's concurrent crises. Online Inf Rev 45(4):656–671

Smith JY, Vanecek MT (1990) Dispersed group decision making using nonsimultaneous computer conferencing. J Manag Inf Syst 7:71–92

Tay YX, Bakar RBA, Kaur B (2021) Hospital training challenges during COVID-19 in Singapore: radiographers' experience of continuing professional development in social distancing mode. J Contin Educ Heal Prof 41(1):13–15

Tay K (2020) COVID-19 in Singapore and Malaysia: rising to the challenges of orthopaedic practice in an evolving pandemic. Malays Orthop J 14(2):7–15

Triantafillidou A, Yannas P (2020) Social media crisis communication in racially charged crises: exploring the effects of social media and image restoration strategies. Comput Hum Behav 106:106269

Ulmer RR, Sellnow TL (2000) Consistent questions of ambiguity in organizational crisis communication: Jack in the Box as a case study. J Bus Ethics 25(2):143–155

Ulmer RR, Sellnow TL, Seeger MW (2017) Effective crisis communication: moving from crisis to opportunity. Sage, London, UK

Vainieri M, Ferrè F, Giacomelli G, Nuti S (2017) Explaining performance in health care: how and when top management competencies make the difference. Health Care Manage Rev 44(4):306–317

Veil SR, Husted RA (2012) Best practices as an assessment for crisis communication. J Commun Manag 16(2):131–145

Veil SR, Buehner T, Palenchar MJ (2011) A work-in-process literature review: incorporating social media in risk and crisis communication. J Contingencies Crisis Manag 19(2):110–122

Weick KE (1988) Enacted sensemaking in crisis situations. J Manage Stud 25(4):305–317

Willan J, King AJ, Jeffery K, Bienz N (2020) Challenges for NHS hospitals during COVID-19 epidemic. BMJ 368:m1117

Xu J (2020) Does the medium matter? A meta-analysis on using social media vs. traditional media in crisis communication. Public Relat Rev 46(4):101947

Rethinking Healthcare Organizations in the Era of Covid-19: Lessons From the Pandemic

Guglielmo Bonaccorsi

Abstract COVID 19 pandemic has abruptly changed our way of living, and concurrently has shown the crisis of the welfare systems and their limits in the responsiveness towards acute as well as non-communicable diseases all over the world. The loss of solidarity and community engagement, together with the progressive impoverishment of the general population, has become evident in the delays of the public health responses and interventions: the healthcare organizations have extremely suffered for the economic cuts and for the effects linked to globalization, for instance in the production and provision of personal protective equipments (PPE), assisted breathing devices, first aid drugs but also in the delays of life-saving surgical and medical interventions due to the need of devoting the scarce human and technological resources available to the fight against SARS-CoV-2. To escape from health emergency and back to building health and safe communities we have to realize different care models, which combine clinical and social care, realign care pathways, roles, sites, and services, and invest in the first richness of all the healthcare systems: the healthcare workforce.

1 Introduction

The recent—and still enduring—COVID-19 pandemic has been determining, worldwide, a deep reflections on our public and private healthcare organizations and whether, or not, they are still capable to forefront the many threats to the citizens' health with appropriate and on-time answers.

The significant challenges posed by the pandemic have shown all the limits of our organizations in terms of resources, capabilities, structures: abruptly, we were forced to review and implement a range of COVID-19 specific care practices, widespread testing, tracing, and surveillance activities in the attempt of mitigating transmission and enable the safe reopening of businesses, schools, and other institutions. All these efforts have been made after years and years during which the welfare systems were

G. Bonaccorsi (✉)
Department of Health Sciences, University of Firenze, Florence, Italy
e-mail: guglielmo.bonaccorsi@unifi.it

N. Persiani et al. (eds.), *Challenges of Healthcare Systems in the Era of COVID-19*, Contributions to Management Science, https://doi.org/10.1007/978-3-031-43114-2_2

living a deep crisis of definancing and scarce attention to the policies of recruitment, education and training of healthcare personnel.

The bio-psycho-social paradigm of Medicine, established during the 70's and 80's of the previous century, has been progressively eroded with the affirmation of globalization and capitalism, in which a more individual vision of health has been pursued in many countries.

This has inevitably led to a different vision of welfare, where the main idea was not (or not yet) "health for all"—as established since 1977 by the World Health Organization—that is, the main social objective of governments would be the achievement by the world's population of a level of health that would allow to lead socially and economically productive lives, but instead a sort of "health for me", where the level of expected health returns to be, as before the Second World War, an affair of individual economic capacities as well as a person's choice to invest—or not—on his/her own health.

As in the previous pandemics (Spanish Flu, only to cite an example) this is not the right approach: investment in health promotion, prevention and capacity building is the only way to effectively forefront any emergence, not only caused by a virus or of acute nature, but also to fight against the pervasive epidemic of chronic diseases which threaten the majority of the populations at all ages, from childhood to aging.

And, as a matter of fact, during the first and the second COVID-19 pandemic waves many of the necessary services to persons with various degrees of chronic diseases have been denied or postponed, with significant effects in terms of loss of health. In fact, if the pandemic has imposed to implement new strategies to maintain continuity of care for patients with ongoing medical and social needs, at the same time, safety concerns have caused a massive drop in elective services and required many organizations to shift quickly to telehealth, not with the same results of in-presence services.

The disruption which affected healthcare services worldwide has often preceded and followed COVID-19 waves, with an impact which has been different and with no clear patterns by country income group or pandemic intensity, which testifies, once again, the axiom that in emergencies "we come out all together or nobody comes out". The consequences have been, and still are, well visible: loss of human lives and suffering; long-lasting psychosocial impact; economic slowdown.

In this picture, the attempt of rethinking healthcare organizations in the era of the Covid-19 seems like *a rhino walking on a thread*: the health care ecosystem and the consumers they serve have faced an unfamiliar world of remote working, virtual doctor visits, and a supply chain marked by shortages of medical supplies, personnel, and services; these areas have been rapidly transforming to meet the new challenges: deploying technology and security protocols to support a newly virtual workforce; swiftly scaling virtual health services for COVID-19 and non-COVID-19 patients alike; forming new partnerships to produce and procure—sometimes desperately—needed capabilities, treatments, and supplies.

2 Methods

Of course, there have been distinctions in the kind and intensity of public answer by the nations involved in the pandemic: we know very well that the "world" has many different speeds according to richness, human rights, social conditions. For this reason, it is fundamental to put a global system in place to prevent rich nations from hoarding vaccines, diagnostics, and medicines in this, as in other potential, future pandemics because health is a human right of all the people who live in this planet.

Even though contingency plans were often already in place, healthcare systems seemed unable to cope with the sudden, intense surge in demand, to absorb and manage swift and persistent pressures on their workload, especially in the settings of acute care. And, finally, this has revealed the importance of attributing more emphasis on preventive measures, remote care, and substantial technological dependence, that is a real recover and rediscovery of "health for all" approach, though in a new perspective and with differing interventions. According to the WHO, "health for all" does not in fact aim to eradicate diseases or disabilities, but aims to evenly distribute health resources so that health care can be accessible to all. The starting point is undoubtedly represented by ensuring sustainable universal health coverage (avoiding the impoverishment of states), which is the basis also for achieving the seventeen Sustainable Development Goals of the Agenda 2030 (UN Organization, 2017).

The past cannot return, and we know very well nowadays that we have to build an expected next, new, normal in healthcare systems: this "normal" must be founded on a set of universal values that cannot be neglected anymore in healthcare, as accessibility, affordability, effectiveness, equitable care, long-term wellbeing and sustainability.

In this process, communication and sharing with all the stakeholders become imperative: we must build trust and bridges with patients and the communities served and make this a measurable strategic priority; this is possible by means of new domains in patients and citizens' engagement as individual Health Literacy, and particularly, Organizational Health Literacy. The first one is the set of knowledge, competencies and motivations which let the persons to acquire the ability to access, understand, appraise and apply health information to make judgments and decisions in everyday life about care, prevention and health promotion pathways to maintain or improve quality of life throughout the entire lifecourse; the second one is the mean to create health literate organizations, that is structures and services which respond to the persons' needs not according to their capacities of expressing their health problems, but instead to the magnitude of the needs to take in charge. In promoting the two dimensions of HL, we can create a pathway and a bridge between individual capacities—to be implemented—and renewed healthcare organizations, which must become easily to be navigated.

3 Discussion

Some keypoints of the future asset of the public health systems appear to be clear: the timing of the responses to be given, with no or less delays; the instance of building long-term health care resiliency; the capacity building in different sectors: in laboratory testing; in the fast-tracked implementation of new technologies, and more; in the answer to the mental health concerns, which are becoming a priority of the new century; the consideration of the ethical concerns, together with the potential rationing of insufficient resources, which risk to creating moral and practical problems; and finally the unsolved criticality linked to the protection of privacy and personal data during times of crises and onwards, especially in relation with the collection, analysis and use of big data to find some common patterns of diseases and cure.

It is here and now that globalization must be transformed from a key to warrant an economic perspective to the markets towards a mean to reach a global health approach, according to a new vision which denies a "my country first" nationalist approach to choose to work cooperatively through shared governance, re-imagining a global health governance and alliance between rich and poor nations: failure to strengthen global governance could lead to permanent nationalist retrenchment and international organization collapse, with enormous negative consequences.

This hazard is attributable also to the impact of the pandemic on the professionals: COVID fatigue is in fact taking an enormous toll on healthcare workers, and as the pandemic has progressed, clinicians and healthcare professionals have had to navigate numerous policy changes, diagnostic discrepancies and treatment developments, which have been hard to manage.

And in the middle of this perfect storm, the impact associated with an aging population and an increased prevalence of noncommunicable diseases (41 million deaths each year, or 71 percent of all deaths globally) make vital that knowledge-driven care has to be standardized and aligned across healthcare organizations in order to improve patient outcomes and alleviate pressures on healthcare systems before, during and after the current pandemic.

No country acting alone can respond effectively to health threats in a globalized world: though international institutions are facing increasing pressures from nationalist governments, detrimental to global solidarity, there is still and stronger a need for a coordinated international approach for future responses to COVID-19: a new governance landscape is crucial to strengthening global public health rising out of crisis to secure a safer future.

In our nation—Italy—as well as in other countries, the new perspective is taken forward by means of the National recovery and resilience plan approach, which foresees the future of the health and healthcare system as depending from other social dimensions (digitalization; green revolution and ecological transition; sustainable mobility; education and research; social inclusion). The keyword of this process is resilience. Resilience let—or should allow—reorganizing the healthcare system by a changing paradigm: from a hospital-centered to a "widespread", territorial, vision, in which each structure has its own dignity, in a perspective which foresees a cross-walk from medical hegemony to a multiprofessional approach, thanks to which the different healthcare professionals can use extensive communication, collaboration, and innovation. A diffuse healthcare system, near to citizens, in which prevention, early diagnosis, patient education are priority choices.

to maintain people healthy, to act on subjects at risk, to take care of the frail and the sick persons—in this hierarchical order. A new hierarchy of needs towards a proactive, instead of waiting, medicine.

4 Conclusion

What do we need, first?

We need more resources: dedicated staffs and workflows to support care coordination and information sharing across providers and settings, including home- and community-based settings; robust data infrastructures enabling population health management, proactive identification of and communication with at-risk patient groups, and continuous monitoring and management of patients with chronic conditions; established telehealth platforms capable of handling quick shifts from in-person care delivery to technology-supported virtual care delivery and management, leveraging existing telehealth platforms and expanding telehealth offerings. That is, resources to implement the new paradigm of health: improving care equity, access to care, overall quality; shifting site of service closer to home and community; developing processes to address social needs.

Moreover: we need to fight against fake news, which in public health produce deaths and ill people. Though health literacy remains a challenge for the majority of citizens and patients all over Europe and worldwide, there is an increasing number of resources available to support breaking barriers of communication between healthcare professionals and citizens and patients, such as patient-centered evidence-based information leaflets (as in the case of COVID-19 symptoms, vaccination effectiveness and side-effects, and many other pieces of info);

Informative content must be delivered in a format that allows citizens/patients to revisit what they have learned to further highlight the risks, side effects and benefits of treatments.

With education and HL being key to acute and chronic disease management, this could help reduce the number of inappropriate hospital admissions (in the shortage of hospital beds causing by COVID-19) and sustain the delivery of quality patient care in a so difficult timeframe.

The obstacles are, of course many: we are calling to solve increasing costs (owing to resource needs for equipment, disposable medical supplies, and personal protective equipment; increase in pharmaceutical costs due to shortages as well as use of specific medications for treatment, see for instance monoclonal antibodies; salaries and wages; digital equipment;…); to develop digital health to support effective prevention, prediction, and disease management; to find the way to use and share data, eliminating data silos and realizing automating data integration to support the recognition of unseen and/or unexpected patterns, to apply new intelligence to service patients and caregivers, creating value across the care continuum and providing data for public health authorities.

Some trajectories have been already traced to pursue these objectives: we need to develop leadership in healthcare organization management, that is to form leaders able to generate the biggest possible impact on the largest number of people at the lowest possible cost; moreover, to attribute the right service to those who are in health needs, we have to implement population segmentation and risk stratification, to tailor prevention and care for/on specific groups. This is still a useful but controversial approach because it raises other questions: what does population segmentation really mean? what is its role in the rethinking of healthcare systems? What are the risks for privacy? Questions to which we must find appropriate and shared answers.

Regarding the repercussions on the healthcare systems beyond the present pandemic, we have to study and experiment new, or different care models and resource financing, enhancing and promoting the best practices used during the critical phases of COVID-19, as for instance better cooperation through public–private partnerships, combining clinical and social care, and taking other measures to realign care pathways, roles, sites, and services; the demand for digital health care, and the use of digital technologies, has rapidly grown among both patients and physicians—see remote patient monitoring (RPM) and home monitoring; and finally, governance and decision making must be founded on solid data and analytics: healthcare systems faced a huge challenge in implementing data and analytics to inform and improve their mitigation measures, but there is a strong need for clarity and standardization in such areas as interoperability, along with data infrastructure and definitions—starting with standard patient outcome definitions.

In conclusion: COVID-19 pandemic revealed to all the stakeholders—the citizens, the healthcare professionals, the management, the politicians—the many problems suffered by our public healthcare systems, greatly known but long ignored and that finally showed us the heavy bill to pay. Rich nations realized they have much to learn from less wealthy nations, including the importance of investing in public health infrastructure, engaging communities in tackling public health crises, and using clear and consistent public health messaging.

But there are also positive elements to promote: we are getting better at fighting scientific misinformation and disinformation; conspiracy theories, bogus remedies, and anti-science ideas have abounded during COVID-19, from the bizarre notion that Bill Gates has put a microchip inside COVID-19 vaccines to the many dangerous assertions by former Presidents, such as his argument that injecting disinfectant or bringing "light inside the body" could cure COVID-19; we are taking steps also in social media communication, in spite of the fact that they have given anti-vaxxers and other science denialists a bigger platform for their dangerous views.

But, first of all, we have rediscovered to possess an extraordinary healthcare workforce: while the pandemic has hit health care workers incredibly hard, they've shown the resiliency and determination to emerge stronger from it. Health care organizations should seize this opportunity to bring human-focused solutions to the center of their recovery and lay the groundwork for a more agile workforce.

Reference

Transforming our world: the 2030 Agenda for Sustainable Development A/RES/70/1, United Nations General Assembly, 21st October, 2015

Italian Health Professions of the Technical, Rehabilitation and Prevention Areas to Support the Reform of Reference Healthcare System After Covid-19 Pandemic

Martina Giusti and Niccolò Persiani

Abstract The 19 Italian health professions of the technical, of rehabilitation and of prevention areas can offer an effective contribution in the identification of the priority interventions to apply in this moment of reform of the healthcare systems. Firstly they had to manage the onset of the COVID-19 pandemic and to control the post-acute phase in the European context. This research aims to support the reform of the Italian healthcare system offering to decision-makers the feedback on the COVID-19 management and the suggestions of reorganization and innovation by the health professions of the technical, of rehabilitation and of prevention areas due to their experience in frontline. The point of view of these health professionals was obtained by the analysis of the position paper written by their most significant associations following the first wave of infections by COVID-19 pandemic in Italy (May 2020). The research group has analysed the considered papers by contents analysis. For the engaged health professions, the strengthening of the Italian healthcare system will start from improving the integrated health and social taking charge of assisted persons by multi-professional teams in all health and social care settings, both in hospitals, in local primary care centres and at the patients' home. It will be possible, if the current essential levels of assistance will be enlarged especially with the inclusion of the services' provison also at home. For doing that in the easiest and the most effective way, the bureaucracy will be reduced. At the end, the work done by all recognized Italian health professions will be adequately valorised making available their specific competences to population in all possible field of action, not exclusively in hospital or in the public sector. At worldwide level, the digital reform of the healthcare system is considered crucial and propaedeutic for the implementation of telemedicine and remote monitoring. This reform is fundamental also in Italy for overcoming the current hospital-centred organization of the healthcare system. These proposals are useful not only for Italy but for all countries that are involved in

M. Giusti (✉) · N. Persiani
Department of Experimental and Clinical Medicine, University of Florence, Florence, Italy
e-mail: martina.giusti@unifi.it

N. Persiani
e-mail: niccolo.persiani@unifi.it

N. Persiani et al. (eds.), *Challenges of Healthcare Systems in the Era of COVID-19*,
Contributions to Management Science, https://doi.org/10.1007/978-3-031-43114-2_3

the reform of the reference healthcare system to be able to respond in the best way to the emerged and the emerging population health needs, especially working on the health prevention and promotion of the wellness and well-being.

Keywords Post COVID-19 · Healthcare system · Reform · Health professions of the technical, of rehabilitation and of prevention areas

JEL classification codes H11 structure · Scope and performance of government · H12 crisis management · I15 health and economic development

1 Introduction

The worldwide COVID-19 pandemic has changed the way of conceiving and experiencing the relationship between patient and healthcare systems in compliance with the common rules of prevention and control of infection's risks (WHO 2020; Filia, Urdiales and Rota 2020). In the first stages of the COVID-19 pandemic, healthcare systems showed to be unprepared to manage this infective emergency both for adequately applying the required actions for contagious' containment at the population level and for the treatment of this new disease as occurred. This led to implement extemporaneous measures aimed only at the response to acute conditions. The informative and educative needs of all population, instead, were not satisfied for a long time, especially in the first COVID-19 pandemic wave. At the forefront, each health professional was called to rethink and to reorganise the own working activity and settings to continue to provide the health care services in safety for patients, colleagues and oneself according to general indications decreed at the international, national and local level. It was possible drawing on the specific professional competences.

Italy was of particular interest to the entire scientific community, compared to other countries, being in temporal order the first western country to be severely hit by COVID-19 infection after China (Remuzzi and Remuzzi 2020; Porcheddu et al. 2020). In Italy, a bed was always guaranteed within hospital settings for all the most serious cases that required hospitalisation for observation, sub-intensive or intensive therapy. It was possible thank to the creation of a national hospitals' network capable of monitoring the demand and directing it towards the offer, wherever it was in the whole national territory. It was permitted by a strong national coordination between the different regional healthcare systems (Pascerella et al. 2020). At the same time, positive asymptomatic or pauci-symptomatic people with all outpatients, who commonly have used health service in primary care centres, nursing houses or in their homes, were abandoned. The Italian healthcare system especially evidenced the limits of a hospital-centred health organization with the critical issues related to the management and the control of taking charge of patients in local health facilities and at home. The local assistance was the weak link in the healthcare chain, since it was not independent from the hospital in the provision of visits, diagnostic examination, rehabilitative treatments and technical-assistance pathways.

These problems favored the discussion for identifying suitable and sustainable proposals for the reform and the reorganisation of the Italian healthcare system. The main goal is the structured, efficient and effective strengthening of the local network of health facilities to lighten the pressure on hospitals. As much as possible the supply of health services must be improved at local level, moving it from hospital to the local network of health facilities. This network will be composed of structures as close as possible to population, if not even at the patients' home. At the same time, taking charge of every person must be responsibility of flexible an resilient multi-professional and multi-disciplinary team, which will include health professionals both of hospital and of local health structures. This organization will be of support to guarantee over time a rapid response to health needs of the population, allowing not to abandon especially more frail subjects. Elderly, patients with chronic diseases, disabled people, both with physic and mental problems, must be, in fact, constantly followed up and monitored for their precarious health conditions. Having to live with the possibility of a constant increase in infections (WHO 2021), the protection of the health of every citizen and the assistance of the current assisted persons require measures capable of identifying emerging needs and preparing timing action plans of reorganization thought the enlargement of the health care network, delocalising at the local level and at the patients' home the provision of health care service and the health assistance (Compagni et al. 2010; Morando et al. 2017; Fantini et al. 2015). It will allow an effective taking charge of general population and people with chronic diseases for follow-up, prevention initiatives, controls and follow-up in all primary health care centres and at home, while in hospitals will be assisted only persons in acute/critical health conditions.

According to this approach, on May 2020 Italian government's with the "Relaunch Decree" (Decree-Law 34/2020) invited Regions and Autonomous Provinces to develop and implement plans to strengthen and reorganise the local health assistance in collaboration with their Prevention Departments, general practitioners, primary care paediatricians and doctors engaged in transitional cares as well as with the special units for continuity of assistance. These plans must move from the proposals made by all health care system stakeholders to not neglect anyone's specific health and social needs and for overcoming critical issues due to the fragmentation of the health care services provision. Among stakeholders, the Italian health professions of the technical, of rehabilitation and of prevention areas (19 of the 22 currently health professionals recognised in Italy) shall be certainly included because they have been a characteristic and multiple point of views on Italian healthcare system, included the private dimension. In fact, these professionals stood out for supporting the management of the outbreak in different fields: from the instrumental diagnosis to the rehabilitative support, from the technical remote supervision of persons at home by tele-assistance to the monitoring of contagioust. They proved to possess both a reactive and proactive approach in relation to evolving needs. It showed their capability to be able to quickly adapt their practices according to emerging changes. Last but not the least, in the last 20 years these health professions have accompanied and promoted the technological and digital evolution of the medical and biomedical sectors that has improved the quality, increased the performance and innovated the healthcare system all over the world. It has expanded the health services offered to the user, not being afraid to get involved for the progress of medicine. For these reasons, the purpose of this work is to collect the feedback about the management of the COVID-19 emergency in the first wave by the health professions of the technical, of rehabilitation and of prevention areas (March–June 2020). Moving from the emerged critical issues, the proposals coming from these professionals will be useful for decision-makers for developing effective reform policies of the Italian healthcare system. In the acute and post-acute phases of the COVID-19. The contribution of these professionals in the planning of the reform projects is crucial for two reasons. On one hand, they have the best knowledge of the state-of-art of the Italian healthcare system, about its limits and its possibilities of improvement and development. On the other hand, they will be among the main actors of the decentralization of the health care services' provision.

2 Method

After the publication of the Decree-Law 34/2020, the Italian National Federation of Orders of Health Professions of the Technical, of Rehabilitation and of Prevention areas formally requested (Rome, Prot. N. 592/2020) to the most representative associations (MRAs) of its 19 health professions the presentation of a contribution, where they offered proposals for reforming the Italian healthcare system in relation to their experience during the COVID-19 pandemic. The Federation suggest to focus on the improvement of the territorial assistance as main goal of the reform, according to its strategy vision of future Italian healthcare system (Krippendorff 1989). In first instance, MRAs were engaged in absence of the national commissions of each profession due to the unavailability to call elections because of the COVID-19 pandemic. Moreover, during all the COVID-19 emergency, the MRAs especially supported health professional in the transposition of the international and national recommendations in the undertaking of their daily work as well as to create opportunities of discussion and comparison about different aspects of the professional sphere.

A qualitative content analysis (Mayring 2004) was conducted on the documents arrived at the Federation by MRAs of the Italian 19 health professions to identify among different feedbacks, coming from heterogeneous experiences, similar detected critical issue and common proposals to support the reform of the Italian healthcare system. In fact, each one of these professions have different mandates (diagnosis, assistance, rehabilitation and prevention) but all contribute together to a single objective, the protection and restoration of public and individual health (Table 1).

The documents received from the MRAs were read in parallel by two researchers to identify the common elements and the different proposals made by the professions for distinctive contexts and specific purposes. At the end of the content analysis

Table 1 Correspondence among Italian health professions of technical, rehabilitation and prevention areas and their most representative associations

Health professions	Most representative associations
Rehabilitation area (Class 2)	
Podiatrist	International mercury podiatrists association (AMPI) and Italian podiatrists association (AIP)
Physiotherapist	Commission of physiotherapists register Italian physiotherapists association (AIFI)
Speech therapist	Italian speech therapists federation (FLI)
Orthoptist/assistant in ophthalmology	Italian orthoptist/assistant in ophthalmology association (AIORAO)
Developmental neuro and psychomotor therapist	Italian development neuro and psychomotor therapists association (AITNE)
Occupational therapist	Italian occupational therapists association (AITO)
Professional educator	
Psychiatric rehabilitation technician	Italian occupational therapists association (AITeRP)
Technical area (Class 3)	
Orthopaedic technician	Italian orthopaedic technicians association (AnTOi) and national orthopaedic techniques operators federation (FIOTO)
Biomedical laboratory technician	Italian biomedical laboratory technicians federation (FITeLaB) and Italian biomedical laboratory technicians association (ANTeL)
Radiographer	Italian radiographers' scientific associations federation (FASTeR)
Audiometric technician	
Hearing aid technician	National hearing aid technicians association (ANAP)
Dietitian	National dietitians association (ANDID)
Neurophysiopathologist	Italian neurophysiopathologist technicians association (AITN)
Technician of cardiocirculatory physiopathology and cardiovascular perfusion	Italian associations of the technicians of cardiocirculatory physiopathology and cardiovascular perfusion (AITeFeP)
Dental hygienist	National dental hygienists union (UNID) and Italian dental hygienists association (AIDI)
Prevention area (Class 4)	

(continued)

Table 1 (continued)

Health professions	Most representative associations
Environmental and workplace prevention technician	National environmental and workplace prevention technicians association (UNPISI) and Italian environmental and workplace prevention technician association (AITeP)
Healthcare assistant	National healthcare assistants association (AsNAS)

and the categorization of the proposals, the two researchers discussed together the divergent results to arrive to a joint decision about them. In this way it will be possible to outline the suggestions by the health professions of the technical, of rehabilitation and of prevention areas about the reorganisation of the Italian healthcare system, strengthening the territorial assistance.

3 Results and Discussion

From the analysis of the MRAs documents, the health professions of the technical, rehabilitation and prevention areas reported seven main critical issues related to the management of the COVID-19 health emergency by the Italian healthcare system (Table 2).

Most of the health professionals identified the chronic shortage of staff as the main problem in the management of the COVID-19 pandemic. This condition brought to satisfy the minimum population health needs already before this emergency with a lot of difficulties mainly related to the lack of time and the impossibility to apply action of optimization and improvement of the practise. The problem was especially attributed to the spending review policies applied in the last 20 years in the Italian public healthcare sector. The consequences were multiple, in particular, the lack of innovation in the health sector and the insufficient availability of positions both in bachelor's and in master's degrees of the health professionals. In fact, in Italy the training positions of each health profession are related to the request of the professionals made by the same Italian healthcare system. This caused the lack of enough trained professionals to be employed during the emergency phase of the COVID-19 pandemic, when there were resources to new hirings. On the other side, the shortage of personnel was due also to the attraction of private health sector. Year by year the private sector offered always higher salaries than public, while the public sector reduced its benefits over time. The under sizing of the offer in comparison with the wide request brings awfully to the spreading of professional abusiveness.

At the same time, the reduction of bureaucracy concerning decision-making and intervention processes in the COVID-19 emergency has been well seen. In fact, it encouraged the greater collaboration among health professions and between the public and private sectors, with the enlargement of available health services for the

Table 2 Critical issues of the Italian healthcare system in the management of the COVID-19 pandemic

Areas	Health professions	Staff shortage	Professional abusiveness	Lack of university training offer and its organization	Reorganisation of taking care models	Bureaucracy	Enlargement of essential levels of assistance	Telemedicine
Rehabilitation	Podiatrist	x	x	x			x	
	Physiotherapist	x						x
	Speech Therapist	x				x	x	
	Orthoptist–assistant in ophthalmology	x			x		x	x
	Developmental neuro and psychomotor therapist	x			x			
	Occupational therapist	x					x	x
	Professional educator	x	x			x	x	
	Psychiatric rehabilitation technician	x			x			
Technical	Orthopaedic technician	x			x	x	x	
	Biomedical laboratory technician							x
	Radiographer				x			x
	Audiometric technician							
	Hearing aid technician			x		x	x	
	Dietitian	x					x	x
	Neurophysiopathologist							x

(continued)

Table 2 (continued)

Areas	Health professions	Staff shortage	Professional abusiveness	Lack of university training offer and its organization	Reorganisation of taking care models	Bureaucracy	Enlargement of essential levels of assistance	Telemedicine
	Technician of cardiocirculatory physiopathology and cardiovascular perfusion							
	Dental hygienist	x						
Prevention	Environmental and workplace prevention technician	x			x			
	Healthcare assistant	x	x		x			

population. The health professionals advocated the maintenance of these positive changes in the post emergency time. Less bureaucracy will make easier the access to some health services that the Italian national healthcare system was already able to offer but which were not included in the national essential levels of assistance yet for the absence of their economic encoding. All regional nomenclatures for outpatient health services or for the provision of protasis supports do not provide all possible health services, in particular of the rehabilitation and of assistence areas. Many professionals of these areas (i.e., podiatrists, speech therapists, orthoptists, occupational therapists, professional educators, orthopaedic technicians, dietitians and hearing care technicians for example) must fight every day against the bureaucratic system to fully perform their work.

It will obviously pass always through the enlargement of the essential level of assistance at national level and their transposition at regional level.

The engaged health professions of the technical, of rehabilitation and of prevention areas perceived the Italian healthcare system as obsolete with its hospital-centred logic. The new architecture of the Italian healthcare system must be based on the integrated social and health taking care of the person by multidisciplinary and multi-professional teams. This will overcome the logic of hyperspecialized medicine and put newly the person at the centre of the healthcare system. The COVID-19 pandemic highlighted how urgent was this change of paradigma into Italian health organizations: from the processes to the patient at the centre of the health care system.

The Italian healthcare system wanted to be in the next future as close as possible not only to the most fragile people but to the entire population in order to ensure the protection and recovery of public health, even during a pandemic. According to this, telemedicine was recognised as an essential tool for the interconnection among all possible health and social assistance settings and the rapid and controlled sharing of health information. It is a matter of moving from the exclusive digitalization of the administrative processes to the inclusion also of the health care pathways. Some health intervention can also be digitalized as well.

Relating the reported seven issues, there were latent needs linked with the characteristics of the field of action and the state of the art of each profession (Fig. 1).

Focusing on each area, the attention of the technical health professions covered spreadly all the identified issues, except for professional abusiveness. There problems were however seen as opportunities for the improvement and the innovation of the Italian healthcare system of tomorrow. The advent of telemedicine was of special interest according to the consolidated experience by these professionals in its implementation, use, and optimization. The professions of the rehabilitation are, indeed, committed to themselves for the full recognition of their work, since essential levels of assistance still did not cover all range of health services that they provide. The inclusion of all their practices will offer wider possibilities of employment, especially in the public sector, both in local health care centres and in hospitals. The current concerns about the chronic shortage of personnel and the absence of integration among taking care models will be overcome.

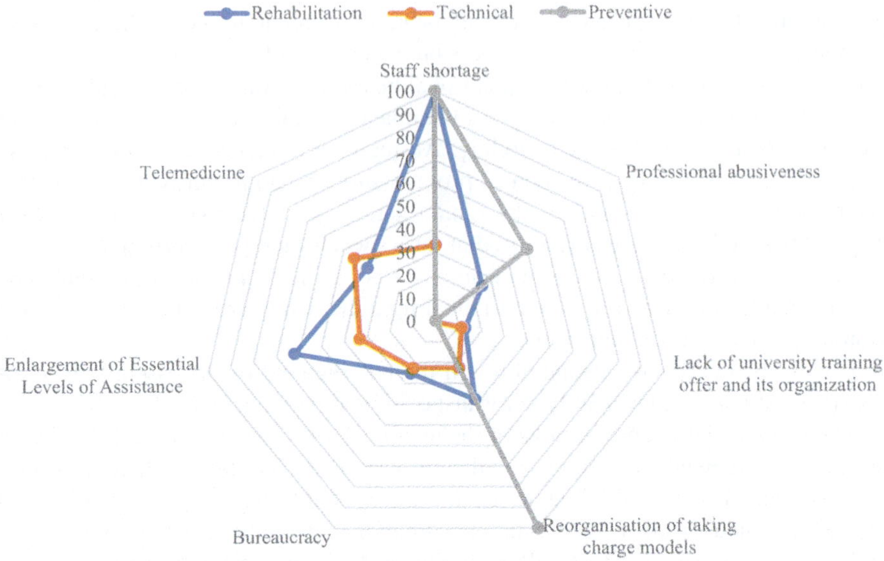

Fig. 1 Critical issues of the Italian healthcare system in the management of the COVID-19 pandemic for professional area (%)

Finally, the professions of prevention area aimed to boost the increase of personnel endowments transposing the law 34/2020, which rightly identified these professionals as the reference figures for the government of the prevention plans for the expertise in their possession, especially after the Covid-19 pandemic.

In relation to the given snapshot of the Italian healthcare system, the 19 engaed health professions of techical, of rehabilitation and of prevention areas purposefully were discussing and rethinking the concept of workplace and professional practice to sustain and simplify the reform process to overcome the hospital-centred organization (Bifulco and Neri 2022). In the next future, they would like to work in every health facility, where their professional competences will be required to satisfy the emerging health needs at hospitals, local districts, outpatients and the patients' home (Ballard et al. 2020). In this way, they will promote the greater garrison of all local health facilities for shortening the distances between population and health care system, processes and health and social needs, health professionals and patients, at the end among people (World Health Organization 2022).

Moreover, the enforcing of local health facilities for these professionals will pass through the strengthening of hospital-territory continuity by the creation of a wider network of multi professional and multi-disciplinary teams. These teams will sustain the timely response outside hospital, although all service are not localetd into the same building but widespread in the territory. The restarting of the health care quality's improvement in health services provision will, in fact, be entrusted to these teams (Franck and O'Brien 2019; Schalkwyk et al. 2020). The mature task-shifting among health professions will be useful to realize effective personalised care paths for accompanying the patient over time, between different assistance settings, and for integrating health and social taking charges (Best and Williams 2019).

At the end, the strengthening of prevention initiatives and campaigns will favor not only the adoption of healthier lifestyles by population and the participation to screening programs for an early diagnosis. They have to increase their impact activating the care of well-being and wellness in the society and the awareness of the fundamental contribution of everyone in the care of the humanity and of the earth according to the "One health" approach (Torales et al. 2020; Lefrançois et al. 2023).

4 Conclusions

The critical analysis of the management of the COVID-19 emergency in Italy by the 19 health professions of the technical, of rehabilitation and of prevention areas offered elements for the proposal of useful suggestions to decision-makers for developing effective reform policies of the Italian healthcare system. In the first acute and post-acute phases of the COVID-19 pandemic, the current organizational structure of the Italian hospital-centric national healthcare system didn't allow the full satisfaction of the health needs of the population by the point of view of the considered professional. Since the reported problems are common in many other countries in all over the world, which have to reform their healthcare system in order to resolve the critical issues encountered, the offered suggestions can be of interested and exploited also in these contexts. The general idea is, in fact, generally approved: the creation of a more resilience, flexiblity and patient-centred healthcare systems in the future based on the integrated health and social taking care of people by multi professional and multidisciplinary team.

To do this, it is necessary to identify a main paths to follow.

The engaged health professions have identified the territorialization of the Italian healthcare system as the strategic and the effective intervention to be close as much as possible to population. It must no longer happen that the health care system leaves alone its users because it is unable to provide a health service outside the hospital or at patient's home. The drivers for this audacious reform process will be mature task-shifting among health professions and the new idea of spread working place in healthcare. Every health professional will lend the health service according to possessed competences and skills in every possible health facility.

Now it is up to the institutional working tables to investigate the made proposals in relation with the economic sustainability of the proposed reform project, the interventions to be promoted for its application, especially for inducing the needed cultural revolution, and the expected positive impact in terms of more efficient provision of the health services, quality improvement, achievement of better health outcomes.

The main limitation of this research was the failure to validate the common proposals, as results of the synthesis carried out by the research group on the data emerging from the parallel reading of the documents received by the MRAs, through focus groups with the representatives of the associations or a sample of professionals. Another limit was the different roles and responsibilities of the considered health professions in each country, which limit the generalisation of the obtained results. Possible developments of this study can be a new analysis of the data collected together with exponents of each profession and an in-depth study of the emerged problems and of the offered proposals. Another interesting development can be the submission of a new survey to the MRAs after sharing their document and this synthesis each other in order to observe whether the identified reference paths are transversally recognized as possible, useful and effective by all 19 Italian health professions of the technical, of rehabilitation and of prevention areas.

Declaration of conflict of interest Nothing to disclosure.

References

Ballard M, Bancroft E, Nesbit J, Johnson A, Holeman I, Foth J, Palazuelos D (2020) Prioritising the role of community health workers in the COVID-19 response. BMJ Glob Health 5(6):e002550

Best S, Williams S (2019) Professional identity in interprofessional teams: findings from a scoping review. J Interprof Care 33(2):170–181

Bifulco L, Neri S (2022) The Italian national health service: universalism, marketization and the fading of territorialization. Forum Soc Econ 51(2):192–206. Routledge

Compagni A, Tediosi F, Tozzi VD (2010) L'integrazione tra ospedale e territorio nelle Aziende Sanitarie in Rapporto OASI 2010. CERGAS Bocconi, Milano, EGE

Decree-Law 19 May 2020, n. 34 of the Italian State Urgent measures regarding health, support for work and the economy, as well as social policies related to the epidemiological emergency from COVID-19. (20G00052) (GU General Series n.128 of 19-05-2020 - Ordinary Supplement n. 21)

DM 666/1994 Podiatrist, https://www.gazzettaufficiale.it/eli/id/1994/12/03/094G0697/sg; DM 741/1994 Physiotherapist, https://www.gazzettaufficiale.it/eli/id/1995/01/09/095G0003/sg; DM 742/1994 Speech Therapist, https://www.gazzettaufficiale.it/eli/id/1995/01/09/095G0004/sg; DM 743/1994 Orthoptist/Assistant in Ophthalmology, https://www.gazzettaufficiale.it/eli/id/1995/01/09/095G0005/sg; DM 56/1997 Developmental Neuro and Psychomotor Therapist, http://www.salute.gov.it/imgs/C_17_normativa_463_allegato.pdf; DM 136/1997 Occupational Therapist, http://www.salute.gov.it/imgs/C_17_normativa_1878_allegato.pdf; DM 520/1998 Professional Educator, https://www.gazzettaufficiale.it/eli/id/1999/04/28/099G0190/sg; DM 182/2001 Psychiatric Rehabilitation Technician, https://www.gazzettaufficiale.it/atto/serie_generale/caricaDettaglioAtto/originario?atto.dataPubblicazioneGazzetta=2001-05-19&atto.codiceRedazionale=001G0233; DM 665/1994 Orthopaedic Technician, https://www.gazzettaufficiale.it/eli/id/1994/12/03/094G0696/sg; DM 745/1994 Biomedical Laboratory Technician, https://www.gazzettaufficiale.it/eli/id/1995/01/09/095G0007/sg; DM 746/1994 Radiographer, http://www.salute.gov.it/imgs/C_17_normativa_1880_allegato.pdf; DM 667/1994 Audiometrist Technician, http://www.salute.gov.it/imgs/C_17_normativa_1865_allegato.pdf; DM 668/1994 Hearing Aid Technician, http://www.salute.gov.it/imgs/C_17_normativa_1869_allegato.pdf; DM 744/1994 Dietitian, https://www.gazzettaufficiale.it/eli/id/1995/01/09/095G0006/sg; DM 183/1995 Neurophysiopathology Technician, https://www.gazzettaufficiale.it/eli/id/1995/05/20/095G0218/sg; DM 316/1998 Technician of Cardiovascular Pathophysiology and Cardiovascular Perfusion, http://www.salute.gov.it/imgs/C_17_normativa_1882_allegato.pdf; DM 137/1999 Dental Hygienist, http://www.salute.gov.it/imgs/C_17_normativa_1874_allegato.pdf; DM 58/1997 Environmental and Workplace Prevention Technician, http://www.salute.gov.it/imgs/C_17_normativa_1877_allegato.pdf; DM 69/1997 Healthcare Assistant, https://www.fnopi.it/archivio_news/leggi/178/DM170197n69.pdf

Fantini MP, Pieri G, Rosa S, Caruso B, Rossi A, Pianori D, Longo F (2015) Definire e programmare le Cure Intermedie nella filiera dei servizi per la fragilità e gli anziani: metodi ed evidenze dal caso della Regione Emilia-Romagna. MECOSAN 93:75–97

Filia A, Urdiales AM, Rota MC (2020) Guida per la ricerca e gestione dei contatti (contact tracing) dei casi di COVID-19. Version on June 25, ii, 41 p. Report ISS COVID-19 n. 53/2020

Franck LS, O'Brien K (2019) The evolution of family-centered care: from supporting parent-delivered interventions to a model of family integrated care. Birth Defects Res 111(15):1044–1059

Krippendorff K (1989) Content analysis

Lefrançois T, Malvy D, Atlani-Duault L, Benamouzig D, Druais PL, Yazdanpanah Y, Lina B (2023) After 2 years of the COVID-19 pandemic, translating one health into action is urgent. Lancet 401(10378):789–794

Mayring P (2004) Qualitative content analysis. A Companion Qual Res 1(2):159–176

Morando V, Prenestini A, Rappini V (2017) Lo sviluppo della Case della Salute: analisi e riflessioni sui risultati del primo censimento nel Servizio Sanitario Nazionale in Rapporto OASI 2017. CERGAS Bocconi, Milano, EGEA.

Pascerella G, Strumia A, Piliego C, Bruno F, Del Buono R, Costa F, Scarlata S, Agrò FE (2020) Covid-19 diagnosis and management: a comprehensive review. J Intern Med 29. https://doi.org/10.1111/joim.13091

Porcheddu R, Serra C, Kelvin D, Kelvin N, Rubino S (2020) Similarity in case fatality rates (CFR) of COVID-19/SARS-COV-2 in Italy and China. Coronavirus pandemic. J Infect Dev Ctries 14(2):125–128. https://doi.org/10.3855/jidc.12600

Remuzzi A, Remuzzi G (2020) COVID-19 and Italy: what next? Lancet 395:1225–1228. https://doi.org/10.1016/S0140-6736(20)30627-9

Torales J, O'Higgins M, Castaldelli-Maia JM, Ventriglio A (2020) The outbreak of COVID-19 coronavirus and its impact on global mental health. Int J Soc Psychiatry 66(4):317–320

van Schalkwyk MC, Bourek A, Kringos DS, Siciliani L, Barry MM, De Maeseneer J, McKee M (2020) The best person (or machine) for the job: rethinking task shifting in healthcare. Health Policy 124(12):1379–1386

World Health Organization (2020) Critical preparedness, readiness and response actions for COVID-19: interim guidance, 7 March 2020 (Available here: https://iris.who.int/handle/10665/331422)

World Health Organization (2021) Framework and toolkit for Infection prevention and control in outbreak preparedness, readiness and response at the national level

World Health Organization (2022) Considerations for integrating COVID-19 vaccination into immunization programmes and primary health care for 2022 and beyond

Location Strategies of Healthcare Facilities: The Case of Private Hospitals in Ankara

Cansu Guller and Cigdem Varol

Abstract The location decision of healthcare facilities is complicated because it is a long-term decision and relocating the facilities can be costly. The study aims to analyze the relative importance of criteria in the locational choices of healthcare facilities. To achieve this, the criteria for the location strategies of private healthcare facilities were examined in different districts of Ankara. Six main criteria, including the demographic structure of the district, environmental factors, building features, locational factors, competition dynamics, and investment costs were determined for private hospital site selection. The relative importance of these criteria was evaluated based on in-depth interviews with the managers of twelve private hospitals selected from different districts regarding their location choices. The findings obtained from the interviews were analyzed by converting them into normalized comparison matrices to make comparisons among the districts. Consequently, the most effective factors in the location strategies of private hospitals in Ankara were determined to be competition dynamics, building features, and investment costs, respectively. It was revealed that the site selection of private hospitals differed depending on the socio-economic characteristics of the districts. The results obtained in this study are crucial for determining effective location strategies for new private or public hospital investments.

Keywords Privatization · Commercialization · Private healthcare facilities · Location of hospitals · Ankara

JEL Classification Codes F68 Economic Impacts of Globalization: Policy · I11 Analysis of Health Care Markets · L22 Firm Organization and Market Structure · P46 Other Economic Systems: Consumer Economics · Health · Education and

---

C. Guller (✉)
Faculty of Architecture and Design, Department of City and Regional Planning, Atatürk University, Erzurum, Turkey
e-mail: cansu.guller@atauni.edu.tr

C. Varol
Faculty of Architecture, Department of City and Regional Planning, Gazi University, Ankara, Turkey
e-mail: cvarol@gazi.edu.tr

N. Persiani et al. (eds.), *Challenges of Healthcare Systems in the Era of COVID-19*, Contributions to Management Science, https://doi.org/10.1007/978-3-031-43114-2_4

Training · Welfare · Income · Wealth · and Poverty · R53 Public Facility Location Analysis • Public Investment and Capital Stock

1 Introduction

Health services are one of the most basic elements that are effective in the social and economic development of a country. It is important to provide these services in terms of quality and quantity, since they have a social nature and concern the entire population. The right to health, which is a fundamental human right, is defined in the World Health Organization (WHO) Convention in 1947 as a state of complete physical, mental and social well-being. In 1948, the Universal Declaration of Human Rights (Article 25) stated that everyone should have adequate living standards for their health and well-being (Universal Declaration of Human Rights 1978). In 1978, at the Alma-Ata International Conference on Primary Health Care Services, it was emphasized that everyone should benefit from health services equally (Alma-Ata International Conference 1978).

The World Health Organization's definition of "health services are a public function even in countries where the economic function of the state is minimal" reveals the public aspect of health services and in relation with this governments are principal responsible for securing human health (WHO 2000). However, today, the private sector is also involved in providing and financing health services in many countries (Altay 2007). The main reason for that is the worldwide economic crisis in the early 1970s. After the economic crisis, there have been many reforms in public expenditures, and privatization has been one of the policy tools used to control the growth rate of public expenditures. Since the mid-1970s, privatization of health services has been realized in many countries (Janssen and Made 1990). As, healthcare services are unique in that they have a direct impact on the well-being of society and can significantly improve the quality of life, they differ from other goods and services produced in the economy. Privatization of healthcare services does not involve the sale or transfer of health institutions to the private sector as is done in other sectors. Instead, it supports the growth and development of private health institutions and private sector investment. It is crucial that public investments in the health sector continue, especially in developing countries like Turkey, where there is a middle-income level and significant income distribution inequalities (Stiglitz 1994).

The locational preferences of healthcare services change due to different criteria. In public services, the necessary conditions for a fair spatial distribution of health services, from family health centers, which is the lowest level of health services, to specialized hospitals, are defined by development plans (Satılmış et al. 2021). However in private services, the investigator determines the site selection considering various criteria evaluating efficiency and competition conditions (Tynkkynen and Vrangbæk 2018).

The state that is responsible for securing the right to health, should provide adequate, sustainable and accessible healthcare. Today, especially with the Covid-19 pandemic, the importance of providing health services and access to these services has increased even more. Unequal spatial distribution of health facilities has caused inequalities in the access to health services (Wang 2012). In this context, it appears as an important issue to evaluate the spatial distribution of health services in the cities and to reveal the factors that affect the location selection decisions, in terms of providing health services equally.

The selection of the optimal hospital location is vital for the efficiency, quality and equity of healthcare services. Irrational location decisions of healthcare services increase the investment and maintenance costs and cause customer dissatisfaction. It also affects the increase in morbidity (disease) and mortality (death) rates (Daskin and Dean 2005). Currently, in the example of Covid-19 pandemic, governments were forced to construct pandemic hospitals in a short period of time to overcome the emergency response problems. Two hospitals were built in ten days to respond to the increasing cases in China, and many countries like Turkey decided to do it in 45 days (Gül and Güneri 2021). In addition, many hospitals served as pandemic hospitals during this time. In this process, the importance of the spatial location decisions of existing hospitals increased even more.

In academic studies the criteria for the selection of hospital sites are grouped under six headings: environmental factors, building characteristics, competition factors, investment costs, location of the building, and demographic characteristics. Environmental factors are mainly defined as governmental regulations for the protection of the environment (Lin et al. 2010; Gül and Güneri 2021; Assad 2019; Wibowo 2014), distance from the noise sources (Abdullahi et al. 2014), proximity to the main roads, and absence of traffic congestion (Soltani and Marandi 2011). Building characteristics are defined as the noticeability of the hospital by users (Organ and Tekin 2017), presence of adequate infrastructure (Pınar and Antmen 2019), land size (Soltani and Marandi 2011; Islam et al. 2016), land uses such as reserve areas (Noon and Hankins 2001; Beheshtifar and Alimoahmmadi 2015; Kim et al. 2015; Kmail et al. 2017; Çelikbilek 2018), and quality of architectural structure (Baran 2018). Competition factors are described as competition with existing hospitals (Chiu and Tsai 2013; Şahin et al. 2019) and distance to existing hospitals (Burkey 2012; Shariff et al. 2012). Investment costs are defined by the criteria of construction regulation costs (Chiu and Tsai 2013), environmental regulation costs (Organ and Tekin 2017), and land costs (Wu et al. 2007; Lin et al. 2010). The location of the building consists of centrality (distance from densely populated areas) (Kaveh et al. 2020) and accessibility (Murad 2007; Burkey 2012; Wu et al. 2012; Daskin and Dean 2005). Demographic characteristics are defined as population density (Vahidnia et al. 2009; Murad 2005), income level (Kim et al. 2015; Wu et al. 2007), and targeted population density (usually population aged 65 and above) (Lee and Moon 2014; Abdullahi et al. 2014; Kahraman et al. 2019) criteria. In academic studies, suitable locations have been determined based on these criteria and models for the site selection of new health services have been developed accordingly. In this article, the spread of the Covid-19 pandemic will be included in the evaluation of location selection decisions of health services as well. When diseases such as pandemics affect the entire population, it is expected that health services will be provided equally to the entire population without any distinction.

Within this context, the aim of this study is to evaluate the most effective criteria for the location preferences of healthcare services based on the private sector and to determine the deficiencies in the provision of health services in Ankara, Turkey. In accordance with this aim, after the introduction, in the second part the development of healthcare services in Turkey is given. The third part consists of the material-method part, which includes the scope and methodology of the study, the fourth part includes the findings of the study, and the fifth part consists of the discussion and conclusion. It is expected that the study will guide for the future site selection models of healthcare services. The determination of the most effective criteria for the private hospital site selection in today's conditions is important in terms of contributing to the policy development of local governments for the provision of health services.

2 Healthcare Service Development in Turkey

The target of privatization of health institutions was initially stated in Turkey's Sixth Development Plan (1990–1994). After that, at the National Health Congress held in 1992 and the Second National Health Congress held in 1993, decisions were taken to privatize hospitals for the restructuring of health services (Kasapoğlu 2016).

The developments in hospital and bed capacity between 1985 and 2018 in Turkey are given in Table 1.

In 1985, the private sector accounted for 16% of the hospitals and 5% of the bed capacity in Turkey, and in 2018, private hospitals increased to 37% of all hospitals and constituted 22% of the bed capacity. While there was an increase of 58% in the number of public hospitals between 1985 and 2018, the number of hospitals in the private sector increased by 400%. When the increase in the number of beds in the

Table 1 Development of public and private sector hospital and bed capacity

Years	Public		Private	
	Number of hospitals	Bed capacity	Number of hospitals	Bed capacity
1985	607	99,044	115	4,874
1990	732	114,508	125	6,230
1995	843	127,138	166	8,934
2002	885	152,084	271	12,387
2005	903	157,096	293	13,876
2010	950	172,176	489	28,063
2015	971	166,003	562	43,645
2018	959	181,717	575	50,196

Source TUIK, Health Statistics (2020)

same period was compared, there was an increase of 83% in the public sector, while the rate of increase in the number of beds in the private sector was 930%.

In Fig. 1, per capita health expenditures of some countries from around the world are given. Despite the liberalization experienced all over the world, the role of the public sector in health expenditures is still significant. The main reason is that the health sector has different characteristics from other goods and services produced in the market. Even in many countries where private market conditions dominate, it is seen that most of the health expenditures are still undertaken by the public. Similar to this trend in the world, the health sector in Turkey is mainly served by the public sector (79%). The share of the private sector in hospital investments is 21% (URL-1). The competent authority for the provision of health services in Turkey is the Ministry of Health of the Republic of Turkey. In addition to the ministry, municipalities and private sector investors also play an important role in the delivery of health services. The health services are provided at three levels in Turkey. The lowest level of healthcare services generally consist of family health centers and pharmacies. The second level of health services consists of public and private hospitals, branch hospitals, district polyclinics and medical laboratories. The highest level of health services consists of education and research hospitals and university hospitals (URL-2). At the beginning of the Covid-19 pandemic, the delivery of health services was carried out in cooperation with national and international institutions and organizations under the coordination of the Ministry of Health. Thanks to these efforts, measures have been taken to prevent the spread of the disease in Turkey and support the treatment (Satılmış et al. 2021). In addition to these measures, some health institutions in cities have been authorized for Covid 19 testing (URL-3) such as public hospitals, private hospitals, university hospitals and medical laboratories.

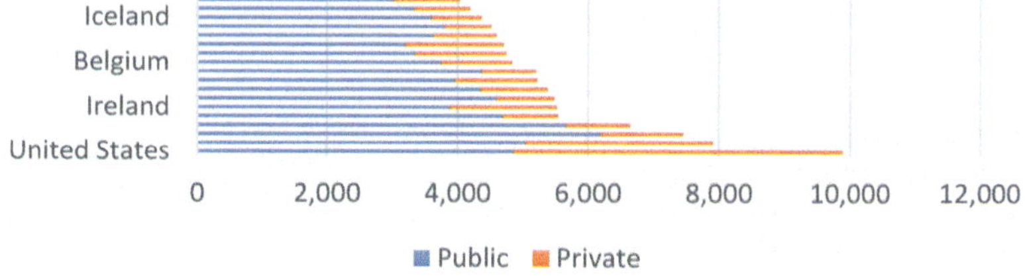

Fig. 1 Public and private health expenditure per capita in selected countries in 2016 (in U.S. dollars) (URL-1)

3 Material and Methods

The locational preferences of healthcare services have become more crucial during the Covid-19 pandemic. Like in other countries around the world, a lockdown was imposed in Turkey in 2020 when the number of Covid-19 cases was the highest. Motor vehicle use was restricted and travel within walking distance was allowed for daily necessities (URL-4). Considering all these experiences, the metropolitan area of Ankara, where the service sector has a great importance due to being the capital of Turkey, has been determined as the study area to analyze the locational preferences of upper level healthcare services focusing on the private sector. The study does not include the family health center, which is the primary healthcare unit but includes the second and third level health units.

In the first stage, to analyze the accessibility of healthcare units and their service areas, the locations of the health facilities were mapped and the service areas were determined based on walking distance and time thresholds of 0–500 m, 500–750 m, 750–1500 m, 1500 m above, and as 0–10 min, 10–15 min, 15–30 min, over 30 min.

- **500 m**: Access distance of services offered in the organization of the neighborhood unit (Ersoy 2015),
- **750 m**: Walkability threshold (Zhou et al. 2021),
- **1500 m**: Maximum thresholds for 30 min walking time from residences to health services (Ersoy 2015).

After the service areas were determined according to the walkability thresholds, in the second stage, the spatial effectiveness of these service areas was evaluated by comparing them with the Covid-19 case density maps. Especially in recent years, the increasing importance of health service delivery with the Covid-19 crisis and the increasing role of the private sector's health services have made it important to determine effective criteria in the selection of the location of these investments.

Ankara is an important field for the study because it is a specialized center in the health services and private hospital sector in Turkey (Table 2).

According to the location quotient analysis (hereafter LQ analysis), Ankara exhibits a specialization in the health sector. The LQ of the health sector for Ankara is greater than 1, which shows this specialization.

Table 2 Distribution of inpatient hospitals in Turkey and Ankara according to their affiliated organizations (2018)

	Turkey	Ankara
Ministry of Health	889	40
University	68	10
Other Public	2	–
Private	575	38
Total	1534	88

Source TUIK (2020)

$$\text{LQ} = \frac{\text{the number of private hospitals in Ankara/the total number of hospitals in Ankara}}{\text{the number of private hospitals in Turkey/the total number of hospitals in Turkey}}$$

$$\text{LQ of Health Sector of Ankara} = [(38/88)/(575/1534) = 1,15]$$

According to the distribution of hospitals in Turkey by regions, it is seen that the total number of hospitals is the highest in Istanbul (15%) and the second in Ankara (5%) (Fig. 2). But when compared by hospitals per 10,000 population, it is observed that both Ankara and İstanbul have equal ratio (0.15). Although the number of hospitals is lowest in east Turkey, the numbers are high in Inner Anatolia, Marmara, Aegean and Mediterranean Regions. Among the 38 private hospitals in the Ankara, interviews were conducted according to the spatial distributions of private hospitals in Ankara. The managers of 4 of 18 hospitals in Çankaya district, 2 of 4 hospitals in Yenimahalle district, and 1 hospital in each of Gölbaşı, Mamak, Altındağ, Keçiören and Sincan districts were interviewed. The factors affecting the locational preferences of private hospitals in the samples were examined under six main headings: environmental factors, building characteristics, competition factors, investment costs, building's location, and demographic characteristics (Fig. 3).

The results obtained in the interviews with hospital administrators were evaluated by Likert scale as very effective, moderately effective, less effective, and ineffective. In the evaluation of the site selection matrix, the scoring method was used to compare the hospitals with each other and to evaluate the criteria among themselves. It was scored as 3 points for very effective, 2 points for moderately effective, 1 point for slightly effective, and 0 points for ineffective. After scoring, the obtained values were transformed into normalized comparison matrices and examined to understand the relative importance among each other.

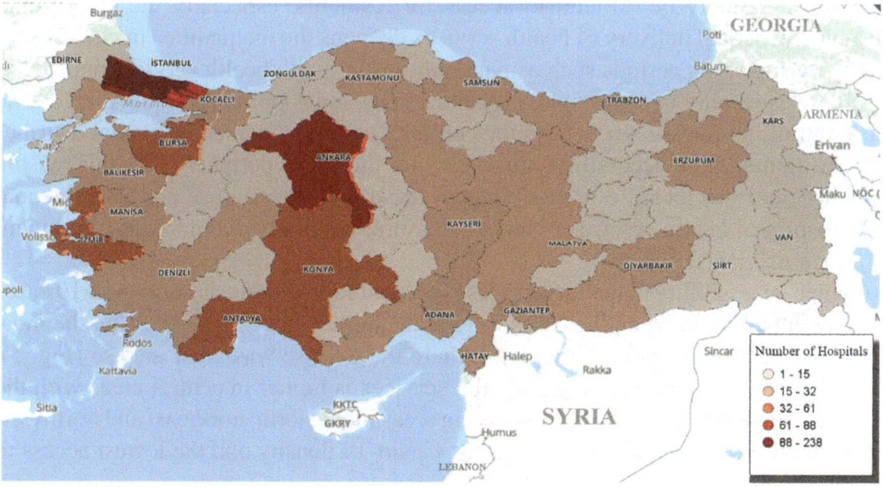

Fig. 2 Number of hospitals in Turkey (TUIK 2020)

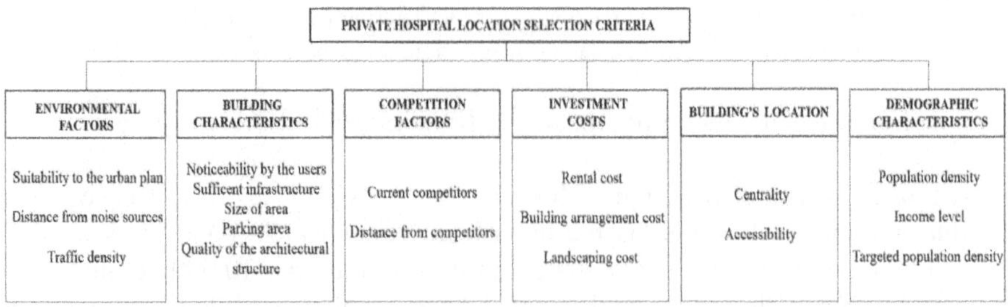

Fig. 3 Private hospitals location selection criteria

4 Results and Discussion

This study, which examined the site selection criteria of private health services in Ankara, was evaluated in two stages. In the first stage, accessibility, which is important for the service of health facilities, was analyzed. Accessibility was measured based on walking distances. In addition, accessibility was compared by the density of the spread of Covid-19 disease. In the second stage of the study, the relationship between hospital location selection and socio-economic structure was examined, and the relative effectiveness of the criteria for the location selection of private hospitals were determined.

Considering the accessibility of inhabitants to the health services, 6.8%, 17.3% and 51.5% of the inhabitants can walk to the nearest second level community health centers in 10 min, 15 min and 30 min respectively. Given the 15-min walk distance threshold for distinguishing well-served or under-served areas, 17.3% of the residents are within a 15-min walk of the nearest community health centers (Fig. 4). This distance may be difficult to access for residents, especially the elderly and disabled. Unequal delivery of health services deepens the inequalities in cities, especially during crisis periods such as pandemics. Access to health services appears to decrease especially in the peripheral regions in the metropolitan area of Ankara. The concentration of health services in the central areas and the unequal spatial distribution bring important accessibility problems for the urban periphery. For this reason, it is necessary to increase accessibility in these peripheral areas and ensure equal distribution of health services in order to ensure the timely diagnosis and treatment of urban residents.

When accessibility to health services is compared to the density of Covid-19 cases in September 2020, when the cases were at the highest level, it is seen that the most inaccessible regions were the regions where the disease was most intense (Fig. 5). It is observed that accessibility to health services is higher in central areas with the lowest disease rate. In particular, the living areas in the north, northeast and northwest of the metropolitan area have the highest Covid-19 density and the lowest access to health services.

Figure 6 shows the Covid-19 case densities by years. It is observed that the densest regions are the similar regions for the three periods of 2020, 2021 and 2022.

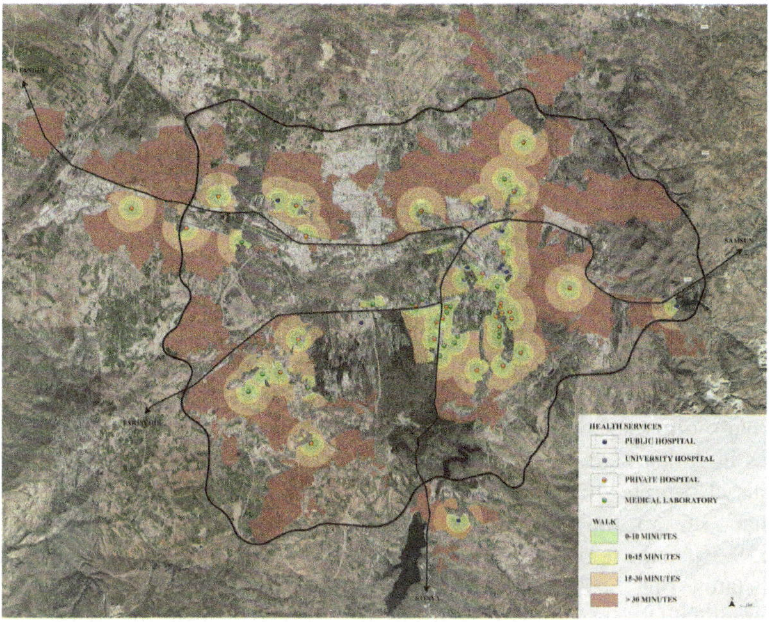

Fig. 4 The walking time thresholds from communities to healthcare services in Ankara

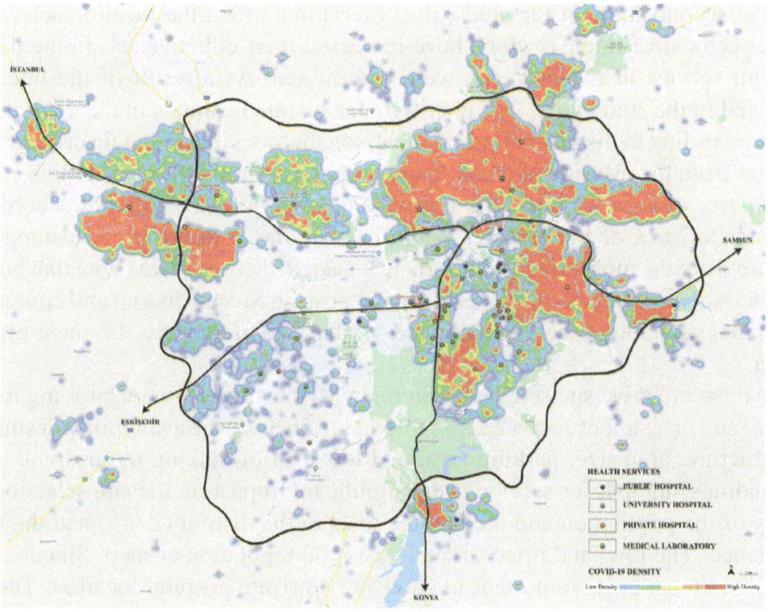

Fig. 5 Covid-19 density in Ankara in September 2020

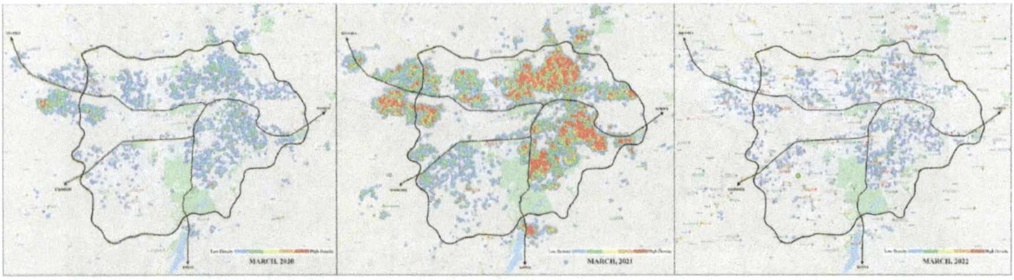

Fig. 6 Covid-19 density in Ankara in March, 2020–2021–2022

It is obvious that access to health services needs to be reconsidered and more attention should be paid to these problematic areas in spatial planning decisions and urban policies. Contrary to the Covid-19 densities, it is seen that the health services in Ankara are concentrated in the central areas. It is observed that private hospitals also prefer to locate in the central and prestigious areas of the city. It is seen that 53.6% of the private hospitals are located in the regions with the highest status, 39.3% in the regions with the medium status, and 7.1% in the regions with the lowest status (Fig. 7). The unequal spatial distribution of health services according to differentiated socio-economic status in the city also deepens the social inequality with spatial inequalities. These inequalities increase especially during crisis periods such as pandemics.

In the second stage of the study, the criteria that affect the location selection of private sector investments, which have increased their effectiveness in the delivery of health service in recent years, were determined. As a result of the interviews conducted in the study area, the subcriteria for private hospitals in the districts were scored according to the normalized comparison matrices and the main criteria values obtained from the average of these scores were compared (Table 3). In this context, the effective criteria for choosing a private hospital location differed according to the characteristics of the district. While the building's location and demographic structure were the most effective criteria in Çankaya district, it was seen that building characteristics in Mamak district, investment costs in Sincan district and competition in Altındağ, Keçiören, Yenimahalle and Gölbaşı districts were the most effective criteria.

The most effective site selection criteria in Mamak district were building features (25.1%) and investment costs (22.2%). In Mamak district, the availability of sufficient infrastructure, area size, parking area, and low cost of making the hospital and its surroundings suitable for service had a significant impact on the site selection. The density of the population and the income level in the district (2.6%) had the lowest importance. The low land prices, rental costs and regulation costs in Sincan district made investment costs important in choosing a private hospital location. The most effective criteria in the district was the investment cost (30.9%). Competition in Altındağ district was seen to be more important than in other districts. The reason for this was that the private hospital here was a specialized hospital (chest hospital). In the districts of Gölbaşı and Keçiören competitive factors were at the forefront, and

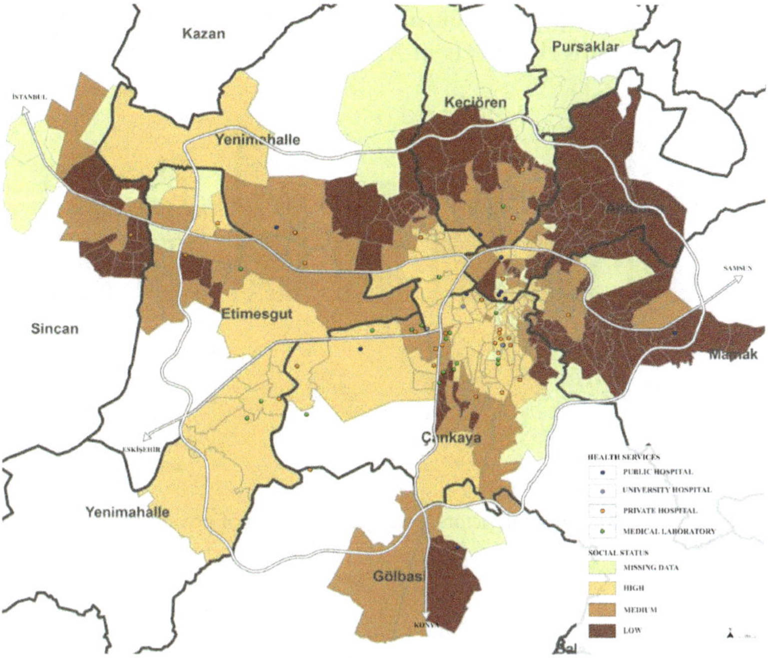

Fig. 7 Social status and hospital location selection

Table 3 Priorities for the location selection of private hospitals in Ankara by districts (%)

Criteria	Mamak	Sincan	Altındağ	Keçiören	Yenimahalle	Gölbaşı	Çankaya
Environmental Factors	16.7	13.7	15.5	17.3	14.7	19.1	13.7
Building features	*25.1*	22.7	8.9	17.3	21.1	21.3	19.7
Competitive factors	16.7	20.6	*27.7*	*23.1*	*22.4*	*24.3*	15.9
Investment Costs	22.2	*30.9*	19.4	19.1	11.5	20.1	6.3
Building's Location	16.7	5.2	13.9	8.7	14.4	6.1	*22.2*
Demographic Characteristics	2.6	6.9	14.7	14.5	16.0	9.1	*22.2*

being far from the city center and other competitors were effective. In the district of Çankaya, which includes the city center and has a high population density and income level, the location of the building and demographic characteristics came to the fore due to the facts of its centrality and population density.

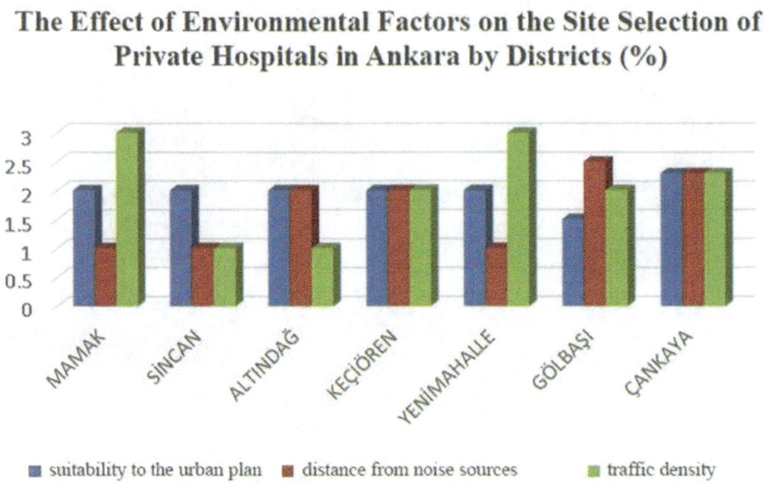

Fig. 8 The effect of environmental factors on the site selection of private hospitals in Ankara by districts (%)

Environmental factors in private hospital location selection were examined under three main headings as suitability to the urban plan, distance from noise sources, traffic density. The importance of proposing the hospital in the urban development plan, being away from the sources that cause noise, and choosing a location with a heavy traffic density in different districts was evaluated (Fig. 8).

The most important environmental factor in Mamak district was seen as traffic density. The fact of the hospital's being on the main road (Nato Road) was the most important factor determining the location of the hospital. In the centrally located district of Yenimahalle, the most important criterion among environmental factors was the high traffic density. When considering the location of Gölbaşı district, which is relatively far from the city center, away from noise sources became the most important environmental factor.

Akyüz and Kılınç (2016) measured traffic congestion as a negative factor in hospital location selection due to the emergence of transportation problems. It was revealed that areas away from city traffic were preferred. In this study, traffic density was seen to have no significant effect on the location of private hospitals in Sincan and Altındağ districts, where traffic density was relatively low. On the contrary, it was determined that the traffic density was the influential factor in the location selection of the private hospital in Mamak district, which was located on the main road and had a relatively higher accessibility. Considering the logic of private hospitals to prefer profitable regions, it is understood that districts with higher accessibility, thus having higher traffic density are more preferred areas.

Building features in private hospital location selection were examined under five main headings as noticeability, infrastructure adequacy, space adequacy, parking space adequacy, and the quality of the architectural structure. The criterisa of the

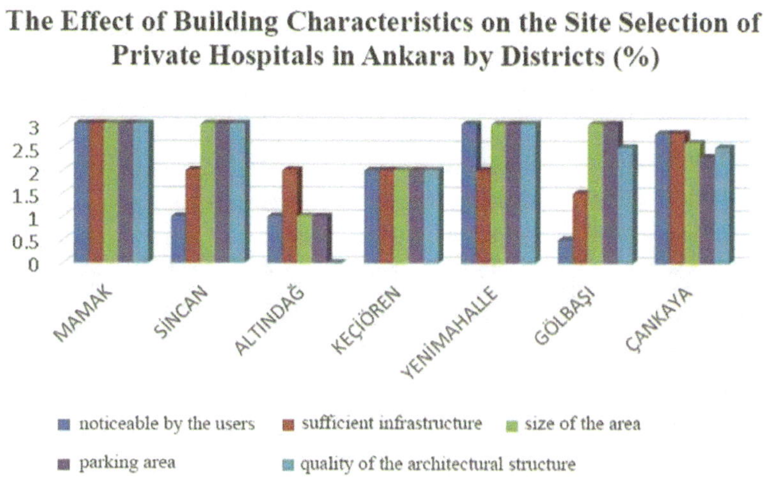

Fig. 9 The effect of building characteristics on the site selection of private hospitals in Ankara by districts (%)

hospital being noticeable by users, sufficient infrastructure in the area, sufficient size of the area required for the hospital function, presence of parking area, and the quality of the architectural structure in the building were evaluated (Fig. 9).

Among private hospitals in Ankara, the district with the most effective building characteristics was Mamak, and the district with the least effective was Altındağ. According to the building characteristics criteria score, Keçiören and Yenimahalle districts had relatively similar subscores. The size of the building, the ownership of the parking area and the quality of the architectural structure had the most effective subcriteria on the location of the private hospital in the district of Sincan, which had a helipad and air ambulance on its roof. In Gölbaşı district, the area required for the hospital and the size of the parking area had the most significant impact. On the other hand, due to the fact that Çankaya district was located in the center and had suitable infrastructure, the most important building feature criteria were identified as being noticeable and having infrastructural adequacy.

Soltani and Marandi (2011) revealed that size of the plot, future plot enlargement possibility, and helicopter access were effective for a professional medicine and cure hospital site selection. The size of the area was determined to be the most effective criterion among the building characteristics criteria in the location selection of the private hospital of the districts of Ankara. On the other hand, Yeşilyurt and Selamzade (2020) revealed that infrastructure adequacy was an effective criterion in hospital location selection. Similarly, the infrastructure adequacy of the districts in Ankara, especially Çankaya and Mamak districts, was determined as an effective criterion for the selection of the hospital location.

Competitive factors in private hospital location selection were evaluated as the number of current competitors and distance from competitors. After privatization in the health services sector, competition between hospitals became an important factor

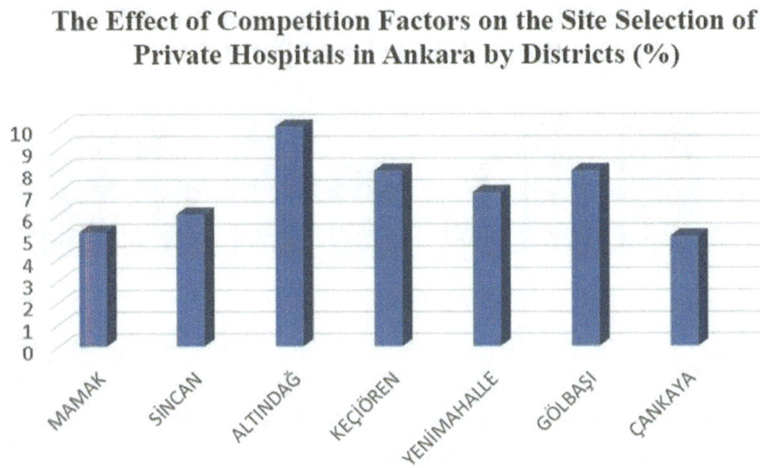

Fig. 10 The effect of competition factors on the site selection of private hospitals in Ankara by districts (%)

and affected the choice of location. Hospital managers began to prefer profitable regions. Within the scope of the study, the degree of importance of the elements of competition according to the districts was evaluated (Fig. 10).

Competitive factors in choosing a private hospital location were most effective in Altındağ. The reason for this is that the privatization law allowed hospitals to be organized in the form of specialized hospitals to gain more profit. Since there was only one specialized private hospital in Altındağ district, competition elements became most effective. In Çankaya district, the presence of many competitive private hospitals caused this criterion to be the least effective in the choice of location. Keçiören and Gölbaşı districts being far from the hospitals in other districts provided an advantage in terms of competition.

Organ and Tekin (2017) determined that the effectiveness of competitors was the most important one among the locational selection criteria of private hospital sites. Besides, Burkey (2012) reported that profits would increase when the number of potential competitors decreased. Therefore, he stated that the distance to potential competitors was effective in the location selection of private firms. The desire of private hospitals to make profit led to the competition as an important criterion in the site selection of private hospitals in Ankara. Especially in Altındağ district, where there was only one private hospital, it was seen that the distance to the competitors was significantly effective.

Investment costs in selecting the location of a private hospital were examined in three groups such as the rental cost, the cost of the building arrangement and the cost of the landscaping (Fig. 11).

Sincan appeared to be the district where investment costs were most effective in choosing a private hospital location. Since costs were cheaper in Altındağ, Mamak, Keçiören and Gölbaşı districts compared to Yenimahalle and Çankaya districts,

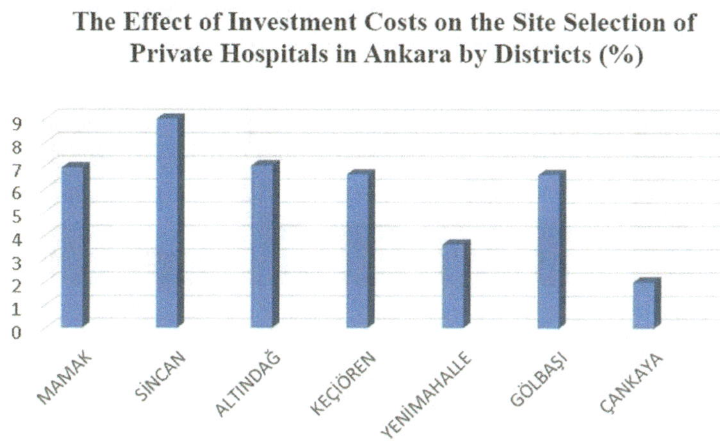

Fig. 11 The effect of investment costs on the site selection of private hospitals in Ankara by districts (%)

investment cost was an effective criterion to choose a hospital location. In districts where investment costs were effective in choosing a private hospital location, the criteria for rent, building arrangement cost and landscaping cost were close to each other.

Önüt et al. (2008) compared the importance of hospital location criteria and found that the most important criterion was land cost. They determined that the district with the lowest land cost and building construction cost was the most suitable field for hospital location selection. In this study, it was seen that the investment costs were high in the city center (Yenimahalle and Çankaya) thus, they had low effect on hospital location selection. The investment cost was more effective in the districts where the land costs were relatively lower.

Within the scope of the study, building features were examined in terms of centrality and accessibility (Fig. 12).

In Çankaya, the location of the building was the most effective criteria for the preferences of a private hospital's location. The central location and easy accessibility of Çankaya district had made the location of the building an important criterion in the selection of hospital location. Compared to other districts, Sincan was the district where the building's location criteria had the least effect on the selection of private hospital location. In Yenimahalle and Mamak districts, on the other hand, the accessibility criterion was seen to have a significant effect on the selection of the location of the private hospital. Since the hospital was located on the main road (Natoyolu) in Mamak, the accessibility was to be the main reason for this. In Yenimahalle district, it was seen that accessibility was effective due to the easy access to hospitals by road. The centrality of the location criterion of the building was seen as more effective in the selection of the location of the private hospital in Altındağ district.

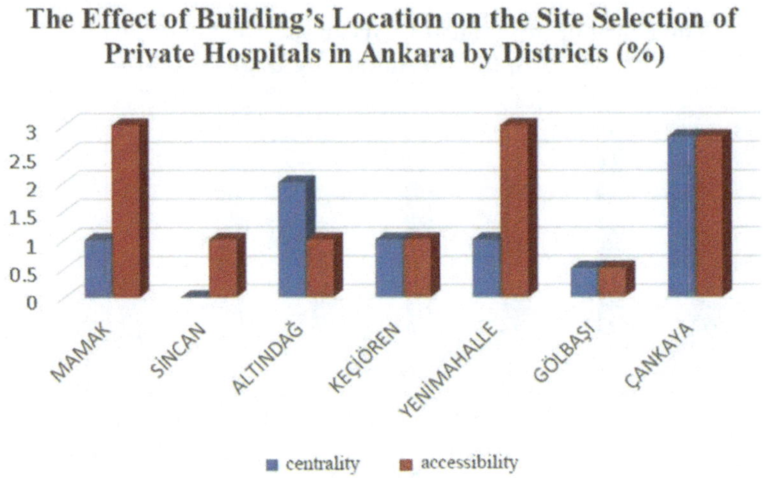

Fig. 12 The effect of building's location on the site selection of private hospitals in Ankara by districts (%)

The demographic structure criteria, which was the demand side factor in the selection of private hospital location, was examined in three groups as population density, income level and targeted population density (Fig. 13).

In Ankara, demographic structure in choosing a private hospital location was most effective in Çankaya district, which is the most central district and has a high income level and population density. The districts where demographic criteria were least effective were Mamak, Sincan and Gölbaşı. It was seen that only the population density was effective among the demographic criteria in Mamak and Sincan districts.

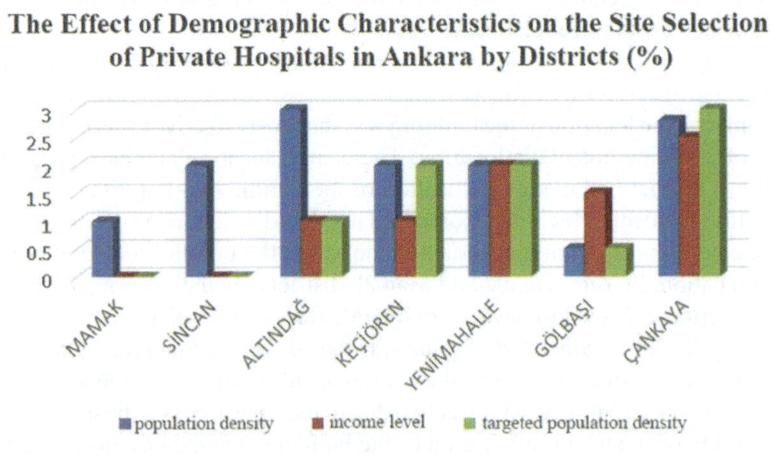

Fig. 13 The effect of demographic characteristics on the site selection of private hospitals in Ankara by districts (%)

In Gölbaşı district, it was seen that the income level was the more effective criterion compared to other districts.

Demirci (2019), Aydın et al. (2009) determined that the most effective criteria for hospital location selection was demographic characteristics. Rahmi (2021), on the other hand, determined that the most important factor among demographic criteria was the density of the population. Similarly, in this study, it was observed that the most important criterion among the demographic characteristics criteria was population density. However, the income level of the population in the Gölbaşı district and the density of the target population in Çankaya district were the most effective criteria in the locational selections of the hospitals.

5 Conclusion

Unequal spatial distribution of health services can cause problems in the functioning of the whole health system, as observed especially during Covid-19 epidemic. Determining the spatial distribution and accessibility of health services in cities constitutes an important basis for the development of health services policies and the development of effective emergency solutions. In the study, it is observed that there are inequalities in the access to health services in Ankara metropolitan area. Especially in the urban peripheries, there are problems in accessing the health services. A 15-min walk of health services does not cover the most residential areas (82.7%) in the study area. However, the importance of providing health services within a walking distance is better understood when measures such as limiting motor vehicle use are taken with crises such as pandemics. The unequal distribution of health services appears to be particularly disadvantageous for vulnerable groups such as the elderly and those with reduced mobility. On the other hand, various campaigns have been launched in many countries, such as "Building a 15-min Community Life Circle" in China (Zhou et al. 2021) and the "15-min City" campaign (URL-5) in Paris, in order to place the facilities within the daily activity area of the residents and to create socio-economically heterogeneous areas.

When the location selection of private hospitals in Ankara is examined, it is seen that the number of hospitals is insufficient in the regions having lowest socio-economic status, where the most intense pandemic cases emerged. Due to the low investments of private hospitals in these regions, it is understood that services are generally provided by public hospitals which are not sufficient for the inhabitants living in these areas. It is observed that the income level of the population has a significant effect on the locational preferences of private hospitals. For this reason, already disadvantaged regions have become even more disadvantaged under pandemic conditions. In addition, it is also understood that the population density in the central areas of the city (e.g. Çankaya) with sufficient infrastructure, accessibility, and noticeable by users are significantly effective for the selection of private hospital locations. It is observed that investments are rare in the peripheries of the city where there are no such conditions and service provision is insufficient. The importance of equitable provision of health services has been further understood in pandemic conditions. It is understood that public health issues should be reconsidered and more attention should be paid in urban planning, especially in emergency conditions such as pandemics.

With the increase in the influence of the private sector in health services investments in recent years, determining the differentiated hospital location selection criteria is important for the implementation of effective strategies in the location selection of new hospital investments. In this study, priorities in the selection of private health institutions in regions with different urban characteristics in Ankara are determined. It is revealed that the criteria affecting the locational preferences of private hospitals, which are distributed in different geographical regions of the Ankara metropolitan area, differ according to the physical, social and economic characteristics of the districts. The location advantage plays an important role in the locational preferences of private hospitals for the Çankaya district, which is located in the center of the city. In Çankaya district, which has a significant population density due to being in the city center, many private hospitals serve the citizens together with their competitors. The most effective criteria in selecting the location of private hospitals in this district are the building's location and demographic characteristics. Accessibility criteria is influential in the selection of the private hospital location for another centrally located district of Yenimahalle, due to the high traffic density and easy access by road. In the districts of Gölbaşı and Keçiören, which are relatively far from the city center, being away from other competitors provided an advantage in choosing a private hospital location. The organization of a private hospital in the form of a specialized hospital in Altındağ district puts the competitive factors in the fore. Since investment costs, rental costs and building arrangement costs are lower in Mamak and Sincan districts compared to other districts, the most effective criteria in the site selection emerge as investment costs.

In the academic literature, many criteria and models have been developed to determine the most suitable location for healthcare services. However, it has been understood in this study that the local characteristics of an area are effective for the location selection of the healthcare service. Although they are in the same province, the criteria affecting the site selection of private hospitals in different districts differ. The locations of the districts, infrastructure conditions, real estate prices, population structures, etc. affect the location choices of private hospitals and enable the hospitals to choose the most profitable and appropriate service areas.

As a result, the study contributes to the academic and practical studies by providing a comprehensive set of criteria for the effective site selection of private hospitals. Considering these datasets determined in this study and the deficiencies related to the spread of Covid-19 disease, new site selection models can be produced bearing in mind the local characteristics in the districts and the equal distribution of health services. In disaster situations like Covid-19, new criteria such as walking distances for differentiated age groups, equal distribution of supporting services, spatial distribution of disease intensity, etc. can be added to the modeling for the selection of hospital locations.

References

Abdullahi S, Mahmud ARB, Pradhan B (2014) Spatial modelling of site suitability assessment for hospitals using geographical information system-based multicriteria approach at Qazvin city, Iran. Geocarto Int 29(2):164–184

Akyüz G, Kılınç E (2016) Kuruluş Yeri Seçiminde Bulanık TOPSIS Yönteminin Kullanımı: Sağlık Sektöründe Bir Uygulama. Akademik Sosyal Araştırmalar Dergisi 4(33):590–608

Altay A (2007) Sağlık Hizmetlerinin Sunumunda Yeni Açılımlar ve Türkiye Açısından Değerlendirilmesi. Sayıştay Dergisi 64:33–58

Assad CAR (2019) Building GIS framework based on multi criteria analysis for hospital site selection in developing countries. Int J Comput Tech 6(4):1–6

Aydın Ö, Öznehir S, Akcali E (2009) Ankara için Optimal Hastane Yeri Seçiminin Analitik Hiyerarşi Süreci ile Modellenmesi. Süleyman Demirel Üniversitesi İktisadi ve İdari Bilimler Fakültesi Dergisi 14(2):69–86

Baran E (2018) An innovative fuzzy TOPSIS method to determine the location of a new hospital. Int J Eng Sci Appl 2(4):133–136

Beheshtifar S, Alimoahmmadi A (2015) A multiobjective optimization approach for location-allocation of clinics. Int Trans Oper Res 22(2):313–328

Burkey ML (2012) Decomposing geographic accessibility into component parts: methods and an application to hospitals. Ann Reg Sci 48(3):783–800

Çelikbilek Y (2018) Group decision making for hospital location selection using VIKOR under Fuzzy environment. İstanbul Gelişim Üniversitesi Sağlık Bilimleri Dergisi 5:435–450

Chiu JE, Tsai HH (2013) Applying analytic hierarchy process to select optimal expansion of hospital location: the case of a regional teaching hospital in Yunlin. In: 10th international conference on service systems and service management. Hong Kong, China, pp 603–606

Daskin MS, Dean LK (2005) Location of health care facilities. Operations Research and Health Care, pp 43–76

Declaration of Alma-Ata (1978) International conference on primary health care. *Alma-Ata*, USSR, pp 6–12

Demirci A (2019) Kuruluş Yeri Seçiminde Analitik Hiyerarşik Süreç Yöntemi: Sağlık Kurumlarında Bir Uygulama. Uluslararası İktisadi ve İdari Bilimler Dergisi 5(1):39–55

Ersoy M (2015) Kentsel planlamada standartlar. Ninova, İstanbul

Gül M, Güneri AF (2021) Hospital location selection: a systematic literature review on methodologies and applications. Math Probl Eng 2021:1–14

Islam MM, Mahmud T, Hossain MS (2016) Belief-rule-based intelligent decision system to select hospital location. Indones J Electr Eng Comput Sci 1(3):607–618

Janssen R, Made J (1990) Privatisation in western European health care a comparative study. Int J Health Sci 2:63–78

Kahraman C, Gundogdu FK, Onar SC, Oztaysi B (2019) Hospital location selection using spherical fuzzy TOPSIS. In: 11th conference of the European society for fuzzy logic and technology (EUSFLAT 2019). Prague, Czech Republic, pp 77–82

Kasapoğlu A (2016) Türkiye'de Sağlık Hizmetlerinin Dönüşümü. J Sociol Res 19:131–174

Kaveh M, Kaveh M, Mesgari MS, Paland RS (2020) Multiple criteria decision-making for hospital location-allocation based on improved genetic algorithm. Appl Geomat 12(3):291–306

Kim JI, Senaratna DM, Ruza J, Kam C, Ng S (2015) Feasibility study on an evidence-based decision-support system for hospital site selection for an aging population. Sustainability 7(3):2730–2744

Kmail A, Jubran J, Sabbah W, Jenin P (2017) Coupling GIS-Based MCA and AHP techniques for hospital site selection. Int J Comput Sci Inf Secur (IJCSIS) 15(12)

Lee KS, Moon KJ (2014) Hospital distribution in a metropolitan city: assessment by a geographical information system grid modelling approach. Geospat Health 8(2):537–544

Lin HY, Liao CJ, Chang YH (2010) Applying fuzzy simple additive weighting system to health examination institution location selection. In: 17th international conference on industrial engineering and engineering management. Xiamen, China, pp 646–650

Murad AA (2005) Using GIS for planning public general hospitals at Jeddah city. Environ Des Sci 3(3):22
Murad AA (2007) Creating a GIS application for health services at Jeddah city. Comput Biol Med 37(6):879–889
Noon CE, Hankins CT (2001) Spatial data visualization in healthcare: supporting a facility location decision via GIS-based market analysis. In: 34th annual Hawaii international conference on system sciences. Maui, USA, p 10
Önüt S, Tuzkaya UR, Kemer B (2008) An analytical network process approach to the choice of hospital location. J Eng Nat Sci 25(4):367–379
Organ A, Tekin B (2017) Şehir Hastanesi Kuruluş Yeri Seçimi için Gri İlişkisel Analiz Yaklaşımı: Denizli İli Örneği. Adnan Menderes Üniversitesi Sosyal Bilimler Enstitüsü Dergisi 4(3):256–278
Pınar MİÇ, Antmen ZF (2019) A healthcare facility location selection problem with fuzzy TOPSIS method for a regional hospital. Avrupa Bilim ve Teknoloji Dergisi 16:750–757
Rahmi B (2021) Özel Bir Hastanenin Yer Seçimi için Bulanık COPRAS Tekniğinin Uygulanması. Bitlis Eren Üniversitesi Fen Bilimleri Dergisi 10(4):1506–1514
Universal Declaration of Human Rights (1948) Official gazette of the republic of Turkey 7217:1–4
Satılmış EŞ, Akkaya İ, Varol Ç (2021) Kent Sağlığı ve Covid-19 Kapsamında Sağlık Hizmetleri Mekansal Yer Seçiminin Değerlendirilmesi: Ankara Çankaya İlçesi Örneği. İdealkent 31(12):268–297
Shariff SR, Moin NH, Omar M (2012) Location allocation modeling for healthcare facility planning in Malaysia. Comput Ind Eng 62(4):1000–1010
Soltani A, Marandi EZ (2011) Hospital site selection using two-stage fuzzy multi-criteria decision making process. J Urban Environ Eng 5(1):32–43
Stiglitz JE (1994) The role of financial markets. The International Bank for Reconstruction and Development, The World Bank, pp 350–351
Şahin T, Ocak S, Top M (2019) Analytic hierarchy process for hospital site selection. Health Policy Technol 8(1):42–50
Tynkkynen LK, Vrangbæk K (2018) Comparing public and private providers: a scoping review of hospital services in Europe. BMC Health Serv Res 18:141–155
TUIK (2020) Health statistics. https://biruni.tuik.gov.tr/medas/?locale=tr. Accessed 28 Dec 2022.
URL-1 https://www.statista.com/statistics/283221/per-capita-health-expenditure-by-country/. Accessed 17 Mar 2020
URL-2 https://shgm.saglik.gov.tr/Eklenti/30975/0/tara0006pdf.pdf. Accessed 04 Jan 2023
URL-3 https://hsgm.saglik.gov.tr/tr/haberler/yetkilendirilmis-covi-d-19-tani-laboratuvarlari.html. Accessed 25 Apr 2022
URL-4 https://www.icisleri.gov.tr/81-il-valiligine-kismi-kapanma-genelgesi-gonderildi. Accessed 03 Jan 2023
URL-5 https://www.theguardian.com/world/2020/feb/07/paris-mayor-unveils-15-minute-city-plan-in-re-election-campaign. Accessed 11 Oct 2020
Vahidnia MH, Alesheikh AA, Alimohammadi A (2009) Hospital site selection using fuzzy AHP and its derivatives. J Environ Manag 90(10):3048–3056
Wang F (2012) Measurement, optimization, and impact of health care accessibility: a methodological review. Ann Assoc Am Geogr 102:1104–1112
WHO (2000) The world health report 2000. Health systems: improving performance, Geneva
Wibowo S (2014) Evaluating and selecting hospital locations using fuzzy multicriteria decision making. Asian J Manag Sci Appl 1(3):278–291
Wu CR, Lin CT, Chen HC (2007) Optimal selection of location for Taiwanese hospitals to ensure a competitive advantage by using the analytic hierarchy process and sensitivity analysis. Build Environ 42(3):1431–1444
Wu WH, Lin CT, Peng KH, Huang CC (2012) Applying hierarchical grey relation clustering analysis to geographical information systems–a case study of the hospitals in Taipei city. Expert Syst Appl 39(8):7247–7254

Yeşilyurt Ö, Selamzade F (2020) Muş İli için Optimal Hastane Yeri Seçiminin Analitik Hiyerarşi Süreci ile Değerlendirilmesi. Anemon Muş Alparslan Üniversitesi Sosyal Bilimler Dergisi 8(5):1361–1367

Zhou Z, Xu Z, Liu A, Zhou S, Mu L, Zhang X (2021) Mapping the accessibility of medical facilities of Wuhan during the COVID-19 pandemic. ISPRS Int J Geo Inf 10(5):318

Corporate Disclosure of Vaccine Producers After Covid-19 Disease

Silvia Fissi, Elena Gori, and Alberto Romolini

Abstract The Covid-19 emergency has rapidly changed the pharmaceutical sectors. A small group of companies have realized the first Covid-19 vaccines in a short time, starting the global distribution of their products. This process has necessarily relevant effects on the global performance of vaccine producers by rapidly improving their global and financial results. In this perspective, the vaccine makers are called upon to provide clear disclosure in their reports regarding their corporate performance and the effects of the vaccine development. The aim of this paper is to investigate whether or not the vaccine producers have changed their disclosures to underline the effects of Covid-19 vaccine production. The research uses a content analysis of the reports provided by the vaccine producers in the last two years (2020 and 2021). After selecting the companies, the research collects the reports of each vaccine producer, such as social and sustainability reports. The data collection will be extended to secondary sources, aiming to obtain a clear picture of the corporate disclosure. The results contribute to opening a discussion about the corporate disclosure of Covid-19 vaccine producers. The need to provide a clear representation of global performance in this sector contributes to the global dialogue about the pharmaceutical sector based on empirical data and analysis. The study has the limitation of being based on an analysis of reports linked to a recent phenomenon; we argue that this research needs to be repeated in the near future after the end of the Covid-19 global emergency. This research has an exploratory nature as, to the best of our knowledge, no previous studies have focused on corporate disclosure of Covid-19 vaccine producers.

Keywords Covid-19 · Vaccine · Pharmaceutical · CSR · Social reporting · Disclosure

S. Fissi · E. Gori
University of Florence, via delle pandette, 9, 50127 Florence, Italy
e-mail: silvia.fissi@unifi.it

E. Gori
e-mail: elena.gori@unifi.it

A. Romolini (✉)
International Telematic University Uninettuno, Corso Vittorio Emanuele II, 39, 00186 Rome, Italy
e-mail: a.romolini@uninettunouniversity.net

N. Persiani et al. (eds.), *Challenges of Healthcare Systems in the Era of COVID-19*,
Contributions to Management Science, https://doi.org/10.1007/978-3-031-43114-2_5

JEL Classification Codes M14 Corporate Culture · Diversity · Social Responsibility · M41 Accounting

1 Introduction

The Covid-19 outbreak created a rapid international emergency after the detection of a new form of coronavirus in the Chinese city of Wuhan. The first case emerged at the end of 2019 and suddenly the emergency spread to more than 114 countries in a few months. On March 11, 2020, the WHO (2020) communicated that Covid-19 was a global pandemic event and, starting from April 2020, many countries in Europe, Asia, Africa, and America rapidly decided to start lockdowns. With a situation never experienced before globally, millions of people were obliged to stay in their homes, living, communicating, and working with the support of new Internet technology tools. In this sense, the impact of Covid-19 has no precedent in history, considering the number of people involved and the countries affected by the virus (Macnamara 2021). Previous emergencies, such as SARS and MERS, did not have similar dramatic effects in terms of human health risk and impacts on the economy and social environment.

During the emergency, many countries needed to deal with a huge number of economic, environmental, and social problems (Rahdari and Anvary Rostamy 2015). In this scenario, private and public companies are experiencing increasing demand from stakeholders for greater disclosure and accountability (Sassen and Azizi 2018). This context appears more complicated for the vaccine producers which are involved in critical work to fight the virus and reduce its negative effects. The design and implementation of sustainable development models and sustainability reports represent a possible response to stakeholders' needs for all kinds of organizations (Leal Filho 2018) and especially for the vaccine producers.

These companies could increase the disclosure of their reports in order to become more accountable for the economic, environmental, and social impacts of their activities (Hahn and Kühnen 2013). In this sense, they will be become more able to respond to stakeholders' expectations, as traditional financial reports do not provide the information required. Companies have indeed started to publish sustainability reports using voluntarily disclosure (Bebbington et al. 2014) as a tool to create dialogue and engagement with their stakeholders (Manetti and Toccafondi 2012).

Looking to previous researches, we can argue that corporate social responsibility (CSR) and social reports are not a recent issue. The first studies on this topic came from the USA in the 1920s (Gay 1927; Donham 1929). These authors constantly referred to the responsibility of businessmen and to the importance of management science as a potential trigger for social wellbeing created through corporate activity. Nonetheless, a univocal and universally accepted definition of CSR has not yet been constructed (Carroll 1999; Thomas and Nowak 2006), and only in recent years have a precise role and a specific evaluation been given to "socially responsible" businesses (Garriga and Melé 2004).

The Covid-19 emergency has rapidly changed the pharmaceutical sectors. A small group of companies (AstraZeneca—UK and Sweden; BioNTech—Germany; Glaxo Smith Kline—UK; Johnson & Johnson—USA; Moderna—USA; Novavax—USA; Pfizer—USA; Sanofi—France) have realized the first vaccines in a short time, starting the global distribution of their products. Moreover, the global vaccine campaign has created a relevant debate about, from one side, the quality and safety of vaccines (Karlsson et al. 2021) and, from the other, the benefits for the pharmaceutical companies in terms of revenues. Indeed, this process has necessarily relevant effects on the global performance of vaccine producers by rapidly improving their global and financial results. Previous studies have also discussed different topics regarding the success of the national vaccine campaigns. Lindholt et al. (2021) identified different factors affecting individual choices regarding people's adherence to national vaccine campaigns, while Machingaidze and Wiysonge (2021) analyzed the problems of access to vaccines in low- and middle-income countries.

In this perspective, the vaccine producers are fully involved in the necessity to disclose the environmental, social, and economic effects of their activities; this necessity is currently more urgent if we consider the role of and attention paid to their work during the recent "pandemic years". In other words, vaccine producers feel the need to disclose to global stakeholders the effects of their activities with the aim of obtaining a full legitimation of their role in the Covid-19 emergency. However, to the best of our knowledge, no previous study has analyzed corporate disclosure in this context.

The aim of this paper is to investigate whether or not vaccine producers have changed their disclosures to underline the effects of Covid-19 vaccine production.

The following sections of this paper are organized as follows. After the literature review, the authors discuss the research method applied in this study and the results of the empirical analysis. Finally, the paper presents the conclusions of this work, underlining its limitations and some possible future research opportunities.

2 Literature Review

In recent years, the need to pay greater attention to sustainability and a demand for a higher level of accountability and transparency regarding the effects of companies' activities on societies and ecosystems have become a fundamental challenge for all types of organizations operating in the public and private spheres (Schaltegger et al. 2014). In this situation, companies have been integrating their traditional reporting with non-financial information such as social, environmental sustainability, and governance information (Kolk 2004, 2010). In the European Union (EU), this situation is also a result of a normative path that started with the Non-Financial Reporting Directive (Directive 2014/95/EU) and with a proposal, in the year 2021, of a new Corporate Sustainability Reporting Directive.

Currently, approaches to non-financial reporting differ. In many cases, this type of reporting appears in the form of addenda to more traditional financial statements.

More recently, non-financial reports have been built as standalone annual reports. Generally, we can argue that non-financial reports are often prepared voluntarily with the aim of demonstrating coherence between business behaviors and social and environmental sustainability (Garcìa-Sanchez et al. 2013).

In recognition of the different approaches used in corporate sustainability reports, it is possible to find several studies focused on different topics of sustainability reporting such as the content, scope, and structure of the reports (Beloe et al. 2006; Slater 2008; Manetti 2011). Reporting practices also differ if we look to the national context. In this perspective, scholars have developed national-level researches over the last 10 years. National-level studies have focused on Austria (Langer 2006), Bangladesh (Sobhani et al. 2009), Canada (Davis and Searcy 2010), Germany (Gamerschlag et al. 2011), Greece (Skouloudis et al. 2010), Italy (Perrini et al. 2006; Secchi 2006), Norway (Vormedal and Ruud 2009), Sweden (Hedberg and von Malmborg 2003), Switzerland (Stiller and Daub 2007), and Thailand (Ratanajongkol et al. 2006). If we analyze the object of the previous studies, we can argue that the majority are focused on assessing the quality of CSR disclosure by evaluating the CSR reporting of stock exchange listed companies. In this type of research, authors apply different analytical approaches such as content analysis, benchmarking analysis, case studies, and so on. However, scholars have reached similar results: the quality of CSR disclosure is quite far from acceptable levels. It needs to be seriously improved to meet international standards and promote effective engagement with stakeholders, instead of merely seeking social legitimacy and increased credibility.

Studies on social reporting are also conducted with regard to different sectors of companies' activities. Dabic et al. (2016) analyzed the academic research on industry-based CSR practices. They identified some sectors that have been widely analyzed, discovering some trends in the study of specific sectors. Unfortunately, they also discovered that the studies are not well distributed between the different industries. In particular, scholars' attention to the practices of the pharmaceutical sector in the field of social reporting research is limited (Cook et al. 2018). Despite the importance of pharmaceutical companies in society and their contribution to individual and public health, studies about increasing corporate responsibility transparency and social accountability are relatively scarce. Some exploratory studies on this industry are very recent and were provided by Cook et al. (2018) and Demir and Ming (2019). For this reason, to the best of our knowledge, it is possible to identify a gap on the pharmaceutical industry. If we consider the role of the pharmaceutical companies in the market and above all in society and the importance of these companies in the prevention of the spread of Covid-19, we understand the need to know more about disclosure in this context and to fill this knowledge gap in the next years.

3 Method

Considering the novelty of the topic, this research has an exploratory nature. Accordingly, we adopted a qualitative approach that is particularly suitable when little is known about a certain phenomenon (Lune and Berg 2017).

The research is exploratory in nature and focuses on sustainability reports produced by companies involved in vaccine production during the Covid-19 emergency. In particular, it considers seven companies that have distributed Covid-19 vaccines in Western countries, in particular in the USA and EU. Specifically, the companies are AstraZeneca, Pfizer, Novavax, Moderna, Johnson & Johnson, GSK, and BioNTech.

The research is structured as follows: First, the authors identify the companies involved in the vaccine production in the EU and USA. After that, the research collects the reports of each vaccine producer such as social and sustainability reports. The reports considered are the last ones published in the years 2020–2021.

From a methodological point of view, the study uses two steps: the first is a content analysis of the reports collected, while the second is an analysis of secondary sources, aiming to obtain a clear picture of the corporate disclosure.

The content analysis is conducted manually in two different ways with the aim of individuating some keywords linked to Covid-19 disclosure. In the first one, the keywords selected are: "Covid-19", "Covid-19 pandemic", "Covid-19 vaccine", "pandemic", and "vaccine". The research considers all the disclosures provided by sustainability reports, discovering the total amount of keywords selected. Moreover, the authors conduct a specific analysis of the CEOs' or presidents' letters in order to discover the impact of Covid-19 vaccine production on the strategy of each company.

In the second method, the authors conduct a content analysis starting with the collection of the sections of the reports where each company discusses the topics "Covid-19" and "vaccine". Moreover, considering that the Sustainability Accounting Standards Board (SASB) model represents a standard generally applied in the pharmaceutical sector, especially in the industry version "Biotechnology & Pharmaceuticals", we identify some material sustainability topics to investigate in the reports. The topics are also identified according to previous researches discussed in the "Introduction" and "Literature Review" sections.

4 Results and Discussion

4.1 An Overview of Vaccine Producers

The research starts with an overview of the seven companies involved in Covid-19 vaccine production. They are all listed companies on different stock exchanges such as London and New York. The companies are based substantially in three countries, the USA, the UK, and Germany, and we observe the presence of one company,

Table 1 Effects of vaccine production on total revenues

Company	Country	Total revenues 2021 (in millions of euros)*	Total revenues 2020 (in millions of euros)*	Variation in total revenues 2021–2020 (%)
AstraZeneca	UK and Sweden	35.9	25.5	41
BioNTech	Germany	18,900	482.3	3,819
GlaxoSmithKline	UK	40.2	40.2	0
Johnson & Johnson	USA	90,147	79,393	14
Moderna	USA	17,755	771.8	2,200
Novavax	USA	1.1	0.45	144
Pfizer	USA	78.1	40.3	94

*The value change is calculated at the date of May 16, 2022

BioNTech, that is active in the European pharmaceutical industry. We conducted an analysis through the annual reports of these companies, comparing the results of the years 2021 and 2020. In particular, we analyzed the consolidated financial reports with the aim of observing the effects of vaccine production on total revenues.

The effects on the financial results are very significant (Table 1): if we look at the total amount of revenues, we can observe that the most of the companies, except for GlaxoSmithKline, experienced strong growth in these performances. The reason for this difference is that GlaxoSmithKline applied for authorization to sell Covid-19 vaccines only at the beginning of 2022. In this sense, we consider the effects of the vaccine production in the 2022 reports. On the other hand, BioNTech and Moderna demonstrate a huge growth of revenues and, in this sense, we can observe that the vaccine production has totally changed their business models.

4.2 *Corporate Social Disclosure on Covid-19 Vaccine Production*

The analysis of corporate social reports demonstrates that the majority of companies (75%) publish a standalone report for social reporting, while, in the other cases, we observe that some information about these topics is integrated in the annual reports and the corporate websites (Table 2).

The corporate social reports have various titles, of which the most frequently applied seems to be the "sustainability report". Regarding the standard applied in the reporting, the analysis shows the general use of different standards with particular attention to the Global Reporting Initiative (GRI), the SASB Index, and the United Nations Global Compact (UNGC). The standards are globally accepted for sustainability disclosure and are used with a "hybrid approach": in other words, each company refers to different standards for each single report. The reports also

Table 2 Corporate social reporting analysis

Company	Sustainability report title	Standard	Pages	Assurance	Specific section
AstraZeneca	Sustainability report 2021	Not available	35	Yes	No
BioNTech	Sustainability report 2020	GRI, SASB Index, UNGC	70	No	No
GlaxoSmithKline	ESG performance report 2020	SASB Index, GRI, UNGC	37	Yes	No
Johnson & Johnson	Health for humanity report	GRI	117	Yes	Yes
Moderna	Impacting human health. 2021 ESG report	SASB	37	No	No
Novavax	Not available	–	–	–	–
Pfizer	Environmental, social and governance report 2020	SASB, GRI, the task force for climate-related financial disclosure	52	Yes	No

have different dimensions in terms of pages: from 35 to 217. Moreover, only one report, published by BioNTech, was not submitted to an external assurance entity in order to verify the application of the accountability principles. This approach can guarantee the quality of the information reported to the external stakeholders. Finally, the general reporting practice is to offer information about the activities of the companies during the Covid-19 emergency in different parts of their reports; only one company (Johnson & Johnson) decided to create a specific section dedicated to Covid-19 disclosure.

The analysis of the reports is enriched by a study of the contents (Table 3). The research has the goal of understanding the disclosure about the role of each company during Covid-19 emergency in a quantitative way. The most frequently used term is "vaccine" (284), which is followed by "Covid-19" (211) and "pandemic" (138); this result confirms the attention of pharmaceutical producers to the disclosure of their role during the health emergency. Moreover, it confirms that social reporting changed after this event with some "terms" that no one had used in previous reports. The other results can be interpreted in the same way with the terms "Covid-19 vaccine" and "Covid-19 pandemic" repeated, respectively, 107 and 103 times in the reports.

The final stage of the analysis is the study of the CEOs' and/or presidents' letters with the aim of understanding whether Covid-19 vaccine production is becoming part of the business strategy (Fig. 1). The word cloud again shows how the reports have changed, as one of the most frequently used terms is now "Covid". In this sense, the pandemic emergency and vaccine production represent the biggest challenges for the future of each company.

Table 3 Keywords analysis of the corporate social reports

Company	Covid-19	Covid-19 pandemic	Covid-19 vaccine	Pandemic	Vaccine
AstraZeneca	7	6	2	5	3
BioNTech	10	7	46	6	82
GlaxoSmithKline	12	2	0	20	86
Johnson & Johnson	126	38	46	71	77
Moderna	39	42	0	26	3
Pfizer	17	8	13	10	33
Total	211	103	107	138	284

Fig. 1 The word cloud

4.3 Sustainability Topics for Vaccine Producers

The research was extended to an analysis of the main topics used in the reports to disclose information related to the role of vaccine producers during the pandemic. For this purpose, in a first step, we conduct a content analysis starting with the collection of the sections where each company discusses the topics "Covid-19" and "vaccine". In the selected sections of the reports, the research aims to identify the disclosures about topics directly connected with the Covid-19 health emergency and the role of the vaccine producers in helping preserve global wellbeing.

For this aim, the authors consider the SASB model applied to "Biotechnology & Pharmaceuticals" (SASB 2018). In more detail, we identify some material sustainability topics that are directly connected with Covid-19 to investigate in the reports. The selected topics used as "keywords" in the content analysis are "clinical trial", "access to vaccine", "vaccine litigation", "vaccine safety", and "employee recruitment, development & retention". These keywords were identified while also considering the previous studies discussed in the "Introduction" and "Literature Review" sections.

The research reveals that the topics discussed more often in the reports concern the protection of employees during the pandemic emergency and the process of the clinical trials. The section dedicated to employees' roles during the development of Covid-19 vaccines aims to disclose the efforts provided in a short time period in response to the health emergency. Moreover, the reports aim to demonstrate the procedures and methodologies applied to protect employees from Covid-19 infection during work hours in the corporate buildings and during periods of working at home. After that, the reports often present a detailed summary of clinical trial procedures with specific attention given to the quality and security of vaccine development and production.

The reports also present each company's strategy for ensuring access to Covid-19 vaccines in low–middle income countries. As global companies, the vaccine producers demonstrate efforts to distribute their products in countries where access to Covid-19 vaccines is difficult or nearly impossible.

The least disclosed issue, however, is "vaccine safety", if this type of information is provided in the sections of the reports dedicated to the clinical trials and product development of the Covid-19 vaccine. The aim of this approach is to ensure affordability and reliability of vaccines diffusion.

Finally, we do not find any information about litigation after the vaccine distribution. This result could be due to the short amount of time that has passed since the marketing of this pharmaceutical product. Probably, we can argue that in the next few years the reports will be obliged to present information about this topic too.

The analysis performed is summarized in Table 4, which shows the topics discussed in the sustainability reports of vaccine producers according to the SASB model.

Table 4 Sustainability topics for vaccine producers

Company	Clinical trial	Access to vaccine	Vaccine litigation	Vaccine safety	Employee recruitment, development and retention
AstraZeneca		X			X
BioNTech	X	X		X	X
GlaxoSmithKline	X	X			X
Johnson & Johnson	X	X		X	X
Moderna	X	X		X	X
Pfizer	X				

5 Conclusion

The Covid-19 emergency represents a global pandemic never experienced before in terms of the number of people and the countries involved. The need to fight this unknown virus has determined the rapid development of vaccines, especially in the USA and EU. The vaccine production has rapidly changed the future and the business models of pharmaceutical companies involved in Covid-19 vaccine production. These companies, after receiving authorization for Covid-19 vaccine commercialization, have experienced a rapid growth in sales and, more generally, in financial performance. Consequently, this research shows that all the listed companies involved in Covid-19 vaccine production demonstrate a huge growth of revenues and a substantial modification of company size and business models.

In this context, vaccine Covid-19 producers play a fundamental new role in global society related to the contribution offered in the long fight against the virus. This new role also determines a new need for disclosure regarding the environmental, social, and economic effects of their activities during the recent "pandemic years". Through an exploratory study, this paper provides the first results about the disclosures of vaccine producers through corporate social reports. According to the SASB model, the analysis reveals that the main topics discussed in the reports are the clinical trials, linked to the whole process of vaccine development and production, the efforts of the companies to protect employees during the pandemic emergency, and the strategies for ensuring global access to vaccines, especially in low- and middle-income countries. The general conclusion is that these companies have substantially changed their approach to the disclosures after the Covid-19 emergency. The content analysis conducted on the social reports of vaccine production companies shows that the words related to Covid-19 are frequently disclosed in all the reports. This type of information has become a basic approach in disclosures, with the aim of showing the efforts in this field.

From a theoretical perspective, this research provides results in two different directions. Firstly, it aims to understand more about the corporate social responsibility and accountability of pharmaceutical companies. Despite the relevant role in public health played by these companies, the pharmaceutical sector remains under-investigated in the area of corporate social reporting. Secondly, it provides the first results concerning the corporate social reporting of Covid-19 vaccine producers. At the same time, the paper also has some managerial implications for pharmaceutical companies. In fact, the managers of this industry have an opportunity to better understand different accountability approaches and best practices for sustainability reporting during and after the pandemic period.

This research has some limitations, that, at the same time, could be seen as opportunities for future development. First, the paper presents an analysis of the effects of vaccine production on the financial results considering only the amount of total revenues. In the near future, we argue that studies should consider other financial and non-financial variables and data. Moreover, researchers should try to study the composition of revenues in more depth in order to isolate the effects of Covid-19 vaccine sales on the total revenues. Finally, future studies could consider a whole time period of observation including some years after the introduction of the vaccine.

References

Bebbington J, Unerman J, O'Dwyer B (eds) (2014) Sustainability accounting and accountability. Routledge, London

Beloe S, Elkington J, Hester KF, Loose M, Zollinger P (2006) Tomorrow's value. The global reporters 2006 survey of corporate sustainability reporting. SustainAbility, London

Carroll AB (1999) Corporate social responsibility: evolution of a definitional construct. Bus Soc 38(3):268–295

Cook L, LaVan H, Zilic I (2018) An exploratory analysis of corporate social responsibility reporting in US pharmaceutical companies. J Commun Manag 22(2):197–211

Dabic M, Colovic A, Lamotte O, Painter-Morland M, Brozovic S, Svensson G, Wood G (2016) Industry-specific CSR: analysis of 20 years of research. Eur Bus Rev 28(3):250–273

Davis G, Searcy C (2010) A review of Canadian corporate sustainable development reports. J Glob Responsib 1(2):316–329

Demir M, Ming M (2019) Consistencies and discrepancies in corporate social responsibility reporting in the pharmaceutical industry. Sustain Account, Manag Policy J 10(2):333–364

Donham WB (Jul 1929) Business ethics–a general survey. Harv Bus Rev, 385–394

Gamerschlag R, Möller K, Verbeeten F (2011) Determinants of voluntary CSR disclosure: empirical evidence from Germany. RMS 5:233–262

Garcìa-Sanchez IM, Frìas-Aceituno JV, Rodriguez-Dominguez L (2013) Determinants of corporate social disclosure in Spanish local governments. J Clean Prod 39:60–72

Garriga E, Melé D (2004) Corporate social responsibility theories: mapping the territory. J Bus Ethics 53:51–71

Gay EF (1927) The founding of the Harvard Business School. Harv Bus Rev, 397–400

Hahn R, Kühnen M (2013) Determinants of sustainability reporting: a review of results, trends, theory, and opportunities in an expanding field of research. J Clean Prod 59(15):5–21

Hedberg CJ, von Malmborg F (2003) The global reporting initiative and corporate sustainability reporting in Swedish Companies. Corp Soc Responsib Environ Manag 10(3):153–164

Karlsson LC, Soveri A, Lewandowsky S, Karlsson L, Karlsson H, Nolvi S, Karukivi M, Lindfelt M, Antfolk J (2021) Fearing the disease or vaccine: the case of COVID-19. Pers Individ Differ 172:110590

Kolk A (2004) A decade of sustainability reporting: developments and significance. Int J Environ Sustain Dev 3(1):51–64

Kolk A (2010) The integration of corporate governance in corporate social responsibility disclosures. Corp Soc Responsib Environ Manag 17(1):15–26

Langer M (2006) Comparability of sustainability reports. A comparative content analysis of Austrian sustainability reports. In: Schaltegger S, Bennet M, Burrit R (eds) Sustainability accounting and reporting. Springer, Dordrecht, pp 581–602

Leal Filho W (ed) (2018) Handbook of sustainability science and research. Springer, Cham

Lindholt MF, Jørgense F, Bor A, Petersen MB (2021) Public acceptance of COVID-19 vaccines: cross-national evidence on levels and individual-level predictors using observational data. BMJ Open 11:1–12

Lune H, Berg BL (2017) Qualitative research methods for the social sciences. Pearson, Boston

Machingaidze S, Wiysonge CS (2021) Understanding COVID-19 vaccine hesitancy. Nat Med 27:1338–1344

Macnamara J (2021) New insights into crisis communication from an 'inside' emic perspective during COVID-19. Public Relat Inq 10(2):237–262

Manetti G (2011) The quality of stakeholder engagement in sustainability reporting: empirical evidence and critical points. Corp Soc Responsib Environ Manag 18(2):110–122

Manetti G, Toccafondi S (2012) The role of stakeholders in sustainability reporting assurance. J Bus Ethics 107:363–377. https://doi.org/10.1007/s10551-011-1044-1

Perrini F, Pogutz S, Tencati A (2006) Corporate social responsibility in Italy: state of the art. J Bus Strat 23(1):65–91

Rahdari AH, Anvary Rostamy AA (2015) Designing a general set of sustainability indicators at the corporate level. J Clean Prod 108:757–771. https://doi.org/10.1016/j.jclepro.2015.05.108

Ratanajongkol S, Davey H, Low M (2006) Corporate social reporting in Thailand: the news is all good and increasing. Qual Res Account Manag 3(1):67–83

SASB–Sustainability Accounting Standards Board (Oct 2018) Biotechnology & Pharmaceuticals. Sustainability Accounting Standard. https://www.sasb.org/standards/download/?lang=en-us

Sassen R, Azizi L (2018) Assessing sustainability reports of US universities. Int J Sustain High Educ 19(7):1158–1184. https://doi.org/10.1108/IJSHE-06-2016-0114

Schaltegger S, Windolph SE, Harms D, Hörisch J (eds) (2014) Corporate sustainability in international comparison. Springer, New York

Secchi D (2006) The Italian in social reporting: an empirical analysis. Corp Soc Responsib Environ Manag 13(3):133–149

Slater A (2008) KPMG international survey of corporate responsibility reporting 2008. KPMG Global Sustainability Services, The Netherlands

Skouloudis A, Evangelinos KI, Kourmousis F (2010) Assessing non-financial reports according to the global reporting initiative guidelines: evidence from Greece. J Clean Prod 18:426–438

Sobhani FA, Amran A, Zainuddin Y (2009) Revisiting the practices of corporate social and environmental disclosure in Bangladesh. Corp Soc Responsib Environ Manag 16(3):167–183

Stiller Y, Daub CH (2007) Paving the way for sustainable communication: evidence from a Swiss study. Bus Strat Environ 16(7):474–486

Thomas G, Nowak M (2006) Corporate social responsibility: a definition. Working paper 62. Curtin University of Technology, Australia

Vormedal I, Ruud A (2009) Sustainability reporting in Norway—an assessment of performance in the context of legal demands and socio-political drivers. Bus Strat Environ 18(4):207–222

WHO (2020) Coronavirus disease 2019 (COVID-19). Situation report–51. https://www.who.int/docs/default-source/coronaviruse/situation-reports/20200311-sitrep-51-covid-19.pdf?sfvrsn 51ba62e57_10. Accessed 30 Mar 2022

The Role of Local Government in the Provision of Health Services with Additional Reference to COVID-19 Pandemic: Evidence from the Croatian Health System

Lana Kordić and Josip Visković

Abstract Objective: The health care system is essential for the functioning of the economy and society, which was particularly evident during the COVID-19 pandemic. Since health care management should be considered as an integral part of economic development management, the objective of this paper is to examine the role of local in supporting health care development, focusing on the city of Split, Croatia. The problem of different responsibilities for health care facilities complicates the role of local government in providing health care to its citizens. This study examines how local government can nevertheless influence and improve the quality of health services provided. Methodology: The study is based on in-depth interviews with all key stakeholders involved in the provision of health services in the city of Split, with a particular focus on the analysis of COVID-19 crisis. Results: The responses obtained provide insights that cannot be gained through the analysis of quantitative data alone, which is the contribution of this study. The paper argues that it is important to shift the focus from local constraints, which primarily concern direct funding of the health care system, to the various ways to support the development of health care infrastructure.

Keywords Healthcare system · Local governance · COVID-19 pandemic · Croatia · Qualitative methodology

JEL Classification Codes H75 · I18 · R50

L. Kordić (✉) · J. Visković
Faculty of Economics, Business and Tourism, University of Split, Cvite Fiskovića 5, 21000 Split, Croatia
e-mail: lkordic@efst.hr

J. Visković
e-mail: josip.viskovic@efst.hr

N. Persiani et al. (eds.), *Challenges of Healthcare Systems in the Era of COVID-19*, Contributions to Management Science, https://doi.org/10.1007/978-3-031-43114-2_6

1 Introduction

In recent decades, health systems in both developed and developing countries have faced various challenges as a result of economic growth and development, which have increased pressure to provide a wider range of quality health services. Health care systems are looking for ways to respond to the increased demand for health care services resulting from aging populations, increased use of medical technology, information asymmetry between patients and health care providers, lifestyles, etc. (Družić, Smolić & Penava, 2009), while coping with resistance to cost increases. Open and heated discussions are taking place about the sustainability, fairness, and effectiveness of these systems (Zhong, 2010). The upcoming changes in the health system should be based on, among other things, greater solidarity in the provision of the means introduced by the reform to exercise health rights, as well as greater equity in their distribution, equality in the exercise of rights for all beneficiaries, ensuring better access, and a transparent and coherent system. In addition to all these changes, these systems must be financially sustainable in the long term (Setnikar Cankar & Petkovšek, 2010).

Given the importance of health infrastructure and its challenges, as explained earlier, and the importance of a bottom-up approach to meeting the needs of citizens in their local communities, the objective of this study is to critically analyze the powers of local authorities in supporting the health system. In doing so, the focus will shift from direct constraints to any indirect means by which local government can promote and build on strengths and opportunities while preventing or minimizing the impact of weaknesses and threats to the health infrastructure in the city it governs, even if that infrastructure is not owned by the local government.

In addition to the analysis of the legal and institutional framework, these relationships were critically analyzed through interviews with the main stakeholders inside and outside the health system in the city of Split, who have an influence on health care in the urban area as part of their activities. The study of subjective attitudes was conducted within the framework of the development strategy of the City of Split until 2030 (City of Split, 2021), with the aim of analyzing the state of the health infrastructure, as the first phase of strategic planning of its development in the urban area. The interviews were conducted in two rounds, the first in 2019 and the second at the end of 2020, to analyze the impact of the pandemic COVID-19. The responses reflect the views of stakeholders working within or for the system and provide insight that cannot be gained through analysis of quantitative data alone. During the research, particular attention was paid to the challenges of managing the health system, which is made up of facilities with varying ownership, and to the role of local government in supporting health facilities that it does not own but that are important to the local community in which they operate. The former is also the contribution of this study.

After defining the concept of health infrastructure and the importance of its role in economic and social development, the next two chapters present the literature review and methodology. The fourth chapter provides an overview of the functioning of the institutions providing health services in the city of Split, and the fifth chapter critically analyzes the direct and indirect role of local government in the development of health infrastructure using the city of Split as an example, with additional focus on the role of local government during the pandemic. The last two chapters discuss the findings and the main conclusions and limitations, leading to recommendations for further research.

2 Literature Review

According to Pašalić (2003), health infrastructure, as an integral part of non-economic infrastructure, forms an economic, technical, and institutional basis of a developed economic system. Pašalić (2003) divides health infrastructure into infrastructure in the narrow and broad sense. The former implies physical assets in health care, while the latter includes infrastructure areas (activities, branches, sectors, and subsectors) that provide infrastructure services, while also including other productive inputs in addition to physical ones to achieve health effects. Yescombe (2010) describes health infrastructure as essential to the functioning of both the economy and society. As opposed to economic activities, infrastructure activities, which in general do not normally have the characteristics of economic activities, are extremely important for the development of each country. The nature of decision-making, the market mechanism, and the degree and form of government intervention vary in the system of infrastructure activities. As a general input, infrastructure activities are a prerequisite for the harmonious economic development of any country.

The purpose of this study is to examine the role of local government in supporting health care development. Although the different responsibilities for health care facilities complicate the role of local government in providing health care services to its citizens, this study examines how local government can nevertheless influence and improve the quality of health care services provided.

Current literature critically analyzes the role of local government in providing public services (Koprić et al. 2016), but also national policies in response to the COVID-19 pandemic as one of the major challenges for health systems (e.g., Calleja et al. 2022; Merkaj and Santolini 2022), which also includes the case of Croatia (Đakula et al. 2022; Koprić 2020).

Furthermore, Schomaker and Bauer (2020) analyzed how local administrations in Austria and Germany confronted the COVID-19 pandemic using surveys among employees of local public administrations. However, they were focused on the perceptions of having bureaucracies coped with the challenges emerging during the pandemic.

Finally, there were studies that analyzed the role of local authorities in health systems, mostly during the pandemic (Jambrović 2021, 2022; Kuković 2021; for more read Nunes Silva 2022). In more detail, Kuković (2021) analyzed the results of the first post-COVID-19 by surveying the mayors of the Slovenian local government. The author presented the results of the first survey of mayors of Slovenian municipalities after the COVID-19 crisis concluding that there is no single and well-established procedure for dealing with a crisis and that the intensity of action depended largely on the commitment, initiative and innovation of the individual mayor. Still, only one part of the stakeholders who are direct or indirectly responsible for providing health services on the local level, are interviewed. Moreover, most studies, which investigated the role of local government during the pandemic, were based on source materials, the sparse literature and/or legal acts (for more read Nunes Silva, 2022).

Similarly, Jambrović (2021) identified and analyzed challenges, responsibilities, and adjustments of Croatian cities during the pandemic, using data content analysis (using strategic documents, legal regulations, and soft law documents). The author concluded that changes in the approach to local governance are necessary for local units not only to better adapt during the crisis but also to effectively solve the problems of the post-crisis period. Furthermore, COVID-19 crisis management in Croatia, with specific emphasis on the contribution of subnational levels of government, was analyzed by Jambrović (2022). Using empirical research that was conducted with data content analysis, the author stressed the role of local and regional units in dealing with the coronavirus crisis. In addition to being able to adapt very quickly organizationally, functionally and effectively implemented the decisions of national institutions, they have made their own contribution to combating the spread of the pandemic (by using guaranteed autonomy and making decisions in accordance with local circumstances).

However, what all previous studies have in common is the conclusion that during the pandemic local governments undertake many innovative activities, slightly changing and upgrading their traditional responsibilities. All of these mentioned provide justification for further research that includes investigating the views of all stakeholders working within or for the health system paying attention to the challenges of managing that system and the role of local government in supporting health facilities in order to provide the most effective health services to the local community.

3 Methodology

In order to achieve the objective of this paper, namely, the critical analysis of the powers of local authorities in supporting the health system, interviews were chosen as sources that can provide appropriate types of data, in addition to the analysis of the legal and institutional framework. Indeed, the overarching purpose of using interviews is to analyze the views of key stakeholders on current integration both within and outside the health system, i.e., to explore different direct and indirect ways to support the development of health care infrastructure. This is to shift the focus from local constraints, which are primarily related to direct financing of the health care system, to the different ways to support the development of health care infrastructure. Therefore, the following research questions were formulated: (1) Strengths, opportunities, weaknesses, and threats of the health care system? (2) In what ways do the main actors in their field of activity contribute to the functioning of the health care system? (3) How familiar are key stakeholders with each other's possibilities for action?

Specifically, a semi-structured approach was used in this study. According to Young et al. (2018), interviews are flexible and allow for in-depth analysis with a relatively small sample size. In addition, semi-structured interviews rely on a pre-designed interview guide that includes standard questions and allows for comparison and maintenance of data quality. Nevertheless, this type of interview allows flexibility, i.e., the interviewer can ask additional questions to analyze complex topics.

As mentioned in the previous chapter, as part of the development strategy of the City of Split until 2030 (City of Split 2021) and for the purpose of analyzing the state of the healthcare infrastructure a first round of interviews was conducted in November 2019. The interviews were conducted with the main stakeholders that affect the provision of healthcare in the urban area, both inside and outside the system. Specifically, the research includes two external stakeholders, one in the City of Split and one in Split-Dalmatia County, whose scope of activities includes healthcare provision in the city area. Furthermore, the study includes five internal stakeholders: directors (or their deputies) of key health institutions in the city area. These are Split-Dalmatia County Public Health Institute, the Split Clinical Hospital Centre and the Split-Dalmatia County Medical Centre, expert from the Croatian Medical Association, and scientific and teaching staff from the Faculty of Medicine at the University of Split, i.e., doctor employed in healthcare institutions in the city of Split.

With the aim of analyzing the state of the healthcare system in the city of Split due to the outbreak of the pandemic, the second round of interviews with the same key stakeholders of the healthcare system in the city was conducted in November 2020. In order to define, based on the situation analysis, the strengths, weaknesses, opportunities, and threats that define the objectives, priorities, and actions for the future development of the health infrastructure, i.e., to make the situation analysis as efficient as possible, it was necessary to interview again the main stakeholders. Moreover, at the end of 2020, no quantitative data were available to analyze the impact of the pandemic on the health system, so the only way to study this impact was to examine the subjective views of key stakeholders.

All stakeholders interviewed were properly briefed on topics such as informed consent to ensure they understood the goals of the project and how their data would be used. An interview protocol (included in the appendix) was used to conduct the survey, which was identical in one section for internal and external stakeholders, but included an additional set of questions for internal stakeholders. After the initial set of questions was created, an interview with colleagues was tested. The first round of interviews was conducted in person, while the second round was supported by video technology, i.e., zoom meetings. In both cases, the average duration of each interview was approximately 30 min. The analysis of the interviews did not include codes.

4 Functioning of Health Care Services in the City of Split

4.1 *Legal and Institutional Framework*

According to McPake et al. (2020), providing of health care services takes place in a series of complex and regulated markets, with existing agencies, oligopolistic or monopolistic organizations, payments through taxation, or social insurance arrangements. A health system is made up of users, payers, providers, and regulators, and due to different possible relations between them, it can take a different form of organization. Furthermore, in it, governments can play a number of different roles as financers, regulators, and/or providers of services. In some health systems, the government is the dominant actor, providing and financing most services. Most health systems are now observed to have a number of sub-components, characterized by different mixes of public and private characteristics and different levels and types of health insurance coverage.

With reference to the legal and institutional framework for health care in the Republic of Croatia, the basic characteristics of the different levels of health care in the city of Split are presented below.

According to the Act on Health Care (Official Gazette, 100/2018), health services of interest to the Republic of Croatia are provided as a public service at the level of primary, secondary, and tertiary care, as well as health care facilities. Specifically, primary health care includes general/family medicine and care for infants and preschool children. Secondary-level health care includes specialist consultation and hospital care. Compared to primary health care, it includes more complex measures and procedures for prevention, diagnosis, and treatment of diseases and injuries. The specialist-consiliary activity can be performed in the day clinic and health center, where laboratory and other diagnostic activities are also provided. Hospital activities include diagnosis, treatment and medical rehabilitation, health care, patient stay and nutrition, and other activities that are part of the performance of the basic activities of health care institutions. Tertiary level health care activity includes the most complex forms of health care, scientific work, and teaching based on contracts with educational institutions. The activity of health care at the tertiary level includes the activity of clinics, clinical hospitals, and clinical hospital centers. Palliative care may also be provided at the tertiary level. The activity of health institutes is a part of health care activity at the primary, secondary, and tertiary levels and includes activity in public health, transfusion medicine, occupational/vocational and sports medicine, toxicology and anti-doping, emergency medicine, and telemedicine. All the above-mentioned levels are interconnected and cooperate with the aim of providing health care to the citizens of the city of Split.

At the same time, health care facilities have different ownership. Clinical hospital centers, clinical hospitals, and state health institutes are state-owned, while general and special hospitals, health centers, polyclinics, pharmacies, emergency medical treatment facilities, home health care facilities, and county public health institutes are county-owned (Official Gazette, 100/2018).

The primary level of health protection in the city of Split is organized and carried out, among others, by the Split-Dalmatia County Medical Centre. Within the Split-Dalmatia County Medical Centre, the departments of general medicine, dentistry, radiology, and specialist and conciliary health care operate (Split-Dalmatia County Medical Centre, 2019).

Split Dental Polyclinic and Rehabilitation Centre for People with Developmental Disabilities in Split are two polyclinics established by Split-Dalmatia County, which participate in specialist conciliar health care in the city of Split.

At the tertiary level, health care for the inhabitants of the city of Split, but also for the inhabitants of other places that gravitate to Split (primarily the inhabitants of the Dalmatian coastal counties and the inhabitants of Bosnia and Herzegovina), is provided by the Split Clinical Hospital Centre, established by the Republic of Croatia. This institution is the largest economic entity in the area, with almost 4,000 employees. Comparing the City of Split with the City of Zagreb, which also has a gravitational area that extends beyond the territorial boundaries of the city, it is obvious that the development of health infrastructure in the City of Split, from the point of view of the possibilities of the local government, is limited by the powers of the City of Split over facilities that are not owned by it. These powers for the territory of the City of Zagreb are much greater since the City of Zagreb is a separate unit of regional self-government, which means that it independently organizes the work of the facilities it creates.

Among the institutes operating in the territory of the city of Split are the Split-Dalmatia County Public Health Institute and the Institute of Emergency Medicine of Split-Dalmatia County. In addition to the above-mentioned institutes, there is also a regional office of the Croatian Institute of Health Insurance in the City of Split.

In addition to public institutions, primary health care is also provided by private health care providers, i.e., private polyclinics and hospitals at the secondary level of health care. In 2018, most of the private companies in the category of health activities in the city of Split were in specialist practices (55 facilities), dental practices (15 facilities), and in the category of other health activities in home health care and rehabilitation (14 facilities). All these categories recorded an increase in the number of registered facilities compared to 2014 and 2018 (Croatian Chamber of Commerce-Digital Chamber, 2020).

4.2 Attitudes About Health Infrastructure—Results from First Round of Interviews with Key Stakeholders Involved in the Provision of Health Services

In addition to listing the facilities according to their level, the following summarizes the subjective views of the interviewed stakeholders on the functioning of the facilities described earlier.

The interviewees emphasized that the facilities at the primary level of health protection are the most important health care facilities in the city of Split. In particular, they emphasized the importance of prevention and the role of the "gatekeeper" that primary health care plays in the health care system. One of the problems faced by the Split-Dalmatia County Medical Center was mentioned as the renting of premises for the provision of healthcare services, which belong to the City of Split, at market prices. Another problem that was highlighted is the uneven availability of primary health care services in different parts of the city. This mainly affects the outskirts of the city, and the trend of population migration could further deepen this gap. In this context, it should be emphasized that there is a lack of statistical data on the provision of health services that also take into account the spatial aspect. The importance of processing this type of data, i.e., analyzing the spatial component, is also emphasized in the Guidelines for the Preparation of the Urban Development Strategy, Monitoring of its Implementation, and Evaluation (Ministry of Regional Development and EU Funds, 2015), suggesting that this type of analytical basis should be provided in the future. In addition, discussions on access to emergency facilities highlighted another problem of stationary traffic.

When discussing the provision of health services at the tertiary level, respondents indicated that trained staff was the greatest strength, while lack of resources (space, equipment, and staff) was cited as a weakness of the Split Clinical Hospital Centre. It was highlighted that the Split Clinical Hospital Centre develops strategic healthcare development projects that serve as a foundation for the development of the healthcare system in the city of Split, Split-Dalmatia County, and beyond. In fact, the facility serves as a general hospital in the city of Split, while as a clinical hospital, it also provides services to residents from a much larger area outside the city of Split. Given its spatial location, it has the role of a strategic facility.

Respondents identified the effective satisfaction of the increased demand for health services at all levels of health care as a challenge for health care facilities in the city of Split, due to the increasing number of tourists staying in Split during the tourist season or coming there in search of health services. According to the OECD recommendations (OECD, 2007) on the provision of alternative sources of funding for the development and maintenance of existing infrastructure, different views have been expressed on the provision of additional funding for health infrastructure through the earmarking of a certain percentage of money from tourism fees, emphasizing the importance of considering other sources of funding. However, the problem of finding an appropriate way to ensure the functioning of the health system during the tourist season remains.

The main health care stakeholders in the city of Split emphasize the need for joint action by authorities at all levels and all health care institutions to ensure quality health care in the city area. The importance of horizontal and vertical integration both within and outside the healthcare system is emphasized, as is a multidisciplinary approach aimed primarily at prevention and then treatment of disease. Particularly encouraging is the desire of all interviewees to understand the role, i.e., the desires and possibilities for action, of the various stakeholders in the health system, as well as the constructive expression of their own views with the aim of finding solutions to the challenges ahead.

5 The Role of the City of Split in the Functioning of Health Infrastructure in the City Area

5.1 The City's Role Within the Given Legislative Framework

The role of the City in relation to the functioning of the health infrastructure in the urban area is largely defined by the Law on Health Care (Official Gazette, 100/2018). Accordingly, the City of Split's Administrative Department of Social Affairs, Health Care and Demography "... performs administrative, professional and other tasks related to the provision of social care for its citizens, meets the local health needs of its residents, proposes measures to improve local social and health protection measures for the population, monitors social and demographic trends and phenomena, proposes the organisation of educational and health measures, prepares expert studies, and cooperates with other authorities to improve the current state ..." (City of Split 2019).

Although the city is legally obligated to provide the aforementioned services, this only affects certain services, and due to the different responsibilities for health facilities, the city has no direct ability to influence the delivery of most health services. On the other hand, there are a number of indirect ways in which local government can support the provision of health services. This was particularly evident during the pandemic and will be discussed in more detail later in the paper, using the city of Split as an example.

In order to analyze the role of the city within the given legal framework, i.e., the involvement of the local government in the financing of health infrastructure we use available data. Namely, Table 1 shows the allocated expenditures for health care of the Administrative Department of Social Affairs, Health Care and Demography of the city of Split in selected years. The focus of the Department is on preventive measures to improve the health of the local population.

5.2 Attitudes About City's Role—Results From First Round of Interviews with Key Stakeholders Involved in the Provision of Health Services

Analyzing possible future investments, the Head of the Administrative Department for Social Affairs, Health Care and Demography emphasized during the interview two points. Firstly, City of Split was included in the Healthy Cities Network (part of the WHO Healthy Cities Project) and secondly the goals of this administrative

Table 1 Expenditure of the administrative department for social welfare and health care of the city of split in HRK

Type of expenditure	Year			
	2013	2016	2017	2018
Improving health of children and young people	841,646.00	900,746.84	750,930.40	871,778.22
Health promotion, disease prevention and risk behavior	877,039.00	1,623,866.94	1,115,743.65	2,159,856.19
Health promotion and support for professional training projects	237,492.00	145,089.25	85,000.00	114,998.00
Psychosocial treatment of people with mental health problems	47,000.00	–	–	–
Combating alcohol addiction and gambling	238,234.00	–	–	270,000.00
Psychosocial treatment of addicts	167,813.00	–	–	–
Primary, secondary, and tertiary prevention of disease and addiction	132,500.00	–	-	–
Preventing and combating the consequences of external causes	54,000.00	–	–	–
Palliative care	0.00	529,110.00	563,932.18	1,341,713.59
Control of addiction	0.00	560,491.78	263,382.00	140,000.00
Prevention and control of chronic and mass non-communicable diseases	0.00	323,175.91	137,329.47	190,330.50
Prevention and control of acute diseases	–	66,000.00	66,100.00	102,814.10

Source City of Split, 2019

department for the next 10 years are to support the development of mental health, early childhood development, palliative care development (through the development of services, mobile palliative teams and contributing to the construction of hospices) and care for the elderly. She emphasized that the City of Split is ready to participate in the co-financing of projects for the development of health infrastructure. Namely, Annex D of the Cohesion Policy Investment Guidelines for Croatia for the period 2021–2027 (European Commission, 2019) states that the development of research and innovation capacities and the use of advanced technologies are among the priority investment needs. According to this document, health outcomes remain inadequate while the healthcare system is inefficient. Therefore, the priority investment needs must be to improve the availability, efficiency, and stability of health and long-term care service delivery (this includes, but is not limited to, developing infrastructure capacity for long-term care and developing health promotion and disease prevention programs). In support of investing in disease prevention, the above report (European Commission, 2019) notes that both smoking and alcohol consumption in the country are above the EU average, increasing cardiovascular and cancer mortality. The above facts provide clear indications of the areas that the European Commission will consider eligible for co-funding, and therefore the City of Split should focus its consideration of its role in the remaining co-funding on these areas.

Although this situation analysis was prepared for the elaboration of the City of Split Development Strategy until 2030, i.e., with the aim of guiding the future work of the City of Split, Split-Dalmatia County or the Republic of Croatia owns most of the healthcare facilities in the city area. However, projects that are the responsibility of the City of Split and focus, for example, on prevention, care for the elderly and disabled, etc., reduce the pressure on the health system.

5.3 The City's Role During COVID-19 Pandemic—Results From Second Round of Interviews with Key Stakeholders Involved in the Provision of Health Services

The consequences of the pandemic caused by the coronavirus (officially known as SARS-CoV-2) COVID-19 have undoubtedly affected the health care system. Given the importance of the health infrastructure and its challenges, as well as the appreciation of the bottom-up approach to meeting the needs of citizens in their local communities, the second objective of this study was to critically analyze the role of local authorities in supporting the health system in their area in the context of the pandemic COVID-19. Indeed, after the initial centralized response to COVID-19, the governance approach in Croatia increasingly involved regional and local authorities in the implementation of measures from May 2020 onwards.

All respondents consider COVID-19 to be an extremely dangerous threat to the general health of the residents of the city of Split (it is perceived as an even more dangerous threat by respondents who also work in the health sector). When evaluating the measures taken at the beginning of the pandemic outbreak by the Government of the Republic of Croatia, line ministries and the National Civil Protection Headquarters to respond to the pandemic, they agreed that the measures were useful. Moreover, some of the interviewees pointed out that they were the best possible measures at the time, considering the available information and knowledge about the virus. Although the measures taken later by the above-mentioned authorities were also useful, and despite the understanding that efforts were made to maintain the balance between pandemic containment and economic viability, some respondents noted that the measures were not sufficient. More specifically, they were considered too soft. On the other hand, some interviewees felt that sanctions should have been imposed on those who did not comply in order to be effective (at the time of the interview, the Law for the Protection of the Population against Infectious Diseases (Official Gazette 2020a), which went into effect on December 5, 2020, had not yet been amended). In addition, some of the interviewees pointed out the inconsistency and non-transparency of the work of the analyzed bodies, which ultimately led to a loss of trust among the population, which in turn contributed to the fact that a significant part of the population did not follow the measures. When analyzing the adequacy of the measures taken by the Split-Dalmatia County Administration at the beginning of the pandemic outbreak as well as at the end of 2020, it was perceived by the respondents as very efficient. Although they positively evaluate the decentralized approach to management, some of the respondents believe that the Split-Dalmatia County Headquarters, although up-to-date in its activities, should have been more proactive. The work of the Regional Office for Civil Protection in Split was also perceived as efficient.

In addition, some interviewees pointed out that all structures related to the protection and prevention of the epidemic have been actively involved in all activities since the beginning of the pandemic. In terms of coordinated actions, it is worth highlighting the good cooperation of all stakeholders in the city of Split, i.e., between the city of Split, Split-Dalmatia County, the Split-Dalmatia County Public Health Institute, the County Medical Centre, the Split Clinical Hospital Centre, and between the different levels of health services. Thus, the County reacted by redirecting financial resources for equipping the facilities it owned with the necessary equipment and by allocating additional staff and acquiring equipment to the Split-Dalmatia County Public Health Institute, an institution that was already operating when the first confirmed case occurred in the world. The epidemiological service found itself in an extremely difficult situation, as its current capacity could not even prepare it for a pandemic of this magnitude. Under the given conditions, the service made sufficient efforts to function under exceptional circumstances, but the increasing influx of patients presented it with new organizational problems. This pandemic has highlighted the importance of the epidemiological service and the need for a stronger presence of this profession.

Moreover, through meetings and continuous monitoring of the situation and discussion of measures to balance economic activities and health protection, the City of Split has supported the health system financially, but also materially, for example, by providing rooms for the accommodation of people in self-quarantine.

The implementation of epidemiological measures and the increasing number of COVID-19 patients have placed significant strain on the functioning of the health care system. By analyzing the functioning of the health care system at each level, we gained insight into the readiness of each level of the health care system in the city of Split to function under the conditions of the COVID-19 pandemic. It is important to emphasize that the majority of respondents believe that the response of all levels of health protection in the city of Split was the best possible given the current possibilities and characteristics of the health system. In order to strengthen the health system and better respond to sudden shocks, it needs to be recognized that no one was able to anticipate the situation related to the outbreak of the pandemic.

In assessing the severity of the impact of the COVID-19 pandemic, respondents agreed that delayed health care due to limited access to health care services, i.e., patients postponing screening or regular checkups during the COVID-19 pandemic for fear of coronavirus, will have a very large impact in the future. Those most affected were the chronically ill, who had difficulty accessing checkups and specialized services, so the risk of malignant disease is likely to increase. The pandemic, i.e., the measures that led to quarantine and reduced social contacts, will have serious consequences for mental health, which will also have an extremely positive impact on the future functioning of the health system in the city of Split. Considering all this, the pressure on the health system without huge financial investments and organizational efforts can immediately be reduced by acting responsibly.

6 Discussion

When considering the role of the city of Split in the development of health infrastructure, it would be wrong and insufficient to limit ourselves only to the present analysis. Taking into account all the above-mentioned legal constraints related to budgeting, i.e., the possibility of financing health infrastructure at the local level, the focus can and should be shifted to the analysis of additional opportunities for the city's participation in the development of health infrastructure. Indeed, as the City has already done, it can and should support health infrastructure development through other areas of activity that do not necessarily fall under the purview of the Department of Social Services, Health and Demographics. These include, for example, amending the land use plan with regard to the conversion of buildings and providing additional land for the development of health infrastructure. The City can also participate in solving the problem of stationary traffic, either on its own or through a public–private partnership. Moreover, it can contribute to accessibility through the development of public transport, provide premises in its ownership for various purposes depending on the needs of the health system or rent them at preferential rates in order to improve the availability and quality of health care. Besides it can help by jointly establishing a kindergarten with a health facility improving working conditions for health personnel and the reputation of the facility where the kindergarten is located. In addition, improving health outcomes for certain categories of residents of the City of Split, e.g., veterans, can also be achieved through the Department for Cooperation with Veterans and Veterans Associations. Namely, the Department can support more effective implementation of the National Programme for Psychosocial and Health Support for Participants and Victims of the Croatian War of Independence, World War II and Returnees from Peacekeeping Missions (Ministry of Veterans Affairs, 2014). Additionally, it can help the implementation of programs, projects, and activities under the Ministry for Croatian Veterans that improve the quality of life and health of said population. At the same time, incentives for the development of health infrastructure can be created by involving the Split Tourist Board in the above development, through membership in the health tourism cluster, etc.

Moreover, by analyzing the role of local authorities in relation to the functioning of the health system during the pandemic, further conclusions can be drawn. Namely, there is a need to build on the strengths, take advantage of the opportunities, manage the weaknesses to minimize them and raise awareness of external threats that negatively impact the health system's functioning. Health system resilience refers to the ability of the health system to successfully adapt to a changing environment, sudden shocks, or crises. This not only includes timely response to short- and long-term challenges and threats in its environment but also refers to the pace of recovery from possible disruptions that threaten its functioning and consequently jeopardize harmonious economic and social development (Ćosić et al. 2017). The goal is to ensure a sustainable healthcare system characterized by proactive, forward-looking management. This also means learning from current crises in order to better respond to future shocks. In this context, respondents are aware of the lack of resources (human and financial) needed to meet a growing number of health needs and therefore emphasize the need to improve organization, i.e., effectiveness and efficiency, while strengthening the capacity to deliver health services.

Finally, the occurrence of a disease such as COVID-19 is not only a problem for health professionals but also for the entire community. However, most citizens behave in a detached, almost negligent manner, as if they were not affected until they themselves become ill. People are also unaware of the indirect damage. At this point, the long-term consequences of the virus are unknown. In addition, the increasing number of COVID-19 patients could hinder the effective functioning of other health services. It also creates negative social pressure on those who comply with the measures and behave responsibly. In the future, the city of Split can and should respond to the aforementioned problems within its legal framework through education, prevention, and support to strengthen mental health.

7 Conclusion

In this paper, health infrastructure is considered as part of the public capital of non-productive infrastructure, which indirectly participates in economic activity through the maintenance, security, and improvement of human capital skills. The paper addresses the role of local government in the development of health infrastructure in its area in general and in particular in the context of the pandemic COVID-19. Thus, the aim of this study was to critically analyze, through the example of the city of Split, the powers of the local administration through which it can contribute to the development of health infrastructure in the urban area it administers, even if it is not directly owned by it.

The study includes an analysis of the legal and institutional framework in the field of health care in the Republic of Croatia, as well as two rounds of interviews with key stakeholders, both inside and outside the health care system, who have an influence on the provision of health care in the city of Split. Therefore, findings reflect the views of stakeholders on the role of the City of Split in supporting the development of health care infrastructure-an insight that could not be gained by analyzing quantitative data alone.

The main conclusion is that it is crucial to shift the focus of local economic policymakers from the limited possibilities of direct funding under the jurisdiction of the Administrative Department of Social Affairs, Health Care and Demography. The focus should be on various ways of supporting the development of health infrastructure through the exercise of its functions under its broad self-government jurisdiction for the benefit of its citizens. More specifically, the City of Split can and should support the development of health infrastructure through the adoption of an appropriate spatial plan, the development of stationary transport, public transport, the provision of city-owned premises at preferential prices, all with the aim of improving the availability and quality of health care. Other options include preventive measures through preschool and primary education, promotion of sports activities, etc. In addition, health promotion, prevention, and mental health development are the direct responsibility of local governments, and they were all identified as critical during the pandemic. Finally, although the key stakeholders are insufficiently aware of each other's responsibilities, they are aware of the importance of joint action, and their desire to work together is encouraging to better understand the different roles of stakeholders in effective joint action.

Finally, pandemic showed that clearer procedures for responsibilities within the health care system as well as capacity building are needed to ensure that all stakeholders at all levels of health care effectively fulfill their roles. The biggest identified weakness of the health system in Split is a lack of capital and medical staff, which has become an even bigger problem during the pandemic. Finally, considering the role of local authorities, a decentralized approach, partnership and co-management in community-led local development must be promoted. The partnership of economic, civil society, and the private sector has an important role to play in addressing local development from the bottom up. This will ensure new sources of capital and quality health care in urban areas. The importance of horizontal and vertical integration within and outside the health system is emphasized, as is a multidisciplinary approach that focuses primarily on prevention and then treatment of disease.

Although this analysis involved only one local case study, it provides relevant policy recommendations. Namely, the responses provide insights that cannot be gained by analyzing quantitative data alone, which is an important contribution of this study. The limitation of the study is its spatial dimension, and although most of the conclusions are applicable to other cities in Croatia, future studies should aim at international comparisons. This could then serve as a basis for proposals to change the legal and institutional framework for local governance actions based on best practices.

Appendix

First round of interviews (November 2019)

As key stakeholders your view of the healthcare system in the Split city area is very important to us. Indeed, in combination with objective indicators based on available statistical databases, it will serve to define the state of health infrastructure in the territory of the city of Split. This study of subjective attitudes is part of the framework of the development strategy of the City of Split until 2030 (City of Split, 2021), with the aim of analyzing the state of the health infrastructure, as the first phase of strategic planning of its development in the city area.

1. I am employed:

- In the primary health care system.
- In specialist healthcare.
- In the hospital inpatient health care system.
- In the department of emergency medicine.
- In the Institute of Public Health.
- In an educational institution.
- In a scientific-educational institution.
- In the administrative department of Split-Dalmatia County.
- In the administrative department of the city of Split.
- Other (please specify where):________________________.

2. How do you see the healthcare system in Split today?
3. Characteristics/elements of the healthcare system in Split today:

THREE BEST	THREE WORST
.	.
.	.
.	.
What is TOO MUCH	What is TOO LITTLE
.	.
.	.
.	.

4. Please, identify the development potential of the level of health care in which you work (primary/secondary/tertiary health care) or for your job if you work in facilities outside of the health care levels listed above

WHAT DO YOU SEE AS POTENTIAL? HOW TO INCREASE /IMPROVE:				
Level or activity	Availability of health services	Quality of health services	Revenue of health facilities	Organization of health service delivery
.	.	.	.	.
.	.	.	.	.
.	.	.	.	.

5. To exploit potential, i.e., to achieve development of health care infrastructure in Split:

WHAT WE HAVE?	WHAT IS STILL NEEDED?
.	.
.	.
.	.

6. How do you see the healthcare system in Split in 10 years (2030)?

Second round of interviews (November 2020)

The standstill caused by the epidemic of the disease COVID-19 has undoubtedly affected the health system, so we can already assume that the recovery will be arduous and will require special short- and even medium-term measures. Certain support measures should be taken as soon as possible, so it is advisable to collect primary data on the state of the health care system (in fact, secondary data are not immediately available). Only after collecting primary data, it will be possible to establish the goals of recovery and further development and determine what the policymakers should do. Therefore, as key stakeholders, your view of the situation is very important to us.

INTRODUCTORY QUESTION

2. I am employed:

- In the primary health care system.
- In specialist healthcare.
- In the hospital inpatient health care system.
- In the department of emergency medicine.
- In the Institute of Public Health.
- In an educational institution.
- In a scientific-educational institution.
- In the administrative department of Split-Dalmatia County.
- In the administrative department of the city of Split.
- Other (please specify where):__________________________.

EVALUATION OF MEASURES

2. What is the Threat of COVID-19 to the General Health of the Inhabitants of the City of Split? (1: Not at All Dangerous, 10: Extremely Dangerous)

.	1	2	3	4	5	6	7	8	9	10	.
Not at all dangerous	.	.	.	.	.	.	.	.	.	.	Extremely dangerous

3. How do you evaluate the measures taken by the Government of the Republic of Croatia, the relevant ministries, and the National Civil Protection Headquarters at the beginning of the epidemic to respond to the epidemic caused by the virus COVID-19?

I evaluate the measures as counterproductive	I rate the measures as useless	I rate measures as neither useful nor unhelpful	I rate measures as useful
.	.	.	.

4. How do you rate the measures currently being taken by the Government of the Republic of Croatia, the relevant ministries, and the National Civil Protection Headquarters to respond to the epidemic caused by the virus COVID-19?

I evaluate the measures as counterproductive	I rate the measures as useless	I rate measures as neither useful nor unhelpful	I rate measures as useful
.	.	.	.

5. How adequately did the Split-Dalmatia County Civil Protection Headquarters respond at the beginning of the outbreak of the epidemic caused by the virus COVID-19? (1: worst possible, 10: best possible).

1	2	3	4	5	6	7	8	9	10
.	.	.	.	.	.	.	.	.	.

6. How adequately is the Split-Dalmatia County Civil Protection Headquarters currently responding to the epidemic caused by the virus COVID-19? (1: worst possible, 10: best possible).

1	2	3	4	5	6	7	8	9	10
.	.	.	.	.	.	.	.	.	.

7. How adequately did the Split Civil Protection Headquarter respond at the beginning of the outbreak of the epidemic caused by the virus COVID-19? (1: worst possible, 10: best possible).

1	2	3	4	5	6	7	8	9	10
.	.	.	.	.	.	.	.	.	.

8. How adequately does the Split Civil Protection Headquarter currently operate in relation to the epidemic caused by the virus COVID-19? (1: worst possible, 10: best possible).

1	2	3	4	5	6	7	8	9	10
.	.	.	.	.	.	.	.	.	.

9. Please comment on your chosen ranking.

FUNCTIONALITY OF HEALTH CARE SYSTEM

10. How do you assess the readiness of primary health care in the area of the city of Split to function in the conditions of the epidemic COVID-19? (1: worst possible, 10: best possible; 0: cannot evaluate).

0	1	2	3	4	5	6	7	8	9	10
.	.	.	.	.	.	.	.	.	.	.

10. Could you comment on your answer in relation to specific activities within primary health care (e.g., general/family medicine, preschool children health care, women health care, health care in the patient's home, outpatient health care, and dental health care):

11. How do you assess the readiness of emergency outpatient medical care in the area of the city of Split to function in the conditions of the epidemic COVID-19? (1: worst possible, 10: best possible; 0: cannot evaluate).

0	1	2	3	4	5	6	7	8	9	10
.	.	.	.	.	.	.	.	.	.	.

12. How would you rate the readiness of emergency departments in Split Clinical Hospital Center to function in the conditions of the COVID-19 epidemic? (1: worst possible, 10: best possible; 0: cannot evaluate).

0	1	2	3	4	5	6	7	8	9	10
.	.	.	.	.	.	.	.	.	.	.

13. How do you evaluate the readiness of the specialized health care system in the area of the city of Split to function under the conditions of an epidemic caused by the virus COVID-19? (1: worst possible, 10: best possible; 0: cannot evaluate).

0	1	2	3	4	5	6	7	8	9	10
.	.	.	.	.	.	.	.	.	.	.

14. How do you evaluate the readiness of hospitals in the area of the city of Split to function in the conditions of the COVID-19 epidemic? (1: worst possible, 10: best possible; 0: cannot evaluate).

0	1	2	3	4	5	6	7	8	9	10
.	.	..	.	.	.	.	.	.	.	.

15. How do you evaluate the general safety measures taken by health professionals during the COVID-19 virus epidemic? (1: not effective at all, 10: most effective possible; 0: cannot evaluate).

0	1	2	3	4	5	6	7	8	9	10
.	.	.	.	.	.	.	.	.	.	.

16. How do you evaluate the readiness of the Split-Dalmatia County Public Health Institute to work in the conditions of the COVID-19 epidemic? (1: worst possible, 10: best possible; 0: cannot evaluate).

0	1	2	3	4	5	6	7	8	9	10
.	.	.	.	.	.	.	.	.	.	.

17. Please comment on your chosen ranking.

FUNCTIONING OF HEALTHCARE IN THE FUTURE (questions for internal stakeholders)

18. How would you rate the extent of health care delays caused by limited access to health care services during the outbreak of COVID-19? (1: not at all significant for the future, 10: will have a very large impact in the future).

.	1	2	3	4	5	6	7	8	9	10	.
Not at all significant for the future	.	.	.	.	.	.	.	.	.	.	Will have a very large impact in the future

19. How would you rate the severity of the impact of the epidemic COVID-19 and the actions that led to the quarantine on mental health? (1: not relevant to the functioning of the health system in the territory of the city of Split, 10: extremely important to the functioning of the health system in the territory of the city of Split).

.	1	2	3	4	5	6	7	8	9	10	.
Not relevant to the functioning of the health system in the territory of the city of Split	.	.	.	.	.	.	.	.	.	.	Extremely important to the functioning of the health system in the territory of the city of Split

20. To what extent did the implementation of epidemiological measures and the increased number of patients with COVID-19 affect the functioning of health care in the city of Split at the beginning of the epidemic? (1: they did not affect the functioning of health care in the territory of the city of Split, 10: they significantly affected the functioning of health care in the territory of the city of Split)

.	1	2	3	4	5	6	7	8	9	10	.
They did not affect the functioning of health care in the territory of the city of Split	.	.	.	.	.	.	.	.	.	.	They significantly affected the functioning of health care in the territory of the city of Split

21. To what extent do the current implementation of epidemiological measures and the increased number of patients with COVID-19 affect the functioning of health care in the city of Split? (1: they do not burden the functioning of health care in the territory of the City of Split, 10: they significantly burden the functioning of health care in the territory of the City of Split).

.	1	2	3	4	5	6	7	8	9	10	.
They do not burden the functioning of health care in the territory of the city of Split	.	.	.	.	.	.	.	.	.	.	They significantly burden the functioning of health care in the territory of the city of Split

22. How do you estimate the severity of the impact of COVID-19 on the functioning of healthcare in the city of Split in the next 18–24 months? (1: will not affect the functioning of health care in the territory of the city of Split, 10: will significantly affect the functioning of health care in the territory of the city of Split).

.	1	2	3	4	5	6	7	8	9	10	.
Will not affect the functioning of health care in the territory of the city of Split	.	.	.	.	.	.	.	.	.	.	Will significantly affect the functioning of health care in the territory of the city of Split

23. Please comment on your chosen rankings.

References

Calleja N et al (2022) Managing COVID-19 in four small countries: initial response to the pandemic in San Marino, Montenegro, Malta and Cyprus. Health Policy 126(4):281–286. https://doi.org/10.1016/j.healthpol.2022.01.008

City of Split (2019) Administrative department for social welfare, health care and demography of the city of Split, city of Split, Croatia. https://www.split.hr/gradska-uprava/upravna-tijela/upravni-odjel-za-socijalnu-skrb-zdravstvenu-zastitu-i-demografiju (10.12.2019)

City of Split (2021) City of Split development strategy until 2030, working paper. City of Split

Ćosić K (2017) Nacionalna sigurnost i društvena rezilijentnost. In: Lipozenčić J et al (eds) Moderne tehnologije: etika korištenja i pravne regulacije Akademija medicinskih znanosti Hrvatske Zagreb, pp 42–46

Croatian Chamber of Commerce—Digital Chamber (2020). Private healthcare facilities. Croatian chamber of commerce—digital chamber, digitalnakomora.hr (10.02.2020)

Đakula A et al (2022) A comparison of health system responses to COVID-19 in Bulgaria, Croatia and Romania in 2020. Health Policy 126(5):456–464. https://doi.org/10.1016/j.healthpol.2022.02.003

Družić I, Smolić Š, Penava M (2009) Health care spending in Croatia and selected EU countries–a panel unit root analysis. Bus Strat Teh Innov Sustain Dev: Creat Glob Prosper Humlty, 369–375.

Europen Commission (2019) Radni dokument službi Komisije, Izvješće za Hrvatsku 2019. s detaljnim preispitivanjem o sprječavanju i uklanjanju makroekonomskih neravnoteža, European Commission. https://eur-lex.europa.eu/legal-content/HR/TXT/HTML/?uri=CELEX:52019SC1010&from=EN (10.12.2019)

Jambrović DD (2021) Croatian cities during the covid-19 crisis: challenges, responses and adjustments. EU Comp Law Issues Chall Ser (ECLIC) (5), 943–966

Jambrović DD (2022) COVID-19 crisis management in Croatia: the contribution of subnational levels of government. In: Nunes Silva C (ed) Local government and the COVID-19 pandemic a global perspective. Springer Cham, pp 405–425. https://doi.org/10.1007/978-3-030-91112-6

Koprić I, Musa A, Đulabić V (2016) Local government and local public services in Croatia. In: Wollmann H, Koprić I, Marcou G (eds) Public and social services in Europe. Governance and public management. Palgrave Macmillan, London. pp 201–2015. https://doi.org/10.1057/978-1-137-57499-2_14

Koprić I (2020) The COVID-19 pandemic: Croatian government response. In: Joyce P, Maron F, Reddy PS (eds) Good public governance in a global pandemic, IIAS public governance series, vol 1, 1st edn. pp 247–257

Kuković S (2021) Local government fighting COVID-19: the case of Slovenian municipalities. Polit Cent Eur 17(4):637–650. https://doi.org/10.2478/pce-2021-0034

McPake B et al (2020) Health economics: an international perspective, 4th edn. Routledge

Medical Centre of Split-Dalmatia County (2019) Medical center's Departments. Medical Centre of Split-Dalmatia County, Split, Croatia, https://dz-sdz.hr/ (10.12. 2019)

Merkaj E, Santolini R (2022) Italian national policies in response to the COVID-19 pandemic: the case of the Friuli-Venezia-Giulia and Umbria Regions. Health Policy 126(4):287–293. https://doi.org/10.1016/j.healthpol.2022.02.004

Ministry of Regional Development and EU Funds (2015) Smjernicama za izradu Strategije razvoja urbanih područja, praćenje njihove provedbe i vrednovanje. Ministry of Regional Development and EU Funds, Zagreb, Croatia

Ministry of Veterans Affairs (2014) Nacionalni program psihosocijalne i zdravstvene pomoći sudionicima i stradalnicima Domovinskog rata, Drugog svjetskog rata te povratnicima iz mirovnih misija, Ministry of Veterans Affairs, Zagreb

Nunes Silva C (eds) (2022) Local government and the COVID-19 pandemic a global perspective. Springer, Cham. https://doi.org/10.1007/978-3-030-91112-6

Official Gazette (2020a) Act on the protection of the population against infectious diseases. 134/2020.OfficialGazette

Official Gazette (2018) Health care act. 100/2018. Official Gazette

Organisation for Economic Co-operationand Development (OECD) (2007) Infrastructure to 2030, vol 2. OECD Publishing

Pašalić Ž (2003) Tržišna valorizacija gospodarske infrastructure. In: Družić I (ed) Hrvatski gospodarski razvoj. Politička kultura, Zagreb, Hrvatska

Schomaker RM, Bauer MW (2020) Mild hit, flexible response: how local administrations in Austria and Germany confronted (first wave) of the COVID-19 pandemic. In: Joyce P, Maron F, Reddy PS (eds) Good public governance in a global pandemic, IIAS public governance series, vol 1, 1st edn. pp 525–533

Setnikar Cankar S, Petkovšek V (2010) Healthcare in Slovenia: changes and analysis 1990–2009. In: Proceedings of the 18th NISPAcee annual conference, Public administrationin times of crisis, Poland

Yescombe ER (2010) Public-private partnerships: principles of policy and finance. Butterworth-Heinemann, London, UK

Young JC et al (2018) A methodological guide to using and reporting on interviews in conservation science research. Methods Ecol Evol 9:10–19. https://doi.org/10.1111/2041-210X.12828
Zhong H (2010) The impact of decentralization of health care administration on equity in health and health care in Canada. Int J Health Care Financ Econ 10:219–237

The Impact of COVID-19 Pandemic on the Health Right in Poland

Monika Urbaniak and Michele Sanfilippo

Abstract This paper analyzes the restrictions on rights and freedoms introduced during the time of coronavirus pandemic. In particular, it focuses on the impact of violation of the basic standards on the protection of human rights in Poland. We analyze whether the functioning of the state in the epidemic regime justified the need to limit the constitutional right to health protection. The right to health protection is one of the fundamental human rights. The decree n. 68 of the Polish Constitution affirms that everyone shall have the right to have his health protected. The protection of this right justified far-reaching restrictions. The actions of public authorities in Poland to manage and prevent the spread of the COVID-19 pandemic highly interfere with human and civil rights, as well as freedom, guaranteed under Constitution. The restrictions imposed by the public authorities to protect the health and life of the citizens violated the standards for the protection of freedoms and rights. Public authorities focused on fighting with the pandemic, and in practice, the actions taken in order to protect public health caused the limitations in access to medical services and especially prevention services. The research aims to present Polish legislation in combating the pandemic. During the pandemic, the health care system has to cope with higher demands. The Polish government has introduced many different solutions to treat COVID-19 patients. During the pandemic, the right to healthcare services has been formally limited. There have been many temporary suspensions of certain services.

Keywords COVID-19 · Fundamental rights · Health right · Pandemic · Infectious diseases · Constitution · Poland

---

M. Urbaniak (✉) · M. Sanfilippo
Poznań University of Medical Sciences, Poznań, Poland
e-mail: Monika.urbaniak@ump.edu.pl

N. Persiani et al. (eds.), *Challenges of Healthcare Systems in the Era of COVID-19*, Contributions to Management Science, https://doi.org/10.1007/978-3-031-43114-2_7

1 Introduction

The novel coronavirus disease outbroke throughout Europe in January 2020. It was first reported at the end of December 2019 in Wuhan, China. The spread of the disease was the cause of a massive global health challenge for the healthcare system capacity.[1] The virus has a very high infectivity, which caused the medical care capacity shortage in many countries.[2] The whole Europe, including Poland has been affected by the pandemic.

In Poland, the first case of the coronavirus infection was confirmed on 4 March 2020. A few days after, the state of epidemic threat because of COVID-19 was introduced on 13 March 2020[3] and remained in force until 20 March 2020. That day the Minister of Health declared the state of epidemic in the Republic of Poland.[4] Art. 5 of the Patients' Rights and the Patients Ombudsman Act of 6 November 2008[5] stipulates possible limitations to the observance of the patients' rights due to a threat of epidemic. When the state of epidemic threat was enforced, the right to limit patients' rights at healthcare centers came in force.

This paper analyzes the restrictions on rights and freedoms introduced during the time of coronavirus pandemic in Poland. It concerns on the method of their implementation and contains the assessment of this process. In particular, it focuses on the impact of violation of the basic standards on the protection of human rights. We analyze whether the functioning of the state in the epidemic regime justified the need to limit the constitutional right to health protection.

2 General Framework Concerning Health Emergency

It's important to start from the law foundations for a comparative analysis of the actions carried out by the Governments of the various countries. If it is true that the pandemic has taken all States by surprise, and it is equally true that the major part of the Constitution provides for the management methods of emergency situations. These methods are usually understood to mean a special manner of exercising public authority and are preceded by specific circumstances, e.g., natural phenomena.[6]

The COVID-19 pandemic has highlighted the problems that had actually already arisen following the terrorist events, the financial crises (especially that of 2008) and

---

1 Lupia et al. (2020).

2 Orzechowska and Bednarek (2020). P. 1.

3 *The Regulation of the Minister of Health of 13 March 2020 on declaration of the state of epidemic threat in the Republic of Poland*, Journal of Laws of 2020, item 433.

4 *The Regulation of the Minister of Health of 20 March 2020 on declaration of the state of epidemic in the Republic of Poland*, Journal of Laws of 2020, item 491.

5 The Patients' Rights and the Patients Ombudsman Act of 6 November 2008, Dz. Ustaw RP 2022 (1876).

6 Chmielnicki et al. (2021).

the technological evolution that allow to control people in a deeper way. In addition, technological evolution has allowed an increase in information, leading to exasperating the issues related to mass society and its manipulability. So, constitutional and legal systems have been severely tested with very strong tensions. There is a sort of "crash test" to check the tightness of the system. At this moment, it still seems premature to make an assessment, but we can fix some issues that can constitute indices and parameters for an assessment to be made at the end of the pandemic event.

Health war and health emergency? An index is determined by the origin of the virus. If it is a natural epidemic situation, the analysis will have to focus on verifying the reactive capacity in identifying and isolating the virus. In the other case, it is essential to identify the function and strategic role of the artificially generated virus.[7] To identify the function, the investigation will focus on the aims of the research in the laboratory, with the related ethical and bioethical issues and subsequently the investigation on the propagation of the virus will follow. Based on the answers to the questions, the policies adopted, and their adequacy will have to be assessed. If the origin of the virus was not natural, a biological "weapon", this action could be considered a war action. And the reactions of the policies would have been those typical of war. The question, however, led to the identification of the real responsible government because currently the international system provides for war between states and not situations where individuals are private individuals who work in projects financed by a plurality of governments.[8] The geopolitical repercussions have been many and particularly penetrating, so much so that we believe that the era of the light-heartedness of globalization is over.[9] The subsequent war in Ukraine opens further strategic issues involving the potential relations between the pandemic and the subsequent invasion of Ukraine. Geopolitical scenarios cannot be disregarded, but which at the moment, it would be premature to analyze them.[10] On the internal front, the responses of the Governments will have to be verified and evaluated in the light of the general scenarios. In any case, some questions and consequent tensions over the democratic seal have opened up. In the constitutional and political sphere, there have always been tensions and open questions regarding the role of information that can condition public opinion and democratic choice and the role of the military in civil contexts that evoke scenarios of military dictatorships.

With the pandemic of COVID-19 arose an important discussion concerning the issue of the relationship between information and consensus that has affected policies of the governments. The issue of the information is fundamental to the formation of a public opinion on which the democratic consensus is based, and which is the consensus to policies adopted by a government. The excess of information, as well as the troublesome, repeated and emotional exposure, creates a situation of a discomfort among the subjects to whom the information is addressed. This makes them even

[7] Capobianchi (a cura di B.Moro), Corona Virus, Castelvecchi, Roma, 2020.

[8] Barnard, L'origine del virus, Chiarelettere, Milano 2021.

[9] L'Altro Virus, LimesRivista italiana di geopolitica, n°1/2022.

[10] La cortina d'acciaio, Limes–Rivista italiana di geopolitica, n°5/2022.

more manipulable, potentially generating what is called by José Ortega Gasset Y Gasset in his book "Movement of the masses",[11] a profile indicative of the decline or crisis of a democratic system.

This phenomenon was so acute that a neologism was issued: "infodemic" composed by the nouns info (rmation) ("information") and (epi) demic ("epidemic"). This phenomenon has actually been known for some time, as it was issued by David J. Rothkopf, who dealt with it in an article that appeared in the Washington Post newspaper, When the Buzz Bites Back (May 11, 2003). But on the occasion of this epidemic, the term "Infodemic" was used in official documents of the World Health Organization.[12] Therefore, the new profiles of constitutional studies are due to open up, as the systems aimed at preventing "Infodemic" from conditioning political choices will have to be found.[13] In Poland, the examples of info demic were manifested in March 2020 by the mass buying of products from stores, repeated rumors of the closure of the cities, and many other uncertainties.[14]

3 The Polish Case

The state of the epidemic is not provided for in the Polish Constitution and thus does not constitute a legal basis for restricting human rights during the COVID-19 pandemic.[15] The introduction of the state of epidemic threat and then the state of the epidemic was associated with the implementation of specific legal measures to combat the coronavirus. These regulations limit the rights and freedoms guaranteed in the Constitution, and sometimes they strike directly at the essence of these freedoms and rights.[16]

The right to health protection has constitutional fundaments in Poland. According to the art. 68(1) of the Polish Constitution, everyone shall have the right to have his health protected. The Constitution states that the equal access to health care services, financed from public funds, shall be ensured by public authorities to citizens, irrespective of their material situation. The conditions for, and scope of, the provision of services shall be established by statute. The regulation of the art. 68(1) of the Constitution derivates from art.30 proclaiming dignity as a source of freedoms and rights art. 38 of the Constitution, which guarantees everyone legal protection of life.[17] Under Article 68(4) of the Constitution, public authorities are obliged to combat epidemic illnesses and prevent the negative health consequences of degradation of the environment. It should be emphasized that the term "epidemic illnesses" used

---

[11] Ortega y Gasset, La ribellione delle masse NEI 1945 1a edizione.

[12] https://www.treccani.it/vocabolario/infodemia_(Neologismi), Antonelli et al. (2020), p. 47–51.

[13] http://blog.terminologiaetc.it/2020/02/03/significato-definizione-infodemia/

[14] Jabłoński et al. (2022).

[15] Gajda (2020). p. 19 ff.

[16] Urbaniak and Urbaniak (2021). p 336.

[17] Grabowska and Urbaniak (2014). p. 97.

in the Constitution is broader than the term "infectious diseases". It also extends to chronic non-contagious diseases. The constitution imposes an obligation on the public authorities to undertake various actions. One has to underline that the actions include also a preventive nature, to control the spread of epidemic illnesses. These activities are aimed at preventing diseases, and not only combating the existing epidemic illnesses.

To combat the epidemic illnesses requires limiting certain freedoms and rights. In accordance with art. 31(3) of the Constitution, any limitation upon the exercise of constitutional freedoms and rights may be imposed only by statute, and only when necessary in a democratic state for the protection of its security or public order, or to protect the natural environment, health or public morals, or the freedoms and rights of other persons. Such limitations shall not violate the essence of freedoms and rights. Combatting an epidemic or a pandemic only such methods of restricting the freedoms and rights are acceptable when they are capable of achieving the goal of controlling the epidemic and preventing further spread of an infectious disease. It is important that the degree of limitations to the sphere of an individual freedom is in proportion to the benefits resulting from the protection of public health.[18]

It is obvious that during the pandemic the health care system has to cope with higher demands. The pandemic time provoked a public debate about the issues concerning the problems of health care system including equipment supply, personnel supply, personal protective equipment, etc. Polish government has introduced many different solutions to treat COVID-19 patients. The focus on fighting the pandemic has resulted in problems of the patients with access to the other healthcare services. In particular, it affected planned procedures and prevention strategies. During the pandemic, the right to healthcare services has been formally limited. There have been many temporary suspensions of certain services. The standards and guidelines published by the state infection control inspectorate and the Supreme Medical Council have pointed out that in-person appointments with specialist doctors must be limited and replaced with telephone consultations.[19]

The term "extraordinary measures" is provided in Chapter XI of the Constitution. In accordance with article 228 of the Constitution of the Republic of Poland, appropriate extraordinary measures may be introduced in situations of particular danger, if ordinary constitutional measures are inadequate. The intention of the legislator was that in the event of sudden and serious threats, both external and internal, to the state and its citizens as well as in the event of natural disasters and catastrophes, it would be possible to cease the "regular" constitutional system of exercising power. Extraordinary measures are a legal instrument to combat extraordinary threats to the security of the state and its citizens.[20] In a democratic state, the introduction of extraordinary measures should only be justified by the occurrence of specific threats

[18] Sroka (2020).

[19] K. Piątkowska, A. Zimmermann, A. Pilarska, Limitation of patients' rights during the COVID-19 pandemic in Poland, European Journal of Translational and Clinical Medicine, 2021, n. 4(1), p. 81.

[20] Dyzenhaus (2012). p. 442; Prokop (2005), p. 9; Brzeziński (2007), p. 48.

for which ordinary constitutional measures are insufficient, and only in order to overcome these threats, serve the common good, protect residents, ensure the effective functioning of the State in a crisis situation and restore the normal functioning of the State.[21]

As a result of the introduction of extraordinary measures, the principles of operation of public authorities are changed, which renders the possibility of introducing special restrictions on the exercise of constitutional freedoms and rights. The Constitution distinguishes between three types of extraordinary measures: martial law, state of emergency, and state of natural disaster. Depending on the situation, the appropriate extraordinary measures may be introduced "if ordinary constitutional measures are inadequate". An emergency is a result of a sudden, rapid, and, usually, unexpected situation that is a direct threat of global phenomenon.[22] In this case, the Council of Ministers must request from the President the introduction of the state of emergency, which is limited in time. President's declared state of emergency can last up to 90 days. What is also important: it can be extended only once for additional 60 days with the consent of the Parliament.[23]

The term "ordinary constitutional measures" referred to in Article 228 of the Constitution shall be understood as all legal norms that can be constructed on the basis of the Constitution, except for Chapter XI thereof.[24] In practice, it covers all possible actions available to public authorities (government and local government) in a regular situation, when no particular danger exists, and there is no need to introduce the extraordinary measures. This includes issuing legal acts, taking individual decisions, as well as taking actual actions within the limits of the competencies conferred upon the authorities.[25] The legislator may also be helpful by defining in statutory acts when ordinary measures should be considered insufficient.[26] Thus, a situation where ordinary constitutional measures are not sufficient takes place when it is not possible to overcome a particular danger without resigning from the application of constitutional norms, in particular without limiting the freedoms and rights of an individual in accordance with Article 31(3) of the Constitution.[27] In other words, if the particular danger can be addressed only by completely abolishing certain freedoms or violating their essence.

The Constitution defines which freedoms and rights may be limited to the extent violating their essence and which may be completely suspended. These catalogs vary, depending on the type of extraordinary measures. In the case of martial law or state of emergency, the Constitution defines a catalog of freedoms and rights that cannot be

---

[21] Gebethner (1982), p. 12; B. Banaszak, L. Garlicki, *Komentarz do art. 31 Konstytucji RP*, [in:] *Konstytucja Rzeczypospolitej Polskiej. Komentarz*, ed. L. Garlicki, Warszawa 2005, p. 1086.

[22] Chmielnicki et al. (2021). p. 81.

[23] Domaradzki (2021). s. 3.

[24] Prokop (2005), pp. 19–20.

[25] Steinborn (2016), p. 1610.

[26] Banaszak, op. cit., p. 1089.

[27] Prokop, op. cit., pp. 19–21; Wojtyczek (1999), pp. 250–51; Steinborn (2016). p. 1610.

suspended or violated, thereby allowing the suspension of the others.[28] In connection with the spreading COVID-19 pandemic, the authorities of individual countries take numerous remedial measures, including extraordinary legal measures limiting the exercise of freedoms and rights in order to protect public health.[29] One of the main problems of the Polish government was to establish an appropriate legal regime in case of emergency, concerning the management of public authorities.[30] It has to be stressed that the method of law-making adopted in Poland was subject to debate both in political and scientific circles. The COVID-19 pandemic has become an element of political struggle between the parliamentary groups, the fight for electoral votes in the presidential elections included.[31] It was proposed to introduce a state of natural disaster, which is provided in the Polish Constitution, but the government has not decided to declare it.[32] In the light of the *Act on the state of natural disaster*, the state of natural disaster is the appropriate measure for preventing the effects of natural disasters, including the mass occurrence of human infectious diseases.[33]

The legal ground for combating pandemic infections in Poland is the *Act of 5 December 2008 on preventing and combating infections and human infectious diseases.*[34] It has to be underlined that this Act did not fully guarantee the health safety of the country's inhabitants during a pandemic.[35] On the basis of this act, numerous restrictive measures were introduced, imposing a lockdown, which was not that much severe than in the other countries attacked by the virus.[36] Later, the *Act of 2 March 2020 on special measures related to the prevention, counteracting and combating COVID-19, other infectious diseases and resulting crisis situations*[37] was introduced. These laws were the basis for many executive acts, including the regulation on the declaration of the state of epidemic.[38] The legal framework has restricted freedoms and rights on a scale comparable to that of a natural disaster,[39]

---

[28] Kaźmierczak (2019), No 4, p. 136; Kaźmierczak (2006), pp. 169–170.

[29] Urbaniak (2020), pp. 10–11.

[30] Zubik and Łukowiak (2020), p. 175.

[31] Serowaniec (2020) p. 170.

[32] Hoffman and Kostrubiec (2022). s. 36.

[33] Art. 3(1)(2) of *the Act of 18 April 2002 on the state of natural disaster*, Journal of Laws, item 1897 (consolidated text).

[34] *Act of 5 December 2008 on preventing and combating infections and human infectious diseases*, Journal of Laws of 2020, item 1845 (consolidated text).

[35] Płonka et al. (2022), p. 55.

[36] Sawicki (2022). Access 19.08.2022.

[37] Until October 2021, the Act was amended 36 times. See.: *Announcement of the Marshal of the Sejm of the Republic of Poland of 29 October 2021 on the declaration of the consolidated text of the Act on special measures related to the prevention, counteracting and combating COVID-19, other infectious diseases and resulting crisis situations* (Journal of Laws of 2021, item 2095).

[38] *The Regulation of the Minister of Health of 20 March 2020 on declaration of the state of epidemic in the Republic of Poland*, Journal of Laws of 2020, item 491.

[39] Bąkowski (2003). p. 77; Bryk (2011), pp. 231–232.

which has led to the situation that is sometimes referred to as the "state of emergency in disguise".[40]

4 Conclusions

The epidemic in the territory of Poland has contributed to a limitation of the health protection right. Especially, the provisions significantly limited the patients' rights during the epidemic threat. As we have seen in Poland as a result of its legislative policy, the government used the regulations issued in the state of epidemic threat and the state of epidemic as legal instruments. Therefore, a state of natural disaster in the substantive sense was introduced. Most of the regulations introduced during pandemic of COVID-19 have been justified, but discussive was the method of their introduction. These restrictions would comply with the Constitution if they had been introduced during a period of introduction of extraordinary measures. It concerned also the right to health protection. The fight with the pandemic should not lead to limiting the right to health protection of all the patients who suffer from the other illnesses. Public authorities focused on fighting with the pandemic. In practice, the actions taken in order to protect public health caused the limitations in access to medical services and especially prevention services. In consequence, it restricted the right to health protection.

References

Ahmed SS (2020) The coronavirus disease 2019 (COVID-19): a review. J Adv Med Med Res 32(4)
Antonelli G (2020) L'influenza delle Parole. Solferino, Corriere della sera, Milano
Bąkowski T (2003) Prawne formy ograniczania wolności oraz praw człowieka i obywatela w ustawie o stanie klęski żywiołowej. Państwo i Prawo 8
Banaszak B (2021) Konstytucja Rzeczypospolitej Polskiej. Komentarz, 2. ed., Wydawnictwo C.H, W. BECKarszawa
Bosek L (2016) Art. 31, [in:] Konstytucja RP. Komentarz, Tom I, ed. M. Safjan, L. Bosek, Wydawnictwo C.H. BECK, Warszawa
Bryk T (2011) Przegląd regulacji stanów nadzwyczajnych w przepisach Konstytucji RP. Przegląd Prawa Konstytucyjnego 1
Brzeziński M (2001) Wybory prezydenckie 2010 r. z perspektywy stanów nadzwyczajnych. Studia Politologiczne 19
Brzeziński M (2007) Stany nadzwyczajne w polskich konstytucjach. Warszawa
Brzeziński M (2009) Pojęcie stanu nadzwyczajnego. In: Błuszkowski J, Zaleśny J (ed) Wielowymiarowość systemów politycznych. Teoretyczne założenia i praktyczne uwarunkowania, Warszawa
Burki TK (2020) Coronavirus in China. Lancet Respir Med 8(3)
Chmielnicki P, Minich D, Rybkowski R, Stachura M, Szocik K (2021) The COVID-19 pandemic as an opportunity for a permanent reduction in civil rights. Studia Iuridica Lublinensia (4)

[40] Pach (2023).

Complak K (2014) Art. 31. Konstytucja Rzeczypospolitej Polskiej. Komentarz. In: Haczkowska M (ed) LexisNexis, Warszawa

Domaradzki S (2021) The polish parliament in the time of coronavirus. Instrumentalizing the pandemic in order to strengthen the grasp on power of the ruling party. Study Robert Shuman Foundation. FRS_Parliament_Poland.pdf (robert-schuman.eu)

Dyzenhaus D (2012) States of emergency. In: Rosenfeld M, Sajó A (ed) The Oxford handbook of comparative constitutional law, Oxford University Press, Oxford

Gajda A (2020) Restrictions on human rights and freedoms during the time of epidemic in Poland. Przegląd Prawa Konstytucyjnego 5(57)

Garlicki L (2005) Komentarz do art. 31 Konstytucji RP, [in:] Konstytucja Rzeczypospolitej Polskiej. Komentarz, ed. L. Garlicki, Warszawa

Gebethner S (1982) Stany szczególnego zagrożenia jako instytucja prawa konstytucyjnego, sPaństwo i Prawo 8

Grabowska S, Urbaniak M (2014) Legal basis of the realization of the rights of health law protection in Poland. Przegląd Prawa Konstytucyjnego 5

Grzywna P (2020) The right to health protection and the actual access of elderly people to medical services in Poland. Przegląd Prawa Konstytucyjnego 5

Hoffman I, Kostrubiec J (2022) Political freedoms and rights in relation to the COVID-19 pandemic in Poland and hungary in a comparative legal perspective. Bialystok Leg Stud 27(2)

Jabłoński M, Kuźnicka–Błaszkowska D (2022) Limiting the right of access to public information in the age of COVID-19–case study of Poland. Bialystok Leg Stud 27(2)

Kaźmierczak M (2005) Zasady funkcjonowania państwa podczas stanu klęski żywiołowej w III RP. Studia Prawnoustrojowe 4

Kaźmierczak M (2006) Zasady funkcjonowania państwa podczas stanu wojennego. Studia Prawnoustrojowe 6

Kaźmierczak M (2019) Limitacja konstytucyjnych praw człowieka podczas stanu wyjątkowego, Radca Prawny. Zeszyty Naukowe 4

van Klink B, Soniewicka M, van den Broeke L (2022) The Utopia of legality: a comparision of the dutch and polish approaches to the regulation of the COVID-19 pandemic. Bialystok Leg Stud 27(2)

Lupia T, Scabini S, Pinna SM, Di Perri G, De Rosa FG, Corcione S (2020) 2019-novel coronavirus outbreak: a new challenge. J Glob Antimicrob Resist 21

Ortega y Gasset, La ribellione delle masse NEI 1945 1a edizione

Orzechowska M, Bednarek AK (2020) Forecasting COVID-19 pandemic in Poland according to government regulations and people behaviour. Retrived from: Medrxiv Preprint https://doi.org/10.1101/2020.05.26.20112458

Pach M (2023) Mamy zakamuflowany stan nadzwyczajny. O naszych prawach podczas epidemii koronawirusa. https://oko.press/mamy-zakamuflowany-stan-nadzwyczajny, 20.01.2023

Płonka–Syroka B, Stych M, Pawlica B (2022) Evolution of the right to health care in Poland during the COVID-19 pandemic. Przegląd Prawa Publicznego 6

Polak P, Trzciński J (2018) Konstytucyjna zasada godności człowieka w świetle orzecznictwa Trybunału Konstytucyjnego. Gdańskie Studia Prawnicze, T. XL

Prokop K (2005) Stany nadzwyczajne w Konstytucji Rzeczypospolitej Polskiej z dnia 2 kwietnia 1997 r., Temida 2, Białystok

Sawicki J (2022) A state of emergency provided in the constitution not declared but implemented. COVID-19 in Poland in the eye of presidential elections, p 3. https://www.nomos-leattualitaneldiritto.it

Serowaniec M, Witkowski Z (2020) Can legislative standards be subject to 'quarantine'? the functioning of the tablet Sejm in Poland in the COVID-19 era. Theory Pract Legis (1–2)

Shereen MA, Khan S, Kazmi A, Bashir N, Siddique R (2020) COVID-19 infection: origin, transmission and characteristics of human coronaviruses. J Adv Res 24

Sroka T (2020) Ograniczenia praw i wolności konstytucyjnych oraz praw pacjenta w związku z wystąpieniem zagrożenia epidemicznego. Ograniczenia praw i wolności konstytucyjnych oraz praw pacjenta w związku z wystąpieniem zagrożenia epidemicznego, Wydanie-6/2020 | Palestra
Steinborn S (2016) Art. 228, [in:] Konstytucja RP. Komentarz, Tom II, ed. M. Safjan, L. Bosek, Wydawnictwo C.H. BECK, Warszawa
Surówka A (2014) Relacja zasad ograniczania wolności i praw człowieka i obywatela w stanach nadzwyczajnych i w stanie normalnego funkcjonowania państwa. Przegląd Prawa konstytucyjnego 4(20)
Tuleja P (2019) Art. 31 (Zasada ochrony wolności, klauzule limitacyjne ograniczenia wolności i praw konstytucyjnych), [in:] Konstytucja Rzeczypospolitej Polskiej. Komentarz, Wolters Kluwer, Warszawa
Urbaniak K, Urbaniak M (2021) Limitation of human and civil rights and freedoms during the pandemic in Poland. Przegląd Prawa Konstytucyjnego 6
Urbaniak M (2020) Lex coronavirus. Włoskie prawo w walce z pandemią. Studia Prawa Publicznego 1(29)
Wojtyczek K (1999) Granice ingerencji ustawodawczej w sferę praw człowieka w Konstytucji RP, Zakamycze
Zubik M, Łukowiak D (2020) COVID-19 and constitutional law: the case of Poland, Universidad Nacional Autónoma de México–Instituto de Investigaciones Jurídicas

Support for SMEs in Greece and Poland During COVID-19

Maciej Woźniak, Simeon Karafolas, and Seweryn Krupnik

Abstract Crises caused by the COVID-19 pandemic lasted much longer than many people previously anticipated, with new waves of coronavirus leading to repeated lockdowns of the economy. Therefore, many governments have decided to help enterprises survive this hard time, particularly small- and medium-sized enterprises (SMEs), which do not have as many sources of financing as large firms. However, there are differences in aid, both in terms of scale and tools, between countries, even if they belong to the European Union (EU). The aim of the paper is to compare support schemes for SMEs in Greece and Poland during the COVID-19 pandemic. In order to describe the effects of the schemes, the article juxtaposes publicly available data on unemployment and evolution of SMEs. The results show that unemployment was controlled in both countries, while the balance between newly created companies and companies that closed during the pandemic was not negative. A significant difference appeared in the evolution of deposits, most likely because of contrast in taking advantage of the Recovery and Resilience Fund. The paper contributes to widening the knowledge of economic crises and public policy, and the results could be interesting for policymakers.

Keywords Small- and medium-sized enterprises · COVID-19 · Support · Unemployment · Deposits

JEL classification Codes · G11 · G24 · J24

M. Woźniak (✉)
AGH University, Krakow, Poland
e-mail: mawozniak@agh.edu.pl

S. Karafolas
University of Western Macedonia, Kozani, Greece
e-mail: skarafolas@uowm.gr

S. Krupnik
Jagiellonian University, Krakow, Poland
e-mail: seweryn.krupnik@uj.edu.pl

N. Persiani et al. (eds.), *Challenges of Healthcare Systems in the Era of COVID-19*,
Contributions to Management Science, https://doi.org/10.1007/978-3-031-43114-2_8

1 Introduction

The COVID-19 pandemic hurts the global economy, negatively impacting many small- and medium-sized enterprises (SMEs), which were particularly vulnerable, as they have fewer financial assets and face more trouble accessing external capital than large companies. SMEs have had to struggle with much lower demand and more supply disruptions since the beginning of 2020 (Oche 2021). In connection to this, support schemes were implemented to mitigate the unexpected problems faced by companies, particularly in sectors connected to social consumption. Moreover, there has been a significant drop in revenues to governments and an increase in spending around the world, particularly in developing countries (Pozhidaev 2022), the results of which include high deficits and significant public debt. Thus, EU funds obtained through the recovery and resilience facility could offer substantial financial aid.

Because of their uniqueness, the impact of COVID-19 on SMEs and the role of relevant public support have attracted the attention of policymakers and researchers. Studies have proposed analytical frameworks instrumental in designing the most effective forms of support (Wang et al. 2021), investigating the support and its effect at the province (Le et al. 2020) or country (Pedauga et al. 2022) level or overviewing the situation at the European level (Juergensen et al. 2020). Finally, some studies aimed to estimate the effectiveness of diverse forms of support (Gourinchas et al. 2020). This article contributes to this literature by comparing the conditions of SMEs, support schemes and macroeconomic indicators for two countries of the European Union (EU), Greece and Poland, during the COVID-19 pandemic. Both countries suffered during previous economic crises, although to different extents (Karafolas and Woźniak 2020), leading to the question of crisis consequences and implemented public policy. The authors considered two main indicators: unemployment and the evolution of SMEs, which were the main targets of the support programs. However, as the lockdown measures reduced consumption, they consequently increased deposits. Thus, the evolution of deposits has, therefore, become a third parameter to examine in this study.

Comparing two countries at a similar development level has been helpful in understanding the implementation and impact of public policies targeting companies (Szczygielski et al. 2017). Poland and Greece are at similar stages of development, as measured by gross domestic product per capita and government effectiveness (Kaufmann et al. 2010), and interestingly, both countries, being members of the EU and having more time than more globalised countries to prepare, had relatively similar reactions to the pandemic itself: they acted relatively quickly (Górniak et al. 2022).

This paper contributes to macroeconomic theory in the areas of fluctuations in economic growth and public policy, and it offers insights into public finance. After the introduction, Sect. 2 refers to measures undertaken through the EU, while Sects. 3 and 4 discuss the measures undertaken in Greece and Poland, respectively, ending with conclusions.

2 Theoretical Background

The results of the analysis presented in this chapter are based on both macroeconomic and public policy theory. The effects of the COVID-19 pandemic on the economy included both demand and supply shocks. Therefore, a decreased GDP and higher unemployment should be expected. According to macroeconomic theory, an expansionary monetary policy should be implemented, but the interest rates in many countries are close to zero—an example of the liquidity trap. Moreover, in the case of SMEs, the effectiveness of monetary policy is lower because of credit rationing. This theory is based on the asymmetry of information between commercial banks and SMEs. Some potential borrowers cannot obtain a loan, even though their assessment by the bank was the same as the companies that received one, while other potential borrowers cannot get a loan even if they agree to a higher interest rate. Rationing is related to the size of the company—it is connected to higher costs of obtaining information and credit assessments, as well as higher risks and information intensity in the case of SMEs (Stiglitz and Weiss 1981). Furthermore, in an oligopolistic market, a restrictive monetary policy that aims to limit access to loans would affect SMEs primarily, according to credit discrimination theory. Large enterprises, however, can negotiate with commercial banks, and they have many more opportunities to finance their activities with equity (Galbraith 1957).

Under such circumstances, the only solution is a fiscal stimulus, which could be achieved by transferring from the budget to companies or reducing taxes. Some authors stated that in the short term, the government should focus on avoiding mass layoffs and bankruptcies (Loayza and Pennings 2020), while stimulation of the economy is recommended only in the medium term (Odendahl and Springford 2020). However, SMEs are not as prepared for such a shock as large enterprises (Shang-Jin 2020).

From a public policy perspective, the reaction to COVID-19 was an example of public administration having to react swiftly under substantial uncertainty. As highlighted by the current literature, public administration often plays the role of risk taker, weighing the consequences of different options (Lazonick and Mazzucato 2013; Mazzucato 2016), and choosing between them often involves trade-offs that should not be ignored (Flanagan and Uyarra 2016). In the case of COVID-19, public administration faced a conflict between saving as many people as possible from COVID-19 and short-term GDP growth, and different countries navigated between these priorities in various ways.

The postulated standard cycle of public policy analysis involves diagnosing the problem, assembling evidence, constructing alternatives, selecting criteria, projecting outcomes, confronting the trade-offs and deciding and communicating the decision (Bardach 2019). Public administration can use different tools categorised into providing resources (equipping), banning undesired behaviours and promoting desired behaviours (Soman 2017). In the context of COVID-19, the cycle of analysis had to be shortened, and the range of possible actions was heavily reduced because the uncertainty about outcomes was extremely high, making the analysis of public administrators' actions and related effects even more important.

3 Measures of Support Decisions Undertaken by the European Union

The EU had to tackle many obstacles, particularly since the economic crisis in 2007. However, the COVID-19 pandemic has been the greatest challenge. Therefore, the EU undertook measures in response to this issue, focusing on the medical but also the economic levels, measures of which involved supporting jobs, businesses and the economy. In April 2020, EU leaders endorsed measures worth €540 billion with respect to maintaining people's jobs, offering guarantees for loans and supporting EU member states. Every measure was undertaken through an operational programme or through EU institutions.

For employment support, a €100-billion package was adopted through the Support to mitigate Unemployment Risks in an Emergency (SURE) initiative, which, as a new EU instrument, must provide up to €100 billion in loans to countries in need to ensure employees receive an income and companies, especially SMEs, retain their staff. This allows people to cover their needs, including rent payments, bills and an acceptable level of consumption for economic stability. EU member states must provide loan guarantees that can help small enterprises in particular to be financed to cover their urgent needs. The SURE initiative would help EU states retain work for employees and the self-employed by supporting short-term job schemes and similar measures, through which companies could reduce temporarily the hours of employees or suspend work to help member states protect jobs, employees and the self-employed from the risks of dismissal and income loss, with income support provided by the state for the hours not worked. Meanwhile, the self-employed received income replacement for the current emergency (Council of the EU 2020a).

Through the European Investment Bank (EIB), a guarantee fund for loans to companies was initiated. In April 2020, the EIB approved a guaranteed fund of €25 billion that could deliver up to €200 billion to support economies and SMEs, in particular. The €25 billion guarantee fund would be funded by EU member states pro rata to their shareholding in the EIB or other institutions (EIB 2020).

Through the European Stability Mechanism, EU members could be supported by €240 billion to face the pandemic crisis. The Eurogroup proposed to establish Pandemic Crisis Support, based on the existing precautionary credit line and adjusted according to specific needs, as a relevant safeguard for Euro-area member states affected by the COVID-19 crisis in the amount of 2% of the respective member's GDP as of year-end 2019, to support the domestic financing of direct and indirect healthcare, cure- and prevention-related costs due to the COVID-19 crisis (Council of the EU 2020b).

Additional actions have been undertaken to redirect EU funds to help member states, including redirecting €37 billion from structural funds to support EU countries and their citizens (Council of the EU 2020c). This included the redirection of up to €800 million through the EU Solidarity Fund, which has been amended to provide support to member states affected by public health crises, such as those caused by COVID-19 (European Commission 2020), and an additional €3.1 billion was unlocked from the 2020 budget to respond to the COVID-19 crisis.

The EU has also increased flexibility in the use of structural funds, which would permit any EU member state the transfer of sources between different funds and regions to respond better to the economic and social needs provoked by COVID-19. Additional measures have been related to flexibility in fiscal rules and state aid to support healthcare systems and businesses and to maintain employment during the crisis.

4 Measures Undertaken in the Greek Case

The COVID-19 pandemic found Greece emerging from a long economic and financial crisis, as well as amidst the restructuring of the financial sector (Karafolas 2019). During COVID-19, Greek enterprises and the self-employed were offered loans, subsidies and suspended tax payables, while the Greek government implemented lockdown-type control measures in March and April 2020, which included closing schools and university classes, cancelling mass events, suspending restaurant/cafe activities, closing shopping and sports centres and imposing travel restrictions. From May, the measures gradually began to be lifted, but during the second wave that came in 2021, restrictive measures were applied again in November 2021 on commerce, restaurants, gyms and beauty salons.

From March 2020, the Greek government announced measures to help the economy using special financial schemes with the support of EU funds. From July 2021, Greece could use EU recovery and resilience funds to help its economy following the COVID-19 fallout (Council of the EU 2022). The Greek government, under the umbrella of the Partnership Agreement for the Development Framework, 2014–2020, financed several sectors of the economy considered to have suffered from COVID-19 (Ministry of Development and Investment 2022). The government budgeted for the allocation of €1.2 billion for an interest subsidy (which reached 100%) on existing loans to SMEs affected by COVID-19 pandemic measures, followed by a second round of €200 million (Ministry of Development and Investment 2022). Around €2 billion was budgeted as guarantees (up to 80%) of new working capital loans for SMEs and large companies (Ministry of Development and Investment 2022), and another €2 billion was allocated as working capital for SMEs with work suspensions or operation restrictions due to COVID-19; 40% would be provided through the Partnership Agreement for the Development Framework and 60% from the banks cooperating with the *Entrepreneurship Fund II* programme. Important allocations were focused on specific targets and sectors.

A specific compensation of €500 million was allocated for business support due to the appearance and spread of COVID-19, and it focused on small enterprises and the self-employed with the offer of an €800 grant for a limited period. Through this measure, about 525,000 compensation recipients were foreseen (Ministry of Development and Investment 2020). Another €680 million was allocated as a working capital subsidy to the service and tourism sectors affected by COVID-19, and around €60 million was allocated to start-up companies. According to Hellenic Development Bank (2022), 16,227 loans totalling €6 billion were offered through guarantees.

5 Measures Undertaken in the Polish Case

Although the first case of COVID-19 in Poland was confirmed on 4 March 2020, the lockdown-type control measures were implemented a week later, including, among others, closures of schools, university classes and offices and cancelling of mass events. These measures were strengthened at the end of March 2020 by limiting non-family gatherings to two people; forbidding non-essential travel; requiring individuals walking in streets to be separated by two meters; and closing parks, boulevards, beaches or hairdressers. In connection to this, the government decided to allocate for SMEs 75 billion zlotys (about €16 billion) in 2020: one-third of the money was intended for microenterprises and the other two-thirds for SMEs. The first support programme was launched in April 2020, consisting primarily of five areas. The first addressed employees' financial safety and job protection, including government-paid social insurance contributions for three months for microenterprises or one-off benefits of about €450 gross (80% of the monthly minimum wage) for self-employed and freelancers. The second area offered finances for businesses, including public co-financing for employee salaries up to 40% of the average monthly wage, if working time was reduced up to 20%; deduction of losses incurred in 2020 from income obtained in 2019, provided that revenue drops by more than 50%; non-repayable loans up to 5,000 zlotys (about €1,100) for microenterprises if they do not lay off employees within the next 6 months; and postponing the deadlines of withholding taxes (www.gov.pl). Moreover, companies could assess creditworthiness based on their previous year's financial statement to extend the repayment terms of business overdrafts. The final areas of support were connected to healthcare and the financial market for reducing capital buffer requirements for commercial banks according to the Financial Stability Committee.

In 2021, the government decided to strengthen the support programme. Companies were offered leasing schemes for trucks, buses and machines, and SMEs could apply for a special loan to cover payrolls. The grace period was up to 12 months. However, the argument between the Polish government and the European Commission about the judiciary system meant the Recovery and Resilience Fund for Poland was suspended. Any changes to this matter could prove significant support for the Polish economy, as the fund may amount to €58 billion.

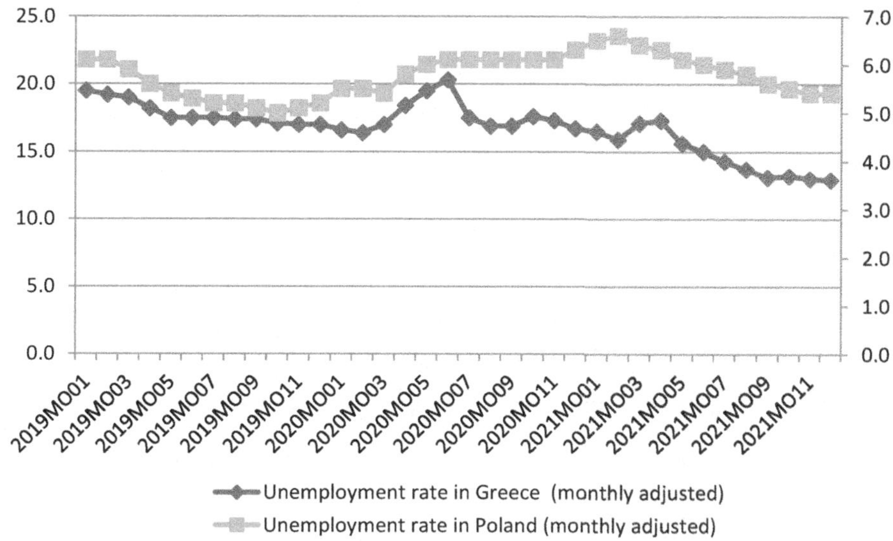

Fig. 1 Monthly evolution of unemployment in Greece[1] and Poland, 2019–2021, (in %).[2] *Sources* a/ Greece, Hellenic Statistical Authority (2022a, b), Employment status and unemployment rate (January 2004–June 2022), https://www.statistics.gr/en/statistics/-/publication/SJO02/. b/ Poland, Central Statistical Office

6 Consequences on Employment and SMES in Greece and Poland

The public funding schemes implemented GreekIt is and Polish governments had some substantial results concerning unemployment, small enterprises and the self-employed. Unemployment in Greece followed a quicker and more substantial decrease compared to Poland in the period 2019–2021. Nevertheless, the unemployment rate in Greece was 3.4 to 2.4 times higher compared to that in Poland during this period. The continuous decrease in unemployment in Greece during 2019 interrupted the second quarter of 2020, after which an important decrease reappeared, from 20.3% in June 2020 to 12.9% in December 2021 (Fig. 1). In the case of Poland, a similar evolution appeared until July 2020; the serious de-escalation of unemployment that appeared in Greece since this month was delayed in Poland for about 9 months beginning in March 2020, rising to 5.4% by the end of 2021.

The difference between new registered companies and companies that closed during this period is positive in favour of new registered companies in both countries

[1] Figures in Greece incorporate the effect of the implementation of Regulation (EU) 2019/1700, which came into force in 2021.

[2] The left axis concerns unemployment in Greece, while the right axis concerns unemployment in Poland.

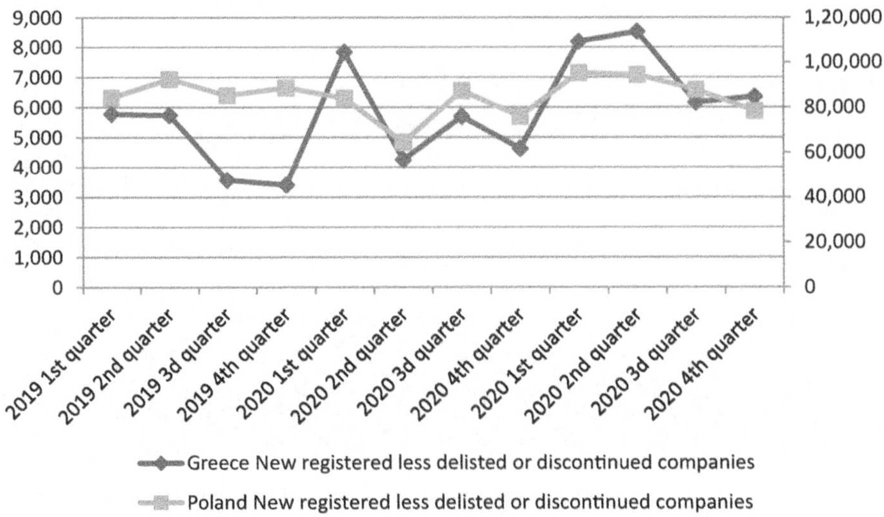

Fig. 2 Quarterly evolution of difference between new and discontinuing companies[3] in Greece and Poland, 2019–2021.[4] *Sources* a/ Greece, General Electronic Commercial Registry of Greece, 2022, creation and stop working companies. b/ Poland, Central Statistical Office

(Fig. 2), which followed a similar evolution, although in the Greek case, quarterly fluctuations were greater than in the Polish one.

The number of new registered companies was situated between 94,000 and 64,000 in the Polish case and 3,400 and 8,500 in the Greek case. In 2019, Greece had a lower number of new less delisted or discontinued companies, while in the case of Poland, the lower positive balance was situated in the first half of 2020 (Fig. 2), and it gradually began to rise until summer 2021 (Fig. 2).

During this period, the phenomenon of increasing deposits appeared in the Greek context (Fig. 3); their growth was 3.8% in the first half of 2020, 9.9% in the second half of 2020 and 4% in the first half of 2021 (Bank of Greece 2022, author's calculations). This phenomenon was due to the decline in consumption observed in other countries as well. However, this was not the case in Poland. The value of deposits, which rose significantly in the last decade in this country, dropped dramatically a year before and during the pandemic (approximately 40%; Fig. 3), which might suggest that entrepreneurs used their own funds to finance costs, particularly during lockdown periods.

[3] Companies on specific dates are a/ Businesses set up, b/ Companies under liquidation, Conciliation procedure, deletion.

[4] The left axis concerns Greece, while the right axis concerns Poland.

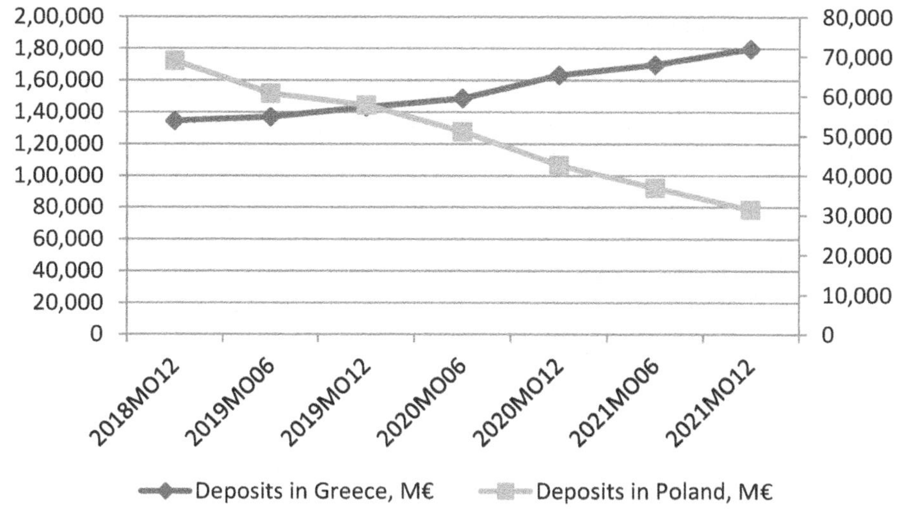

Fig. 3 Evolution of bank deposits in Greece and Poland (Million €)[5] *Source* a/ Greece, Bank of Greece, 2022. b/ Poland Source: https://businessinsider.com.pl based on Central Statistical Office

7 Conclusions

The COVID-19 pandemic affected the economic activity of countries in the EU, which then undertook measures to fund programmes to reduce negative economic and social consequences. The COVID-19 crisis found the two countries of Greece and Poland in different economic conjunctures because in the previous decade, Greece faced an extensive economic recession in contrast to Poland. The two countries reacted to the economic and social consequences of the COVID-19 pandemic by using the measures agreed upon in the EU. They paid particular attention to SMEs with measures to tackle unemployment, financed SMEs through loan guarantees and offered favourable loan interest rates. Contrary to Greece, which took significant advantage of EU aid measures, the Recovery and Resilience Fund for Poland was suspended in Poland because of disagreement with the EU over the country's judiciary system.

The financial results show that unemployment was controlled in this period in both countries compared to the previous period, while the balance between newly created companies and companies that closed during the pandemic was not negative, especially in Greece. A significant difference appeared in the evolution of deposits during this period. In Greece, deposits increased primarily due to reduced consumption within the country, while in Poland, deposits fell sharply, which can be attributed to the use of funds by companies to refinance their needs and, at the same time, to reduce financial assistance from the EU due to the differences between the Polish legal system and that of the EU.

[5] The left axis concerns deposits in Greece, while the right axis concerns deposits in Poland.

The paper contributes to widening the knowledge of economic crises and public policy, and the results could be interesting for policymakers, whether in Poland or Greece. However, the paper has some limitations. It could be enriched by the use of other economic parameters, such as inflation and the evolution of investment during this period. Nevertheless, the results may be used as an example of comparative work between EU countries, to show the reaction of countries to EU financial assistance measures, and non-EU countries that are ineligible for financial assistance.

Acknowledgements The research on the Polish example was financially supported by the AGH University of Science and Technology in Kraków (grant for maintaining research potential). The contribution of one of the authors (Seweryn Krupnik) was financed by the Polish National Science Center (Project 2019/35/B/HS5/04238).

References

Bank of Greece (2022) Bank deposits. https://www.bankofgreece.gr/en/statistics/monetary-and-banking-statistics/deposits
Bardach E (2019) A practical guide for policy analysis: the eightfold path to more effective problem solving, 6th edn. CQ Press
Businessinsider (2022) Bank deposits in Poland. https://businessinsider.com.pl. 5 April 2022
Council of the EU (2020a) Council Regulation (EU) 2020/672 of 19 May 2020 on the establishment of a European instrument for temporary support to mitigate unemployment risks in an emergency (SURE) following the COVID-19 outbreak. https://eur-lex.europa.eu/legal-content/en/TXT/?qid=1589957881511&uri=CELEX:32020R0672
Council of the EU (2020b) Eurogroup statement on the pandemic crisis support. https://www.consilium.europa.eu/en/press/press-releases/2020/05/08/eurogroup-statement-on-the-pandemic-crisis-support/
Council of the EU (2020c) COVID-19 - Council adopts measures for immediate release of funds. https://www.consilium.europa.eu/en/press/press-releases/2020/03/30/covid-19-council-adopts-measures-for-immediate-release-of-funds/
Council of the EU (2022) COVID-19: the EU's response to the economic fallout. https://www.consilium.europa.eu/en/policies/coronavirus/covid-19-economy/
European Commission (2020) State aid: commission adopts temporary framework to enable member states to further support the economy in the COVID-19 outbreak. https://ec.europa.eu/commission/presscorner/detail/en/IP_20_496
European Investment Bank (2020) Coronavirus outbreak: EIB Group's response. https://www.eib.org/en/about/initiatives/covid-19-response/index.htm
Flanagan K, Uyarra E (2016) Four dangers in innovation policy studies—and how to avoid them. Ind Innov 23(2):177–188. https://doi.org/10.1080/13662716.2016.1146126
Galbraith JK (1957) Market structure and stabilization policy. Rev Econ Stat 124–133
General Electronic Commercial Registry (2022) Businesses report. http://backoffice.businessportal.gr/stats/publicity/opening
Górniak J, Krupnik S, Koniewski M (2022) Public policy responses to the pandemic. A comparative perspective. In: Kossowska M, Letki N, Zaleśkiewicz T et al (eds) Human behaviour in pandemics, 1st edn. Routledge, London, UK
Gourinchas P-O, Kalemli-Özcan Ş, Penciakova V et al (2020) COVID-19 and SME failures. http://mpoc.org.my/malaysian-palm-oil-industry/.

Hellenic Development Bank (2022) Guarantee fund COVID-19. https://hdb.gr/tameio-egguodosia-covid/

Hellenic Statistical Authority (2022a) Gross domestic product. https://www.statistics.gr/en/statistics/-/publication/SEL84/

Hellenic Statistical Authority (2022b) Employment status and unemployment rate. https://www.statistics.gr/en/statistics/-/publication/SJO02/

Juergensen J, Guimón J, Narula R (2020) European SMEs amidst the COVID-19 crisis: assessing impact and policy responses. J Indus Bus Econ 47(3):499–510. https://doi.org/10.1007/s40812-020-00169-4

Karafolas S (2019) Crisis consequences on the structure of the Greek banking system. Financ Stud 23(4):1–20

Karafolas S, Woźniak M (2020) The development of small enterprises during and after crisis: comparative analysis of Greece and Poland. Int J Bus Econ Sci Appl Res 13(2):30–38

Kaufmann D, Kraay A, Mastruzzi M (2010) The worldwide governance indicators: methodology and analytical issues. World Bank Policy Research Working Paper No. 5430. https://ssrn.com/abstract=1682130

Lazonick W, Mazzucato M (2013) The risk-reward nexus in the innovation-inequality relationship: who takes the risks? Who gets the rewards? Ind Corp Chang 22(4):1093–1128. https://doi.org/10.1093/ICC/DTT019

Le HBH, Nguyen TL, Ngo CT et al (2020) Policy related factors affecting the survival and development of SMEs in the context of Covid 19 pandemic. Manag Sci Lett 10(15):3683–3692. https://doi.org/10.5267/j.msl.2020.6.025

Loayza N, Pennings SM (2020) Macroeconomic policy in the time of COVID-19: a primer for developing countries. World Bank Research and Policy Briefs, p 147291

Mazzucato M (2016) From market fixing to market-creating: a new framework for innovation policy. Ind Innov 23(2):140–156. https://doi.org/10.1080/13662716.2016.1146124

Ministry of Development and Investment (2020) Inclusion of the act "Measures to support society due to the suspension of operations to reduce the risk of dispersal of COVID-19/Special Purpose Compensation" with OPS Code 5069407 in the Operational Program "Human Resources Development, Education and Lifelong Learning 2014–2020"

Ministry of Development and Investment (2022) Partnership agreement for the development framework, entrepreneurship support due to the COVID-19 disease pandemic. https://www.espa.gr/el/Pages/espa_covid.aspx

Oche E (2021) Entrepreneuship and COVID-19: challenges and opportunities. Academia Lett

Odendahl C, Springford J (2020) Three ways COVID-19 will cause economic divergence in Europe. CER Policy Paper

Pedauga L, Sáez F, Delgado-Márquez BL (2022) Macroeconomic lockdown and SMEs: the impact of the COVID-19 pandemic in Spain. Small Bus Econ 58(2):665–688. https://doi.org/10.1007/s11187-021-00476-7

Polish Central Statistical Office (2022a) Unemployment in Poland. https://stat.gov.pl. 5 April 2022

Polish Central Statistical Office (2022b) Enterprises in Poland. https://stat.gov.pl. 30 April 2022

Pozhidaev D (2022) COVID-19 and inequality in developing economies: what do we know? Academia Lett

Shang-Jin W (2020) Ten keys to beating back COVID-19 and the associated economic pandemic. In: Baldwin R, di Mauro BW (eds) Mitigating the COVID economic crisis: act fast and do whatever it takes. CEPR Press, London, pp 71–76

Soman D (2017) The last mile. Creating social and economic value from behavioral insights. University of Toronto Press, Toronto, Canada

Stiglitz JE, Weiss A (1981) Credit rationing in markets with imperfect information. Am Econ Rev 71(3):393–410

Szczygielski K, Grabowski W, Pamukcu MT et al (2017) Does government support for private innovation matter? Firm-level evidence from two catching-up countries. Res Policy 46(1):219–237. https://doi.org/10.1016/j.respol.2016.10.009
Wang SS, Goh JR, Sornette D et al (2021) Government support for SMEs in response to COVID-19: theoretical model using Wang transform. China Financ Rev Int 11(3):406–433. https://doi.org/10.1108/CFRI-05-2021-0088

Financing and Performance

COVID-19 Costs and National Financing System: Evidence from Italy

Ilaria Elisa Vannini and Niccolò Persiani

Abstract For the past 2 years, healthcare systems have been judged on their ability to afford the costs of the COVID-19 pandemic. There was a need to face the imposed state of emergency and implement flexible approaches to adapt to a changing context. Economic and managerial aspects also came under the spotlight after the pandemic outbreak. This study promotes a reflection on the impact of the pandemic and its effects on the financing system, expenditure trends, and economic data incurred by Italian public healthcare organisations in the year of the pandemic outbreak in Italy, which was the first Western country to be involved in the COVID-19 crisis. As a starting point, the study focuses on national data and then turns to data from two Italian regions significantly stressed by the pandemic (Lombardy and Veneto). Data analysis shows that the Italian healthcare financing system—based on the per-capita share—was able to cover the costs incurred by the pandemic. The resources allocated to healthcare organisations were sufficient to cope with the structural change in services provided and changes in national health mobility data.

Keywords COVID-19 pandemic · Costs · Consolidated income statement · National health financing system · Regional healthcare systems

1 Health Systems in the Face of Pandemic Crises

In the last 2 years, healthcare services have been hit by a pandemic crisis affecting all economies of the world (IMHE 2021; Liu et al. 2020; Lu 2020). The need to cope with this pandemic necessitated the activation of reorganisational responses capable of adapting to a changing context whose boundaries were, and are still being

I. E. Vannini (✉) · N. Persiani
Department of Experimental and Clinical Medicine, University of Florence, Florence, Italy
e-mail: ilariaelisa.vannini@unifi.it

N. Persiani
e-mail: niccolo.persiani@unifi.it

N. Persiani et al. (eds.), *Challenges of Healthcare Systems in the Era of COVID-19*, Contributions to Management Science, https://doi.org/10.1007/978-3-031-43114-2_9

defined day by day (Lloyd-Smith 2020; Nadarajan et al. 2020; Norris et al. 2020; Pallivathukkal 2021; Thurmer et al. 2020).

The pandemic has generated new costs and financial requirements for health services (Gates 2020), especially the intervention of new players who have enriched the pre-existing interaction between Public Administration, the market and civil society (Cepiku et al. 2006; Reichard 2001; Meneguzzo 1996; Rhodes 2000; Kooiman and van Vliet 1993) and the need to respond to new health needs (Hatswell 2020) that could ensure economic balance over the following years.

Since Italy was the first Western country to be overwhelmed by the pandemic and suffered dramatically from its impact (Nadarajan et al. 2020), our study on the effect of the pandemic on the costs of the Italian public healthcare sector can serve as an example for other countries.

To cope with the emergency situation by injecting financial resources into the Italian National Healthcare System (hereafter INHS), the central government instructed healthcare organisations to adopt a Cost Centre dedicated to the costs caused by the emergency (D.L. 17 March 2020, n. 18, art. 18, co. 1). This accounting of actual resources consumed would be the basis for all the subsequent funding decisions. The aforementioned Cost Centre allowed the regions to recognise, by consolidating data from each healthcare organisation, the direct and indirect costs (Anthony et al. 2005; Brusa 2000), thus ensuring "a distinct perimeter" of accounting data related to the management of the state of emergency until a separate accounting procedure is activated (Anthony et al. 2005; Brusa 2000).

Thus, these data provide a starting point for reflection on the costs of the pandemic in healthcare organisations and on the role of the national healthcare financing system.

The aim of this study is to investigate the impact of the pandemic on the costs incurred by the INHS, as well as the effect on its financing system. The work was conducted with reference to the Italian experience; specific attention was paid to two Regional Healthcare Systems (hereinafter RHS) significantly stressed by the pandemic (Veneto RHS and Lombardy RHS). Starting with national data, the study analyses data from the COVID Cost Centre adopted by the regions focusing on the costs most affected by the pandemic. Finally, it brings a reflection on the Italian financing system.

2 Materials and Methodology

This paper presents the results of an analysis conducted primarily with national data on health care spending and financing, while also focusing on two RHSs, namely, Veneto RHS and Lombardy RHS, which were affected first, and most dramatically, by the pandemic.

The case selection strategy was guided by theoretical arguments. Case studies (Yin 2003) were chosen through the use of purposive sampling to illustrate the objectives of the study (Eisenhardt and Graebner 2007; Van Thiel 2014, p. 90). At the regional level, it is possible to isolate the impact of the pandemic through detailed monitoring of costs as well as outputs and health outcomes. Because the selected RHSs were the first in Europe to be involved in the COVID-19 crisis, they are representative of the pandemic's cost impact at the organisational level and are not affected by different pandemic phases in other settings.

Starting from the analysis of national data of health expenditure trends in the period 2017–2020, the analysis was interested in 2020 versus 2019, and the 3-year average in the period 2017–2019 was considered a significant parameter to appreciate the impact of pandemic on costs. National data (average of RHSs' data) were previously compared with those of Northern, Central and Southern Italy, each including RHSs by territorial basins. In order to understand any deviations in the regional data, with these RHSs being the first to be impacted by the pandemic in Italy, a comparison was made with the national data and those from the North (territorially closer).

Considering those cost items affected by variance and the distinction between COVID-19 cases and non-COVID-19 cases, most significant in the year of the outbreak of the pandemic, we have analysed the consolidated financial statements of two Italian RHSs: Lombardy RHS and Veneto RHS. They represent two of the main Italian regional healthcare systems: 25% of the Italian population reside in these areas (ISTAT, Population Census and Demographic Dynamics 2020), and there are 81 public hospitalisation facilities, equal to 15.7% of the total (Ministry of Health, Statistical Yearbook of the National Health Service 2020); they also manage 1/4 of the national per-capita health fund, and there are approximately 147,275 NHS personnel, equal to 23.85% of the total (Ministry of Health, Statistical Yearbook of the National Health Service 2020). Lombardy and Veneto were first, and significantly, affected by COVID-19.

It should be underlined that, in Italy, the management operations of public healthcare organisations are recognised by full accrual consolidated (Andrei and Fellegara 2020; Pisani and Giunta 2018) and the Income Statement, in particular, includes costs and revenues of each organisation. It is a scheme adopted by all of the healthcare organisations in the INHS, consolidated at the regional level. Consequently, with regard to Lombardy RHS and Veneto RHS, we collected regional healthcare consolidated financial statements for 2019 and 2020; the former year was considered an important point of comparison in order to evaluate the pandemic's impact on costs and revenues. We analysed the consolidated financial statements so as to isolate the COVID-19 impact within a specific Cost Centre which provides detailed information on costs (Anthony et al. 2005; Brusa 2000) for 2020. Indeed, we also reclassified the consolidated financial statements to deepen the analysis of those costs and revenues which were more significant with regard to the COVID-19 pandemic. The analysis stimulated the construction of specific indicators to capture the percentage increase or decrease of the same costs and revenues.

3 Results

The analysis started with the preliminary observation of health expenditure at the national level for the period 2017–2020 (MEF 2021). In order to capture the economic and financial impact of the pandemic in the different areas of Italy, the data relating to Northern, Central, Southern Italy were analysed and compared with 2019 and, jointly, with the 3-year period 2017–2019.

Current health expenditure shows an increase of 5.59% in 2020 over 2019 (Table 1) distributed as follows: in the northern regions, it is 5.50%, in the central regions, 7.51%, and in the southern regions, 4.07%. This increase is particularly significant when compared with that recorded in 2019 compared with the average of the previous 3 years, as shown in Table 1. In fact, in 2019, compared to the 2017–2019 average, the overall growth is 1.11% at national level, divided between North, Centre and South, respectively in 1.41%, 0.72% and 1.06%.

In the year of the pandemic outbreak, the growth in expenditure is more significant in the Centre than in the North, where the clinical-epidemiological impact was greatest.

The 5.59% increase in Italian current health expenditure in 2020 is particularly influenced by certain aggregates directly attributable to typical health management: personnel, pharmaceutical products and other social services in kind from private operators/bodies/organisations. Personnel expenses—comprising the health role, professional role, technical role and administrative role—(Table 2) show an increase (3.33% on 2019), which is more relevant in the Centre (4.94%) than in the North (3.40%). There is an even more marked increase compared to the previous 3 years—by 5.07% overall.

Moreover, the category pharmaceutical products (Table 3) shows an increase (6.18% at the national level), which, however, is particularly significant in the South (7.91%). It should be noted that the aggregate grows over the broader period 2012–2020 by more than 50%, going from 7.856 to 12.131 million euros, with an average annual increase of 5.6% (MEF 2021). Only in 2019, it is characterised by a contraction, primarily due to the collection of pay-backs for the period 2013–2017 following the resolution of administrative disputes with pharmaceutical companies.

Table 1 Italian healthcare expenditure—years 2017–2020

	Absolute values (millions of euros)			Variation %	
	2017–2019 (average)	2019	2020	2020 on 2019 (%)	2020 on the average of the previous 3 years (%)
North	45.984,83	46.631,5	49.196,3	5.50	6.98
Centre	31.904,05	32.135,1	34.549,5	7.51	8.29
South	37.760,74	38.161,5	39.713,4	4.07	5.17
Italy	115.649,61	116.928,0	123.459,3	5.59	6.75

Table 2 Personnel expenses

	Absolute values (millions of euros)			Variation %	
	2017–2019 (average)	2019	2020	2020 on 2019 (%)	2020 on the average of the previous 3 years (%)
North	13.807,03	14.086,56	14.564,97	3.40	5.49
Centre	9.927,32	10.113,97	10.613,39	4.94	6.91
South	11.159,08	11.281,13	11.485,79	1.81	2.93
Italy	11.631,15	11.827,22	12.221,38	3.33	5.07

Table 3 Pharmaceutical products

	Absolute values (millions of euros)			Variation (%)	
	2017–2019 (average)	2019	2020	2020 on 2019 (%)	2020 on the average of the previous 3 years (%)
North	4.049,69	4.204,65	4.444,05	5.69	9.74
Centre	3.309,48	3.276,00	3.430,85	4.73	3.67
South	4.031,36	3.944,57	4.256,64	7.91	5.59
Italy	3.796,84	3.808,40	4.043,85	6.18	6.51

Finally, the category other social services in kind from private operators (Table 4) includes purchases of hospital, specialist, rehabilitative, supplementary, prosthetic and other services from private operators accredited with the INHS. At the national level, there is a contraction (−3.25%, Table 4), which is substantially aligned with the South (−3.68%). The North (−6.58%) and the Centre, where there is even an increase (2.63%), differ considerably from the national average. Looking at the broader period 2012–2020, this aggregate at the national level shows an increase of 7.4% (from 22.534 to 24.195 million euros, corresponding to an average annual growth of 0.9%). The increase up to 2019 is offset by the decrease in 2020 due to the lower number of assistance services provided because of the restrictions associated with the COVID-19 health emergency. This decline is different in the Italian regions. In most of them, a decrease is observed (MEF 2021), and it reaches higher values in Abruzzo (−12.1%), in Molise (−11.7%) and in Lombardy (−10.8%). On the other hand, the most consistent positive rates of change are in Lazio (+5.4%), Umbria (+2.9%) and Marche (+2.6%).

By observing national data, it is not possible to understand how the increase in expenditure is specifically attributable to COVID-19. This is the reason why we analysed the regional consolidated financial statements and those dedicated to COVID-19 for Lombardy RHS and Veneto RHS. Both belong to Northern Italy, where the variation in expenditure (national data) is perfectly in line with the national average (5.59% national, 5.50% North).

Table 4 Other social services in kind from private operators

	Absolute values (millions of euros)			Variation (%)	
	2017–2019 (average)	2019	2020	2020 on 2019 (%)	2020 on the average of the previous 3 years (%)
North	10.007,18	10.139,68	9.472,62	−6.58	−5.34
Centre	6.174,67	6.367,34	6.534,74	2.63	5.83
South	8.308,17	8.500,77	8.187,66	−3.68	−1.45
Italy	8.163,34	8.335,93	8.065,00	−3.25	−1.20

To cope with the emerging needs of the pandemic, the Italian central government requested that the public healthcare organisations create a special Cost Centre—referred to as COVID-20. It is dedicated to the costs generated by the pandemic and it is useful for their accounting and reporting closely linked to the funding specifically provided by the central government (D.L. 17 March 2020, n. 18, art. 18, co. 1). This Cost Centre, including direct and indirect costs (Anthony et al. 2005, 96-ss.), guarantees “a distinct perimeter of accounting events” related to the management of the pandemic up to the activation of a real “separate accounting”.

The analysis of the main cost aggregates of the two regions was preceded by the reclassification of their consolidated health income statements for 2020 and for the previous year. It was also determined for the year of the outbreak of the pandemic the COVID/no COVID incidence (Tables 5 and 6).

In Lombardy RHS, the 4.49% increase in production costs can be ascribed, in particular, to the increased costs of purchasing healthcare and non-healthcare goods (2.94%) and to the increase in personnel costs (3.29%, in line with the national data for Northern Italy). Considering the COVID/no COVID incidence, it is 0.53% for purchases of health and non-health goods and 2.09% for personnel costs.

The increase in production costs of 4.49% is offset by the increase in the value of production of 4.30%, which is particularly affected by the increase of extra funds paid for the pandemic emergency.

Considering the core business as a whole, it produces an EBITDA increase of 47.11%, with a COVID/no COVID incidence of 17.32%.

In Veneto RHS (Table 6), the rise in production costs (7.23%) is determined, in particular, by the increase in the purchasing of health and non-healthcare goods (24.41%) and the increase in personnel costs (4.20%, which is higher than the national data for Northern Italy). With regard to the COVID/no COVID incidence, it is 21% for purchases of health and non-health goods and 3.10% for personnel costs.

The increase in production costs (7.23%) is offset by the 6.87% increase in the value of production, which is particularly affected by the increase in extra funds paid for the pandemic emergency.

Table 5 Lombardy RHS—consolidated income statement: reclassification

	2019	2020	2020 COVID	2020 NO COVID	2019 on 2020 (%)	COVID/no COVID Incidence
Value of production	21.294.696.607	22.210.617.928	808.552.603	21.402.065.325	4.30	3.78
Costs of goods (health)	2.760.902.033	2.842.704.433	13.423.456	2.829.280.977	2.96	0.47
Costs of goods (non-health)	55.676.180	56.806.172	1.961.530	54.844.642	2.03	3.58
Changes in inventories of raw materials	−12.450.880	−78.771.550	−174.471	−78.597.079	532.66	0.22
Cost of external services (health)	9.475.029.317	9.274.263.155	240.978.024	9.033.285.131	−2.12	2.67
Cost of external services (non-health)	1.540.825.246	1.514.640.204	4.947.844	1.509.692.360	−1.70	0.33
Use of third-party assets	209.799.032	214.680.109	386.534	214.293.575	2.33	0.18
Other operating expenses	134.692.756	135.811.354	27.794	135.783.560	0.83	0.02
Added value	7.130.222.923	8.250.484.051	547.001.892	7.703.482.159	15.71	7.10
Cost of personnel—health role	3.978.990.668	4.112.292.082	89.650.366	4.022.641.716	3.35	2.23
Cost of personnel—professional role	20.595.985	21.866.626	157.958	21.708.668	6.17	0.73
Cost of personnel—technical role	665.958.990	688.613.036	14.930.379	673.682.657	3.40	2.22
Cost of personnel—administrative role	444.027.644	455.147.811	3.333.577	451.814.234	2.50	0.74
Salaries and wages (total amount)	5.109.573.287	5.277.919.555	108.072.280	5.169.847.275	3.29	2.09
Earnings before income taxes, depreciation and amortization (EBITDA)	2.020.649.636	2.972.564.496	438.929.612	2.533.634.884	47.11	17.32

(continued)

Table 5 (continued)

	2019	2020	2020 COVID	2020 NO COVID	2019 on 2020 (%)	COVID/no COVID Incidence
Amortisation	415.532.854	435.220.368	748.037	434.472.331	4.74	0.17
Share of capital contributions allocated during the year	0	0	0	0	0.00	0.00
Provisions	1.325.788.786	2.285.609.934	429.326.989	1.856.282.945	72.40	23.13
Earnings before interest and taxes (EBIT)	279.327.996	251.734.194	8.854.586	242.879.608	−9.88	3.65
Financial income	235.915	134.906	0	134.906	−42.82	0.00
Financial charges	3.323.304	2.650.677	0	2.650.677	−20.24	0.00
Ordinary result	276.240.607	249.218.423	8.854.586	240.363.837	−9.78	3.68
Extraordinary income and expenses	96.313.333	137.911.298	830.000	137.081.298	43.19	0.61
Earnings before tax (EBT)	372.553.940	387.129.721	9.684.586	377.445.135	3.91	2.57
Taxes	366.222.115	375.876.574	9.684.586	366.191.988	2.64	2.64
Net income (loss)	6.331.825	11.253.147	0	11.253.147	77.72	0.00

Table 6 Veneto RHS—consolidated income statement: reclassification

	2019	2020	2020 COVID	2020 NO COVID	2019 on 2020 (%)	COVID/no COVID incidence (%)
Value of production	10.051.039.206	10.741.137.848	595.315.712	10.145.822.135	6.87	5.87
Costs of goods (health)	1.576.862.683	1.965.926.048	343.525.286	1.622.400.762	24.67	21.17
Costs of goods (non-health)	26.088.816	28.275.873	2.621.092	25.654.781	8.38	10.22
Changes in inventories of raw materials	−15.504.538	−138.409.022	−99.945.801	−38.463.222	792.70	259.85
Cost of external services (health)	3.836.764.089	3.877.802.737	115.022.191	3.762.780.546	1.07	3.06
Cost of external services (non-health)	931.600.279	956.628.319	38.858.688	917.769.631	2.69	4.23
Use of third-party assets	128.179.256	127.533.145	1.867.958	125.665.188	−0.50	1.49
Other operating expenses	39.165.053	48.800.224	6.784.736	42.015.487	24.60	16.15
Added value	3.527.883.568	3.874.580.524	186.581.562	3.687.998.962	9.83	5.06
Cost of personnel—health role	2.204.703.788	2.289.880.252	64.545.485	2.225.334.766	3.86	2.90
Cost of personnel—professional role	7.455.978	7.913.469	102.002	7.811.466	6.14	1.31
Cost of personnel—technical role	372.085.739	404.935.728	20.285.406	384.650.323	8.83	5.27
Cost of personnel—administrative role	205.658.586	204.294.655	2.423.134	201.871.521	−0.66	1.20
Salaries and Wages (Total Amount)	2.789.904.091	2.907.024.103	87.356.027	2.819.668.076	4.20	3.10
Earnings Before Income Taxes, Depreciation and Amortization (EBITDA)	737.979.478	967.556.420	99.225.535	868.330.886	31.11	11.43
Amortisation	239.745.631	253.123.238	7.241.601	245.881.637	5.58	2.95
Share of capital contributions allocated during the year	192.079.953	208.848.423	7.242.229	201.606.194	8.73	3.59
Provisions	493.228.321	745.264.800	240.141.552	505.123.248	51.10	47.54
Earnings Before Interest and Taxes (EBIT)	197.085.479	178.016.806	−140.915.389	318.932.195	−9.68	−44.18

(continued)

Table 6 (continued)

	2019	2020	2020 COVID	2020 NO COVID	2019 on 2020 (%)	COVID/no COVID incidence (%)
Financial income	128.479	83.200	0	83.200	−35.24	0.00
Financial charges	2.303.665	1.692.662	0	1.692.662	−26.52	0.00
Ordinary result	194.910.293	176.407.343	−140.915.389	317.322.733	−9.49	−44.41
Extraordinary income and expenses	38.207.779	41.798.832	6.220.531	35.578.301	9.40	17.48
Earnings Before Tax (EBT)	233.118.071	218.206.175	−134.694.859	352.901.034	−6.40	−38.17
Taxes	204.572.272	212.522.732	8.418.098	204.104.634	3.89	4.12
Net income (loss)	28.545.799	5.683.443	−143.112.957	148.796.400	−80.09	−96.18

EBITDA also increases significantly in Veneto (31.11%), with a COVID/no COVID incidence of 11.43%, although the annual result is affected by a significant contraction compared to 2019 (−80.69%).

Net income determined by the various areas in Veneto RHS shows an overall decrease of 80.69%, with a COVID/no COVID incidence of −96.18%.

4 Discussion

The increase in national health expenditure in 2020 (5.59% divided as follows: 5.50% North, 7.51% Centre, 4.07% South) is easily attributable to COVID-19, considering that the current healthcare expenditure from 2012 to 2019 shows a significantly lower average annual increase (0.8%).

In the North, where the case studies are located, the increase in expenditure is in line with the national average; the fact that it is not the highest at national level can be ascribed to the widespread presence, in the North, of private hospitals that historically attract patient flows. Due to collapsing active mobility in the Northern Regions, as a consequence of government restrictions on travel (lockdown) and the same focus of hospitals on COVID-19 care activities, there are lower expenses for ordinary activities. In other words, the fact that it is not the highest can be attributed to a compensatory effect.

The increase in expenditure is linked to greater specific funding for the management of the emergency status: in 2020, when the costs related to the pandemic weigh on, the funding disbursed by the central government increases (5.45%, Table 7) as follows: 5.09% North, 7.09% Centre and 4.49% South. It can be observed that there is a substantial alignment in the North (but also in the other two areas) with the variation in health expenditure.

This alignment inevitably influences the annual results in the year of the outbreak of the pandemic compared to 2019.

The analysis of the data relating to the funding disbursed by the central level made it possible to understand the system responses that contributed to addressing the health emergency and to determine the annual result.

Table 7 Funding provided by the state level

	Absolute values (millions of euros)			Variation (%)	
	2017–2019 (average)	2019	2020	2020 on 2019 (%)	2020 on the average of the previous 3 years (%)
North	45.607,47	46.164,9	48.514,7	5.09	6.37
Centre	32.072,56	32.365,52	34.660,15	7.09	8.07
South	37.394,70	37.704,4	39.397,5	4.49	5.36
Italy	115.074,73	116.234,90	122.572,37	5.45	6.52

Regional consolidated data supported the analysis of the effect of COVID-19 costs on health expenditure through an examination of the COVID-20 Cost Centre. However, this Cost Centre risks being only partially capable of allowing the accounting of the actual cost incurred for the pandemic and scarcely able to form the basis for effective and complete reporting of the pandemic.

The increase in costs accounted for the COVID Centre is significant, but lower than we would expect in a dramatic situation. However, it must be considered that in the same year with equal financing—net of COVID—ordinary activity is substantially interrupted. These data (which emerge from the comparison of costs for health services and the other costs NO-COVID 2020 and 2019) made it possible to pour the available resources (financial, professional, etc.) into pandemic care.

The per-capita financing system, disbursed on the basis of the assistants regardless of the services provided, made it possible to face the crisis with an unexpected elasticity, not guaranteed by an insurance system.

Of course, our reflection applies to the short term. In fact, already in 2021, in Italy, there was a thorough re-thinking to address a problem that certainly can no longer be considered temporary.

On the other hand, the complexity of the phenomenon and the difficulty in predicting its duration and evolution make necessary a more articulated reporting model (based on a more sophisticated accounting), capable of understanding all the aspects of such a complex problem. Indeed, it seems reasonable to think that the health system that emerged from the pandemic crisis will need a new financing and reporting model, which takes into account the many changes that the system has undergone and the new articulation it will have to assume. The approach has a shortcoming regarding the request for the reporting of a limited series of costs generated in the first phase of the health emergency, as it risks neglecting multiple economic effects related to its evolution that can be better represented by an accounting per order approach (Combattente 2001).

In order to include in the analysis all the costs and their evolution in the different phases of the crisis, and to compare the behaviours of the organisations operating in the national public health system, it is relevant to address the issue of accounting and consequent reporting of costs, considering the moment in which they occur in relation to the evolution of the pandemic event and its different phases, namely, pre-crisis, crisis and post-crisis (Coombs 2015; König et al. 2020).

5 Conclusions

The study shows that the pandemic impact, although present, was modest: the indicators determined using consolidated economic data demonstrate the Italian national healthcare system's resilience (Sutcliffe and Vogus 2003) and the elasticity of its financing system based on the per-capita share.

Indeed, there was a need to cope with the emergency status imposed and to implement flexible approaches to adapt healthcare systems in a continuously changing context. Economic and managerial aspects also came into the spotlight with the onset of the pandemic. Starting from national consolidated data, the analysis of those two Italian regions significantly stressed by the pandemic (Lombardy RHS and Veneto RHS) underlines the modest pandemic impact as well as its effects on the financing system, on expenses trends, and on economic data incurred by public healthcare organisations in the year of the pandemic outbreak in Italy.

Based on per-capita share, the INHS was able to cover those costs generated by the pandemic. The resources allocated to healthcare organisations were sufficient to cope with the structural modification of the services provided and the changes in national health mobility data.

It follows that COVID-19 has taught us many lessons certainly valid in the short term. One of these pertains to the importance of public health. Another lesson relates to the national financing system and healthcare system's resilience as a great opportunity to strengthen the toolbox of public health economics for pandemic outbreaks. It emerges that the regions selected maintained their balanced budget thanks to the Italian healthcare financing system. By virtue of this, all costs were kept at a reasonable level to allow the system to provide health services.

Acknowledgements We would like to thank the management of the two Italian regions which shared data for their interest in the research project.

References

Andrei P, Fellegara A (2020) Contabilità generale e bilancio d'impresa. Giappichelli, Torino

Anthony R, Hawkins DF, Macrì DM, Merchant KA (2005) Sistemi di controllo. Analisi economiche per le decisioni aziendali. McGraw-Hill, Milano

Brusa L (2000) Sistemi manageriali di programmazione e controllo. Giuffrè

Cepiku D, Ferrari D, Greco A (2006) Governance e Coordinamento Strategico Delle Reti Di Aziende Sanitarie. Mecosan 57:17–36

Claeys AS, Cauberghe V (2012) Crisis response and crisis timing strategies, two sides of the same coin. Public Relat Rev 38(1):83–88

Combattente A (2001) Il controllo di gestione nelle imprese che producono su commessa. Amministrazione & Finanza 6:33–39

Comfort LK (2007) Crisis management in hindsight: Cognition, communication, coordination, and control. Public Adm Rev 67(1):189–197

Coombs WT (2015) Ongoing crisis communication: planning, managing, and responding, 4th edn. Sage, Thousand Oaks, CA

Eisenhardt KM, Graebner ME (2007) Theory building from cases: opportunities and challenges. Acad Manag J 50(1):25–32

Gates B (2020) Responding to Covid-19. A once-in-a-century pandemic? New Engl J Med 382(18):1677–1679

Hatswell AJ (2020) Learnings for health economics from the early stages of the COVID-19 pandemic. Pharmaco Econ Open 4:203–205

Institute for Metrics Health and Evaluations (IMHE) (2021) Spending for COVID-19

ISTAT (2020) Censimento della Popolazione e Dinamica Demografica. Anno

König A, Graf-Vlachy L, Bundy J, Little LM (2020) A blessing and a curse: how CEO's trait empathy affects their management of organizational crises. Acad Manag Rev 45(1):130–153
Kooiman JP, van Vliet M (1993) Governance and public management. Managing public organizations: lessons from contemporary European experience, pp 58–72
Liu H, Manzoor A, Wang C, Zhang L, Manzoor Z (2020) The COVID-19 outbreak and affected countries stock markets response. Int J Environ Res Public Health 17(8):2800
Lloyd-Smith M (2020) The COVID-19 pandemic: resilient organisational response to a low-chance, high-impact event. BMJ Leader 1–4. https://doi.org/10.1136/leader-2020-000245
Lu M (2020) This chart shows how debt-to-GDP is rising around the world. World Economic Forum. 14 Dec 2020. https://www.weforum.org/agenda/2020/12/global-debt-gdp-covid19/. Accessed 14 Jan 2021
Meneguzzo M (ed) (1996) Strategia e gestione di reti di aziende sanitarie. Egea, Milano
Ministero dell'Economia e delle Finanze (2021) Il monitoraggio della spesa sanitaria. Studi e Pubblicazioni, Rapporto n. 8. Roma
Ministero della Salute (2020) Annuario Statistico del Servizio Sanitario Nazionale. Anno
Nadarajan GD, Omar E, Abella BS, Hoe PS, Do Shin S, Ma MH-M, Ong MEH (2020) A conceptual framework for emergency department design in a pandemic. Scand J Trauma, Resuscitation Emerg Med
Norris JI, Casa de Calvo M, Mather R (2020) Managing an existential threat: how a global crisis contaminates organizational decision-making. Manag Decis 58(10):2117–2138
Pallivathukkal J (2021) Healthcare leadership in times of crisis. An overview of COVID-19 crisis management and its effect on economy. Ann R.S.C.B. 25(5):3777–3785
Pisani M, Giunta F (2018) La contabilità generale. Maggioli Editore, Bologna
Reichard C (2001) New approaches to public management. In: König K, Siedentopf H (eds) Public administration in Germany. Nomos, Baden-Baden
Rhodes RAW (2000) Governance and public administration. In: Pierre J (ed) Debating governance: authority, steering and democracy. Oxford, Oxford University Press
Sutcliffe KM, Vogus TJ (2003) Organizing for resilience. In: Cameron K, Dutton JE, Quinn RE (eds) Positive organizational scholarship. Berrett-Koehler, San Francisco, pp 94–110
Thurmer JL, Wieber F, Gollwitz PM (2020) Management in times of crisis: can collective plans prepare teams to make and implement good decisions? Manag Decis 58(10):2155–2176
Van Thiel S (2014) Research methods in public administration and public management: an introduction. Routledge
Yin RK (2003) Case study research: design and methods. Sage Publications, Thousand Oaks

Factors Affecting the Health Care Expenditure in Albania: A Macroeconomic Analysis

Ermira H. Kalaj and Kelt Kalaj

Abstract Using time-series data for Albania for the period 2000–2020, the study investigates the effect of various macroeconomic factors on health care expenditure. Health care expenditure measured as percentage of GDP, out-of-pocket expenses, domestic private health expenditure and external health expenditure per capita. The central point of this study is to understand which factors are driving health expenditures. In the study, explanatory variables are divided into two groups: demographic and socio-economic determinants. Findings indicate that health expenditure are negatively affected by deposit interest rate, and positively influenced by population aged 65 and over, life expectancy, mortality rate, and number of physicians for 1,000 people. These results are comparable with similar research in other Eastern European countries. On the other hand, remittances positively affect the household out-of-pocket expenditure and external health expenditure. Remittance flows are significant in driving health care expenditures when compared to income such as GDP per capita. These income flows may contribute to stabilization in the use of health care services by poorer households. These results may be used from policymakers to better use and management of remittances from abroad to reinforce their role in the increased well-being of households.

Keywords Health care expenditure · Out-of-pocket expenses · Remittances

JEL Classification Codes I11 · I15 · F24

E. H. Kalaj (✉)
University of Shkodra "Luigj Gurakuqi", Shkodër, Albania
e-mail: ermira.kalaj@unishk.edu.al

K. Kalaj
University of Medicine, Tirana, Albania

N. Persiani et al. (eds.), *Challenges of Healthcare Systems in the Era of COVID-19*,
Contributions to Management Science, https://doi.org/10.1007/978-3-031-43114-2_10

1 Introduction

Health care expenditure analyses have become central recently due to the pandemic crises of COVID-19. Nevertheless, the debate on the nature of health care expenditure if it belongs to the group of luxury or necessity goods is quite older (Parkin et al. 1987; Blomqvist and Carter 1997; Getzen 2000; Sen 2005; Costa-Font et al. 2011). Using different data and methodologies, previous empirical studies have investigated on the income elasticity of health care expenditure both at the micro and macroeconomic level of analyses.

Utilizing research from both developed and developing countries results show that the variance in per capita health care expenditure can be explained by variation in per capita GDP or income, and that health care expenditure results with the elasticity greater than 1 (Clemente et al. 2004; Wang and Rettenmaier 2007). Still, there are few studies showing that the elasticity of income is lower than 1 (Baltagi and Moscone 2010; Mehrara et al. 2012). Besides income level behind health care expenditure, there is a myriad of factors acting both at the micro and macro level such as public expenditure, inflation rate, life expectancy, birth rate, technological development, individual characteristics, etc.

Since theoretical and empirical analyses on the factors affecting health care expenditure are controversial, it is crucial to further investigate on the causes behind the behaviour of health care expenditure in development context such as Albania. The paper contributes to the limited empirical literature on the factors driving health care expenditure in Albania, including, and testing new macroeconomic variables in the model. Health care coverage is provided through the mandatory health insurance system administered by a single purchasing agency, the Mandatory Health Insurance Fund (MHIF). The MHIF covers only around two thirds of the population. Uninsured people are entitled to free emergency care (since 2013), a free basic health check-up once a year and free visits to general physicians. They must pay out of pocket for all other health services. According to INSTAT (2020), informal payments are widespread, particularly for inpatient treatment, and impose an important financial burden on poorer households.

The paper is organized as follows. A brief introduction is represented in the first section. The second section provides a literature review on the factors affecting health care expenditure. Data and methodology are described in the third section. While the fourth section discusses the empirical results. Conclusions and discussions are presented in the fifth section of the study.

2 Literature Review

According to EUROSTAT (2022), health care expenditures for Albania are among the lowest in Europe, and this trend continued in the pandemic year 2020. Nominal expenditures per capita in the health sector, the second lowest in Europe after Northern

Macedonia (EUR 255) and almost 10 times less than the European Union average (27 countries) of EUR 2,614. The outbreak of the COVID-19 pandemic has had a large effect on Albania, both in the economy and in managing the health situation of the population.

At the microeconomic level, the current literature on determinants of health care expenditure has widely focused on studying the topic principally using survey data. Bredenkamp et al. (2011) use Living Standards and Measurement Surveys (LSMS) period 2000–2005 for Albania, Bosnia and Herzegovina, Montenegro, Serbia, and Kosovo to investigate the influence of health care expenditure on household welfare. They find that catastrophic and the impoverishing effects of health care expenditures are serious in Albania and Kosovo. In Albania and Serbia, transportation expenditure accounts for a large share of total health care expenditures. Informal payments are considerable in all Western Balkan countries and tend to be high in Albania. Using household surveys, Kalaj (2015) investigates on the impact of remittances on health care expenditure through instrumental variable and propensity score matching methodology. The findings indicate that households increase their expenditure for medicines and other health services in the presence of remittance income. The positive effect is significant in the case of remittance-receiving households living in the rural area. Using cross-sectional data survey of 2526 patients from all the Italian regions, Ruggeri et al. (2020) investigate on the determinants of health care expenditures. In their study, Italian regions were clustered according to three criteria: geographic, income- and performance-based. They use Heckman decomposition and controlling for age, education and severity, individual health care expenditures have the tendency to increase in southern regions where per capita income and the performance of the health care services are lower if compared to the rest of Italy.

From the macroeconomic point of view, empirical studies link the health care expenditure to economic and social variables. The relationship between per capita health expenditures and income, Di Matteo (2005), assesses age distribution and time. Real per capita health expenditures are positively related to income, time, and an ageing population for time series from USA and Canada. Simple models of health expenditures find that the increase in the percentage of population aged 65 and over is the reason of the increase in health spending. Models that use a more complex specification for age and time indicator variables find that time is more important variable. Grigorakis et al. (2018) use panel data for the period 1995–2013 for 26 OECD countries to examine macroeconomic determinants on health care financing. Using fixed/random effects and dynamic panel data techniques, the authors demonstrated that public spending and unemployment have beneficial effects on health care finance. A comparative analysis of the link between gross domestic product and health expenditure growth is realized by Stepovic et al. (2020) in Balkan and East European countries. Among other findings, they notice that the median value in out-of-pocket payment was the highest in Albania and Ukraine, while the largest decrease in trend was noticed in Albania and Bosnia and Herzegovina. The causality between economic growth and health care expenditure is in the centre of the study of Xhindi (2020). They use data for Albania for the period 1996–2017. ARDL Bounds testing approach for co-integration and Granger causality test are the methodologies used to give answer to the research question. The ARDL model estimations confirm the positive relationship between the two variables.

In times of pandemic challenges, there is a growing interest in investigating the effects of health expenditure on household well-being all over the world and especially in developing countries. In this context, further analysis is needed to better understand factors affecting health care expenditure in Albania.

3 Data and Methodology

In our study, we use time series from Albania for the period from 2000 to 2020, in Tables 1 and 2, the variables and respective sources are described. Primary care, secondary hospital care and tertiary care are the three levels of the Albanian health system. The public sector provides most health services, while the private sector handles things like pharmaceutical, dentistry, specialist clinics and hospitals. During 2020, the budget expenditures to cope with the effects of the COVID-19 pandemic on the economy and health were EUR 134.8 million. This amount was 3.1% of the total budget expenditures for 2020. From the total funds (EUR 134 million) allocated to face the pandemic effects, only 19% were used to finance the health needs, while 11 million EUR were used to support the economy through two relief packages. The budget that finances the health needs in 2021 was 6.1% higher than the actual expenditures of 2020 (INSTAT 2021).

Table 1 Description of dependent variables

Dependent variable	Source	Description
Current health expenditure (% of GDP)	World health organization	Level of current health expenditure expressed as a percentage of GDP. Estimates of current health expenditures include healthcare goods and services consumed during each year. This indicator does not include capital health expenditures such as buildings, machinery, IT and stocks of vaccines for emergency or outbreaks
Out-of-pocket expenditure		Share of out-of-pocket payments of total current health expenditures. Out-of-pocket payments are spending on health directly out-of-pocket by households
Domestic private health expenditure		Share of current health expenditures funded from domestic private sources. Domestic private sources include funds from households, corporations and non-profit organizations
External health expenditure per capita		External sources are composed of direct foreign transfers and foreign transfers distributed by government encompassing all financial inflows into the national health system from outside the country

Table 2 Description of explanatory variables

Explanatory variables	Source	Description
Demographic indicators		
Population growth (annual %)	World Bank	Annual population growth rate for year t is the exponential rate of growth of midyear population from year t-1 to t, expressed as a percentage. Population is based on the de facto definition of population, which counts all residents regardless of legal status or citizenship
Population ages 65 and above		Population ages 65 and above as a percentage of the total population. Population is based on the de facto definition of population, which counts all residents regardless of legal status or citizenship
Life expectancy at birth		Life expectancy at birth indicates the number of years a newborn infant would live if prevailing patterns of mortality at the time of its birth were to stay the same throughout its life
Mortality rate, infant		Infant mortality rate is the number of infants dying before reaching 1 year of age, per 1,000 live births in a given year
Socio-economic indicators		
GDP per capita		GDP per capita is gross domestic product divided by midyear population. GDP is the sum of gross value added by all resident producers in the economy plus any product taxes and minus any subsidies not included in the value of the products
Inflation, GDP deflator		Inflation as measured by the annual growth rate of the GDP implicit deflator shows the rate of price change in the economy. The GDP implicit deflator is the ratio of GDP in current local currency to GDP in constant local currency
Deposit interest rate		Deposit interest rate is the rate paid by commercial or similar banks for demand, time or savings deposits. The terms and conditions attached to these rates differ by country, however, limiting their comparability
Personal remittances (% of GDP)		Personal remittances comprise personal transfers and compensation of employees as a percentage of GDP. Personal transfers consist of all current transfers in cash or in kind made or received by resident households to or from non-resident households. Personal transfers thus include all current transfers between resident and non-resident individuals
Exchange rate (LCU per US$)		Official exchange rate refers to the exchange rate determined by national authorities or to the rate determined in the legally sanctioned exchange market. It is calculated as an annual average based on monthly averages (local currency units relative to the U.S. dollar)
Physicians (per 1,000 people)		Physicians include generalist and specialist medical practitioners

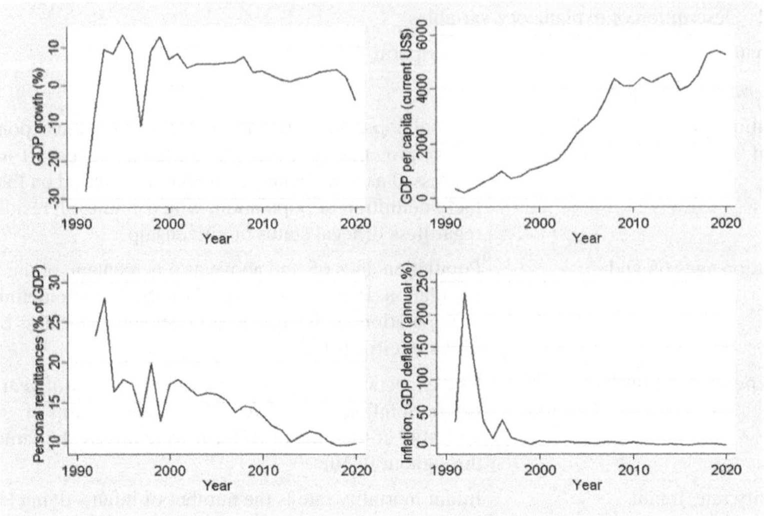

Fig. 1 Main economic indicators period 1991–2020. *Source* Authors' calculation

Main economic indicators and their trend are shown in Fig. 1. GDP growth and GDP per capita are estimators of the economic performance of the country. From the figure, we can depict the increasing tendency of both indicators over time. Since the 90s Albania experienced a massive migration with around one third of the population living abroad. Consequently, the level of remittances has been substantially exceeding by three-fold the level of FDI received in the country (Duval and Wolff 2010). However, remittances have a cyclical behaviour and tend to decrease over time as shown in Fig. 1.

The health service in Albania is organized into three levels: primary care, secondary hospital care and tertiary care. Mostly, the health service is offered by the public sector while the private sector covers services such as pharmaceutical, dental, speciality clinics and hospitals. Health expenditure per capita has been increasing in nominal terms as shown in Fig. 2, however, health care expenditure measured as a share of the GDP remains low if compared to the neighbouring countries.

In Fig. 3, we represented the main demographic indicators for the period 1991–2020. After the fall of communist regime during 1990, Albania experienced important economic and social changes. The transition from central economy to the open market economy affected the dynamics of Albanian population in terms of massive migration, births and deaths. As we can see, the annual population growth results negative since 1991. These changes affected the Albanian median age of population, which has increased by sex: to 36.8 for males and 38.6 for females in 2021.

According to INSTAT (2022), in 2021, the population of Albania was 2.83 million with a decrease of around 2.7% if compared to the year 2011. Life expectancy at birth has been increasing during 2019, with 75.2 years for male and 79.6 years for

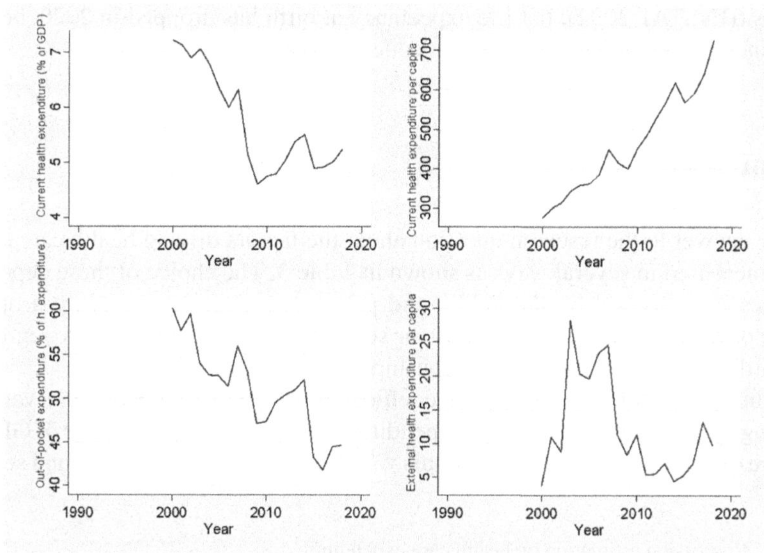

Fig. 2 Main health care indicators period 1991–2020. *Source* Authors' calculation

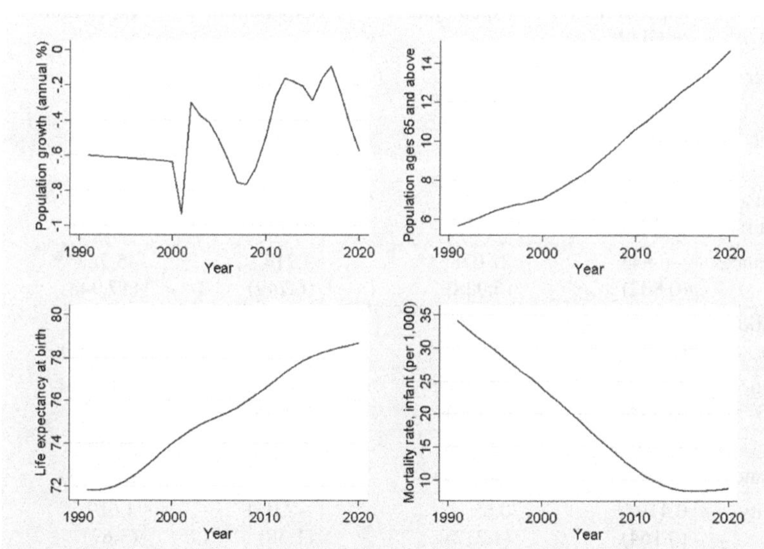

Fig. 3 Main demographic indicators period 1991–2020. *Source* Authors' calculation

females ((INSTAT 2022), but life expectancy at birth has dropped in 2020, because of the increase in the number of deaths due to COVID-19 pandemic.

4 Empirical Results

To give answer to the research question about the factors driving health care expenditure measured in several ways as shown in Table 3. The choice of these dependent variables is motivated by the public and private perspective to capture a broader picture of health care expenditure. In our study, we estimate multivariate regression to identify the macroeconomic relationship.

In the first column, we find the coefficients for the socio-economic variables affecting the level of current health expenditure expressed as a percentage of GDP. As we have explained earlier in the text, this variable includes health goods and services

Table 3 Regression estimation on health care expenditure

Dependent variable	(1)	(2)	(3)	(4)
	Health expenditure (% of GDP)	Out-of-pocket expenditure	Domestic private expenditure	External health expenditure
GDP per capita	0.001 (0)	0.01*** (0.002)	−0.007** (0.003)	−0.008 (0.007)
Inflation	0.096 (0.084)	0.28 (0.617)	−0.919 (0.703)	2.527 (1.869)
Deposit interest rate	−0.171* (0.086)	−0.016 (0.639)	0.278 (0.728)	−1.318 (1.935)
Remittances (log)	−0.943 (0.802)	22.078*** (5.928)	9.714 (6.749)	45.288** (17.948)
Population growth	−0.574 (0.55)	−2.401 (4.061)	3.073 (4.624)	−1.748 (12.296)
Population over 65	1.797** (0.694)	12.384** (5.126)	16.68** (5.836)	−11.214 (15.52)
Life expectancy	3.144* (1.501)	13.238 (11.089)	23.977* (12.625)	31.292 (33.574)
Mortality rate	0.419** (0.164)	0.65 (1.212)	−2.051 (1.38)	4.619 (3.67)
Physicians	32.509** (13.638)	3.144* (1.501)	0.12 (0.297)	0.419** (0.164)
_Cons	−203.782 (116.151)	−414.769 (858.318)	1559.475 (977.234)	−3250.052 (2598.825)
Observations	21	21	21	21
R-squared	0.952	0.921	0.93	0.63

*** $p < 0.01$, ** $p < 0.05$, * $p < 0.1$

but excludes the capital health expenditure such as buildings, machinery, IT, etc. The only statistically significant coefficients are those deposit interest rate, population aged 65 and over, life expectancy, mortality rate and number of physicians for 1,000 people. The positive relationship with the former coefficients is straightforward and is in line with the literature. From the economic point of view, the negative sign for the deposit interest rate finds the rationale to the increased cost of capital for the government inducing in the health care expenditure cut in the public sector.

The determinants are different when we investigate the share of out-of-pocket payments of total current health expenditures. Out-of-pocket payments are spending on health paid directly by the households. Coefficients show that there is a positively significant relationship with GDP per capita and remittances received from abroad. The magnitude of remittances on household health expenditure is evident and greater if compared to the income per capita. During 2021, remittances were worth 184 million euros, an increase by 8.9% compared to the first quarter of last year (BoA 2022). This value also represents the highest level recorded for this period of the year, since 2008.

According to the Bank of Albania, about a quarter of Albanian households receive remittances, while about 6% of households declare remittances as the only source of income. Meanwhile, households receiving remittances spend about 69% of their monthly income in food a similar goods. In this context, we can presume that for many Albanian families, remittances are resource of income that guarantees survival. This positive correlation between remittances and health expenditure is validated in other countries as well (Kalaj 2009; Amuedo-Dorantes and Pozo 2011).

For the estimates of domestic private health expenditure and external health expenditure per capita, we obtain similar direction of association with remittances received, life expectancy to birth and population over 65 remaining statistically significant.

5 Conclusions

In our analyses of determinants, health care expenditure measured as percentage of GDP and out-of-pocket expenses, we use time-series data for the period 2000–2020 for Albania. Following previous literature on the topic, the explanatory variables are divided in two groups: demographic and socio-economic factors. Regression results for health expenditure measured as percentage to GDP show that income level measured in terms of GDP per capita is statistically significant but the magnitude is quite low. Life expectancy to birth, population over age 65 and number of physicians have positive and statistically significant effect on the health care expenditure by the public sector. Interesting is the negative and significant effect of deposit interest rate. The rationale for this relationship can be found in the public finance reasoning since Albanian public debt has reached levels of 80.1% of GDP in 2021 establishing a record in three decades.

On the other side, remittances positively affect the household out-of-pocket expenditure and external health expenditure. Remittance flows are significant in driving health care expenditures when compared to income such as GDP per capita. This income from abroad may contribute to stabilization in the use of health care services by poorer households or those households lacking health care coverage. According to the literature, in countries where they are received, remittances have a significant role in determining access to healthcare. Furthermore, remittances cause the middle-income class to move from using public to private health care services. These findings imply that measures intended for increasing remittances are appropriate for developing countries.

According to the theory, the increased share of population of age 65 and above is reflected in higher health expenditure. This is confirmed in our model as well. When population growth is taken into account, controversial coefficients appear to be negative. However, this result is explained by the negative population rate growth since 1991. Increased number of doctors per thousand people is positively affecting health care expenditure either in governmental level or private level.

Empirical results of our study shed light on policy implications first related to the public debt decrease since as we have noticed cost of capital expenditure is concurrent with health care expenditure. Second, a better use and management of remittances from abroad to reinforce their role in the increased well-being of households. Still further investigation is needed to evaluate factors affecting health care expenditure by using alternative methods such as ARDL model or including variables that capture medical technological changes or health care informal payments.

References

Amuedo-Dorantes C, Pozo S (2011) New evidence on the role of remittances on healthcare expenditures by Mexican households. Rev Econ Household 1(9):69–98

Baltagi BH, Moscone F (2010) Health care expenditure and income in the OECD reconsidered: evidence from panel data. Econ Model 4(27):804–811

Blomqvist ÅG, Carter RA (1997) Is health care really a luxury? J Health Econ 2(16):207–229

BoA (2022) Annual report. Bank of Albania, Tirana

Bredenkamp C, Mendola M, Gragnolati M (2011) Catastrophic and impoverishing effects of health expenditure: new evidence from the Western Balkans. Health Policy Plan 4(26):349–356

Clemente J, Marcuello C, Montañés A, Pueyo F (2004) On the international stability of health care expenditure functions: are government and private functions similar? J Health Econ 3(23):589–613

Costa-Font J, Gemmill M, Rubert G (2011) Biases in the healthcare luxury good hypothesis? A meta-regression analysis. J R Stat Soc A Stat Soc 1(174):95–107

Di Matteo L (2005) The macro determinants of health expenditure in the United States and Canada: assessing the impact of income, age distribution and time. Health Policy 1(71):23–42

Duval L, Wolff FC (2010) Remittances matter: longitudinal evidence from Albania. Post-Communist Econ 1(22):73–97

EUROSTAT (2022) Healthcare expenditure statistics. Statistics explained: EU

Getzen TE (2000) Health care is an individual necessity and a national luxury: applying multilevel decision models to the analysis of health care expenditures. J Health Econ 2(19):259–270

Grigorakis N, Floros C, Tsangari H, Tsoukatos E (2018) Macroeconomic and financing determinants of out-of-pocket payments in health care: evidence from selected OECD countries. J Policy Model (6):1290–1312
INSTAT (2020) Public health indicators. Instituti i Statistikave, Tirana
INSTAT (2021) Public Health Indicators
INSTAT (2022) Population in Albania. Republika e Shqipërisë, Instituti i Statistikave
Kalaj EH (2009) Do remittances alter labor market participation? A study of Albania
Kalaj EH (2015) A Micro-level analysis of the effect of remittances on health expenditures: evidence from Albania. Mediterr J Soc Sci 1(6):660–665
Mehrara M, Fazaeli AA, Fazaeli AA, Fazaeli AR (2012) The relationship between health expenditures and economic growth in Middle East & North Africa (MENA) countries. Int J Bus Manag Econ Res 1(3):425–428
Parkin D, McGuire A, Yule B (1987) Aggregate health care expenditures and national income: is health care a luxury good? J Health Econ 2(6):109–127
Ruggeri M, Drago C, Cadeddu C, Armuzzi A, Leone S, Marchetti M (2020) The determinants of out-of-pocket expenditure in IBD Italian patients. Results from the AMICI survey. Int J Environ Res Public Health 17(21):8156
Sen A (2005) Is health care a luxury? New evidence from OECD data. Int J Health Care Finance Econ 2(5):147–164
Stepovic M, Rancic N, Vekic B, Dragojevic-Simic V, Vekic S, Ratkovic N, Jakovljevic M (2020) Gross domestic product and health expenditure growth in Balkan and East European countries—three-decade horizon. Front Public Health 8:492–503
Wang Z, Rettenmaier A (2007) A note on cointegration of health expenditures and income. Health Econ 6(16):559–578
Xhindi TK (2020) Causality between economic growth and health expenditure: a time series analysis from 1996 till 2017 in Albania. WSEAS Trans Environ Dev 16–29

The Challenges of Measuring Performance in Pandemic Times. Evidence from Italy

Milena Vainieri and Federico Vola

Abstract This contribution informs the functioning of performance management measurement systems during the pandemic from the specific standpoint of Italy, one of the first countries affected by it. As those management control systems must reflect the context in which they operate, they also have to change in relation to them. For this reason, strategies had to be put in place to balance two sometimes mutually exclusive needs, that of timeliness and accuracy of data. These last, respectively serve to support the operation management and strategic planning processes. The "resilience dimension" (i.e., the healthcare organizations' capacity to proactively foresee, absorb, and adapt to shocks) was conceptualized and strictly monitored. Real-time information systems based on a few indicators and information related to COVID-19 became routinely addressed at all governance levels (central, regional, and local), also to meet the pressing demands of the media on the state of the pandemic. In the light of lessons learned and considerations made, two main threads of further research arise: the necessity to perform an in-depth analysis of what happened during the emergency period and the necessity to identify potential innovations to be made in the healthcare performance evaluation process.

1 Introduction

The recent COVID-19 epidemic made more evident what eminent management scholars already stated a few decades ago: management control systems (namely performance measurement systems) must evolve in relation to the context (Ferreira and Otley 2009; Chenall 2003).

Since the introduction of performance measurement systems in health care at the end of the 80 s, these systems evolved, by passing from merely focusing on

M. Vainieri (✉) · F. Vola
Sant'Anna School of Advanced Studies, Pisa, Italy
e-mail: milena.vainieri@santannapisa.it

F. Vola
e-mail: federico.vola@santannapisa.it

N. Persiani et al. (eds.), *Challenges of Healthcare Systems in the Era of COVID-19*, Contributions to Management Science, https://doi.org/10.1007/978-3-031-43114-2_11

financial performance tools to the inclusion of several dimensions such as quality, responsiveness, and safety (Bititci et al. 2012; Nuti et al. 2021).

In the last decade, health care management scholars have also advocated the inclusion of other dimensions such as the patient voice and the population health perspective, and finally the concepts of sustainability and resilience (Vainieri 2020). In particular, the resilience domain of health care systems has become of primary importance during the pandemic.

On the one side, several daily surveillance systems were born to measure COVID-19-related indicators, e.g. epidemiological impact, the response, the resources (Ivanković et al. 2021), with the aim to provide prompt information on the basis of which taking decisions upon the introduction of restrictive measures (Testa et al. 2021; Barbazza et al. 2022), or helping health care managers to allocate patients (especially the COVID-19 ones) among hospitals (Damone et al. 2022).

On the other side, these new surveillance systems overshadowed traditional performance measurement systems which had a lag time with real-time information required by the pandemic, especially in 2020. Moreover, in a decentralized system, like the Italian one, there was also an argument of conflict between the central and regional health systems. Yet, at the time of writing (September 2022), the national performance assessment made by the Italian government regarding the regional health system has not been published. However, Italy provides interesting examples of how to measure performance during the pandemic. Actually, the National Agency for Regional Health Services (Agenas) monitored, in a transparent way (by publicly disclosing the results on its website), the 2020 outcome performance (Agenas 2021a) and the capacity of each Italian region to ensure the necessary health care services (Vola et al. 2022; Nuti et al. 2021a). In addition, since 2008, there has been an inter-regional collaborative network that has been sharing the same performance evaluation system and voluntarily measures its performances in benchmarking (Nuti et al. 2016, 2018). This system has kept measuring performance during the pandemic by mainly focusing attention on non-communicable diseases—NCDs (Vola et al. 2022).

Based on the Italian multilevel experience in performance evaluation, this paper sums up the evolution of these systems in 2020 and 2021 to provide some general considerations on the role of performance evaluation systems during pandemic times.

2 The Dynamic of the "Traditional" Italian Performance Evaluation Systems Under the Pandemic

The Italian National Health Service was founded in 1978 (Law number 833/78) on the principles of universal and equal access to all health care services for all citizens and it is a tax-based system. Since the early 1990s, the Italian regions have been granted powers to plan, organize, and finance health care services locally, by transferring power from the central government to the regions (through the so-called "regionalization reform"); other reforms were subsequently implemented, aiming at introducing efficiency in the system, such as the prospective payment system through tariffs (Ricciardi and Tarricone 2021).

This decentralized system tried to transform the organization from a political model to a managerial and professional one, by introducing internal and external control systems to assess performance (Fattore 1999; Tediosi et al. 2009) at different levels of governance. Actually, at least three main systems converge in assessing the National health system's (NHS) performance: (i) monitoring provision of essential levels of health care (*Griglia LEA, Nuovo Sistema di Garanzia—NSG*[1]), (ii) the national outcome evaluation program (Programma Nazionale Esiti—PNE[2]), and (iii) the inter-regional performance evaluation system (IRPES[3]) (Expert Group on Health Systems Performance Assessment 2016).

Table 1 compares the characteristics of the three systems, before the pandemic, by distinguishing the institution that was in charge of conducting the process (**who**); the granularity of the performance assessment (**units**); the approach adopted (**approach**); the domains analyzed (**what**); the period and timeliness of analysis (**time**) and the main references.

Italy has been one of the first European countries to be hit by the COVID-19 wave and became one of the most affected countries in Europe: around 6 million cases were reported from 24/02/2020 to 31/12/2021, with a death toll up to more than 130 thousand (data extracted from ourworldindata.org). The capacity to transfer the national recommendations into regional strategies as well as the overall reaction of the regional governments to cope with the pandemic was different (Bosa et al. 2021a). In particular, some authors argued that the management of non-communicable diseases has become crucial for preserving both short- and long-term health and economic outcomes leading to a 'twin epidemic' alongside COVID-19 (Bosa et al. 2021b; Sheldon and Wright 2020) which should be tackled by endorsing a "syndemic approach" (Horton 2020).

The pandemic was a tsunami that drastically changed the normal way of providing services and governing the health care systems, also by modifying the use of health information systems and the way of controlling performance.

Real-time information systems based on a few indicators and information related to COVID-19 (e.g. number of cases, number of hospitalizations, vaccination coverage…) became routine. All the levels of governance (central, regional, and local) use to daily provide comments on these data also under the pressure of the media. How did the three above-mentioned systems react to the new context?

---

[1] https://www.salute.gov.it/portale/lea/dettaglioContenutiLea.jsp?lingua=italiano&id=5238&area=Lea&menu=monitoraggioLea.

[2] https://pne.agenas.it.

[3] https://performance.santannapisa.it/pes/start/start.php.

Table 1 The three performance evaluation systems in 2019

	The three performance evaluation systems		
Reference	EAL (essential assistance levels) and new system of guarantee on the healthcare levels (Ministero della Salute 2021)	PNE 2020 (Agenas 2021a)	IRPES (Nuti et al. 2020)
Government level	National	National	Regional
Who is in charge?	Ministry of Health through the Department of Health	Ministry of Health throughout the Agenas (Agenzia Nazionale dei Servizi Sanitari)	Regions through Management and Health Lab
Unit of analysis	Regions	Hospitals and Provinces	Regions, Health Authorities and Autonomous Hospitals
Purpose and approach	Financial award and autonomy penalty—mandatory	Mainly for professional audit and feedback—mandatory	Internal benchmarking, regional tool—voluntary
What is measured	Prevention; Acute care; District level of care and long-term care	Outcome and intermediary outcome	Multiple dimensions (efficiency, quality, pharmaceuticals…)
Timeliness of release	Annual release. 2019 released in May 2021	Annual release. 2019 released in March 2021	Annual release. 2019 released in July 2020

2.1 The Reaction of the Inter-Regional Performance Evaluation System (IRPES)

The first performance evaluation system that changed was the IRPES. Indeed, by considering that under the pandemic the responses to the NCDs differed among the regions, those adhering to the IRPES decided to take up the comparison of 2020 performance, by introducing new indicators and anticipating the normal timeline. Actually, starting from the second semester of 2020, the twelve regions undertook an innovative trajectory along which they remodeled the evaluation system (Vola et al. 2022). The main innovations of the collaborative network can be grouped into three main actions: (i) suspending indicators that were too affected by the pandemic, (ii) introducing new indicators to capture the relevant phenomena of the new context, and (iii) calculating infra-annual measures for a specific subset of indicators (those measuring the health systems' resilience). Concerning the first step, the indicators and the dimensions frozen are the ones that lose their relevance or clarity in the interpretation. This is the case of the hospitalization rates. For instance, hospitalization rates for ambulatory care sensitive conditions are usually considered as indirect measures of good primary health care and community care systems; however, during the pandemic, this interpretation turned out unrealistic. Indeed, because of the lockdown, the reduction of hospitalizations for non-urgent reasons and the fear of access to the hospitals and outpatient clinics, as well as the closures of community services, could be more representative of a lack of supply instead than of a good response of primary health care services.

For the second group of changes, the inter-regional collaborative network introduced the "resilience" dimension. Although resilience was a dimension already considered in some health system performance assessments (see for instance the EU health status profile), it has often been included in the funding dimensions (Blanchet et al. 2017; Adger 2006). The IRPES network decided instead to use the operational definition provided by the expert panel of effective investment in health care: "Health system resilience describes the capacity of a health system to (a) proactively foresee, (b) absorb, and (c) adapt to shocks and structural changes in a way that allows it to (i) sustain required operations, (ii) resume optimal performance as quickly as possible, (iii) transform its structure and functions to strengthen the system, and (possibly) (iv) reduce its vulnerability to similar shocks and structural changes in the future" (EXPH 2020). In particular, in 2020, IRPES focused on the first and second sub-domains. More in detail, starting from the population's needs, the indicators introduced in 2020 to assess resilience were mainly based on the comparison of volumes supplied in 2020 and 2019. These differences can be representative of unmet needs. They referred to (i) non-deferrable activities, which mainly pertain to the oncological and cardiovascular fields; (ii) quality of care, which mainly refers to intermediary outcomes such as the proportion of femoral neck fractures operated within two days and the proportion of caesarean sections; (iii) reductions (and backlogs) for outpatients follow up visits and drug consumption (especially those related to chronic diseases).

The results of the resilience dimension assessment were shared among the regional governments adhering to the IRPES through specific summaries, which rejected the assumption that the Regions most affected by the virus were those recording greater levels of contraction of services, thus highlighting the important role of the recovery capacity played by both the regional and the local government.

Overall, the 2020 release of the IRPES consisted of around 400 indicators showing that when people had already been taken in charge of the system (they had a diagnosis and/or they were treated), the response in terms of quality, efficiency, and appropriateness was stable or improved for more than half of the indicators (56%) with the respect to 2019 (Vola et al. 2022). Moreover, the pandemic triggered some silent (and long-lasting implementation of) innovation, such as e-prescription and e-health; reduced the consumption of antibiotics among the population; increased the coverage of dormant vaccinations (flu vaccination for elderly and for health care workforce) and provided a stimulus to revise the plan of potentially inappropriate surgical intervention (Vainieri et al. 2022) as well as reduced access to the emergency departments.

In 2021, the inter-regional collaborative network added also the last sub-domain of the EXPH definition of resilience—the one related to the reduction of the vulnerability of the health care system—although this aspect was measured mainly through the vaccination coverage for COVID-19 for different target populations (health care workforce; nursing homes workforce and users; elderly and the whole population). Other indicators that can be referred to in the above cited sub-dimension of resilience concern the digital health. Digital health indicators, already in place in the IRPES, have been expanded, by including indicators referring to the digitization of the electronic patient clinical records (Fascicolo Sanitario Elettronico), e-prescriptions, and virtual follow up visits.

The 2021 was characterized by the huge effort related to the vaccination campaign as well as the attempt to come back to the normal provision of the services by trying to recover the activities suspended in 2020. Overall, 2021 confirmed to have capitalized the good heritage of the pandemic period for the digital health (e-prescription, virtual follow up visits) and the consumption of antibiotics in the population, while the effort put by the whole system to achieve high Covid-19 vaccination coverage led to reduced attention (and related access) to the flu vaccination in elderly and health care workforce. In addition, the emergency department accesses increased (although they did not achieve 2019 levels yet).

In terms of the re-launch of the health system, the 2021 comparison of 2021–2019 and 2020–2019 per region highlighted the capacity of the regions to improve or maintain the level of service provision.

Table 2 shows the relation between contractions in service provision registered in 2021 (compared to 2019) and those recorded in 2020. "Rebound effect" did not seem to apply: regional health care systems that contracted their activity the most in 2020 did not seem able to react and recover in 2021, and did show a case of "managerial hysteresis", so to speak. Again, the pandemic seems to have been an eloquent stress test for different managerial skills across regions.

The resilience dimension, although presented through specific maps or charts, was also included in the final overall graphical representation of the target diagram. Figure 1 shows the usual graphical representation of the IRPES with a spotlight on the resilience dimension. The indicators related to the differences of volumes in percentage terms were assessed on the basis of average performance of the regions and then plotted into the target.

2.2 The Reaction of the National Performance Evaluation System Managed by Agenas (PNE)

At the national level, Agenas added an ad hoc analysis to measure the regional capacity to respond to the pandemic through the comparison of 2019 and 2020 volumes, by using the indicators developed by IRPES and coming from the hospital discharge records.

Figure 2 reports the Italian example of the 2020 performance results about resilience. The graph shows the indicators of resilience selected, their distribution in terms of the percentage of the difference of volumes with respect to 2019 (with

Table 2 Regression analysis on the contraction in healthcare service provision in 2021 compared to the service provision in 2019. As can be seen from the negative sign of the coefficients of all the regions except the first, in the year 2021 the gap of the previous year was not closed, if not for a small part of it was closed

Contraction 2021 vs 2019	Coef	Std. Err	T	P > |t|	95% conf. interval	
Region 1	0.9117803	0.0728627	12.51	0.000	0.7683498	1.055211
Region 2	−4.061865	5.033944	−0.81	0.420	−13.9712	5.84747
Region 3	−17.33381	5.001402	−3.47	0.001	−27.17908	−7.488534
Region 4	−8.200128	4.80159	−1.71	0.089	−17.65207	1.251818
Region 5	−9.882798	4.976418	−1.99	0.048	−19.67889	−0.0867038
Region 6	−9.967808	5.017712	−1.99	0.048	−19.84519	−0.0904258
Region 7	−2.881334	5.131825	−0.56	0.575	−12.98335	7.220681
Region 8	−9.015428	4.932305	−1.83	0.069	−18.72469	0.6938298
Region 9	−4.654181	4.899083	−0.95	0.343	−14.29804	4.989679
Region 10	−13.99268	4.832777	−2.90	0.004	−23.50602	−4.479343
Region 11	−12.517	4.970876	−2.52	0.012	−22.30218	−2.731814
Constant, Y	17.94263	4.147865	4.33	0.000	9.777542	26.10771

Source Our elaboration on IRPES website data. The participant regions are: Toscana, Lombardia, Basilicata, Puglia, PA Trento, PA Bolzano, Umbria, Liguria, Friuli-Venezia Giulia, Marche, Veneto, Piemonte

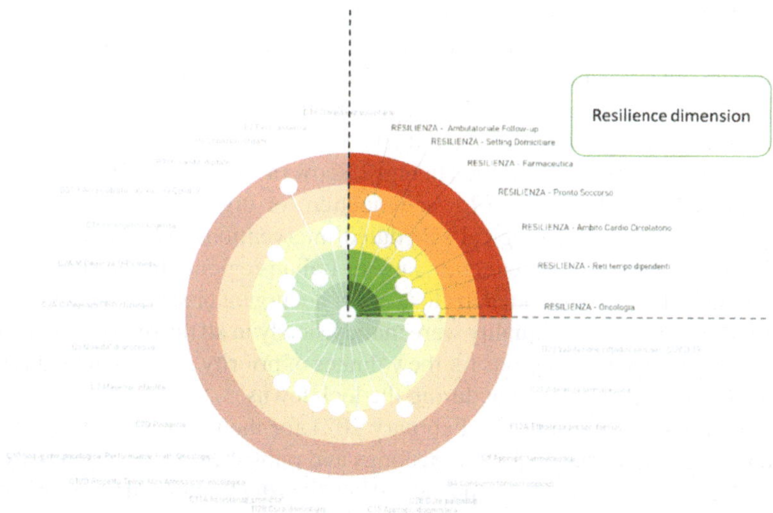

Fig. 1 Example of overall performance with a spotlight on the resilience dimension that includes these performance indicators: variation of services provided on (i) outpatient and follow up dimension, (ii) homecare dimension, (iii) pharmaceutical appropriateness, (iv) Emergency Department, (v) oncology services, (vi) time-dependent rescue networks, (vii) cardiovascular dimension. *Source* IRPES presentation on the 10th of June 2022

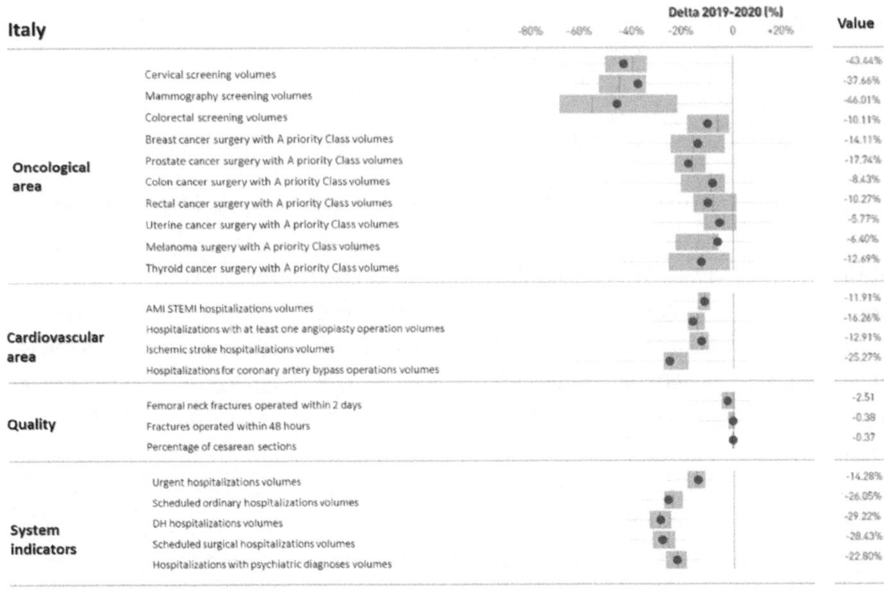

Fig. 2 Sums up the distribution at national level and the variation across the regions (the grey box). *Source* English translation of Agenas and Mes (2021) report

the exception of the percentage of femur fractures and the percentage of cesarean sections whose values are differences of indicator values and not the difference of volumes), and the variation across regions. The grey box plots show the distribution of regional values, and the blue dots represent the Italian values (or the regional values when reporting the regional exhibit).

Overall, the performance reported in Fig. 2, shows a reduction of 26% of the scheduled ordinary hospitalizations, a lower reduction for urgent hospitalization (14%) but a higher reduction for surgical scheduled interventions. The grey boxes show a relatively low variation in reduction among Italian regions. In the first wave, the Ministry of Health recommended to close down not urgent or strictly necessary acute care activities. The levels of quality were mainly steady in all the regions, while wider variation occurred among regions for the volumes of priority A surgical interventions which had to be guaranteed even during the lockdowns.

This analysis was presented in February 2021 for the first semester of 2020 and in June for the whole year in public meetings and published on the Agenas website.

This was a very fast reaction, especially if considering the normal time gap (around 7 months after the end of the year) applied to present the annual releases of the PNE.

In addition, in mid of December 2021, Agenas updated the PNE system by revising its structure (Agenas 2021b). In particular, new indicators were included, also adding the dimension of equity, that investigates the gender differences in terms of quality of care and appropriateness. Agenas eventually changed the granularity of the provision of information for indicators related to population, passing from the provinces to the local level of governance. These innovations were already discussed among the representatives of the regions and the other experts involved in the scientific committee of the PNE. However, the dimension of resilience was not included yet in this already established performance evaluation system. It should be recalled that PNE aims to focus on the outcome dimension and not to build up a comprehensive system.

2.3 The Reaction of the National Performance Evaluation System Managed by the Department of Health (Griglia LEA-NSG)

The third system (Griglia LEA—Nuovo Sistema di Garanzia) managed by the Department of Health at the national level was instead provisionally suspended. After many years of discussion and study among experts, as well as regional and national government representatives, the regions and the state defined the new national system to assess the performance of regional health services that should have substituted the one applied until 2019, just in 2020. A very unlikely moment to start a new assessment with a traditional and already set package of indicators. Due to the objections of some regional governments to be evaluated during the pandemic period through a monitoring system built to capture the performance of non-emergency time, at the end of August 2022, the assessment of 2020 was not publicly disclosed yet. Instead, some monitoring indicators related to specific health care paths were published at the end of July 2022.

3 Discussions

Some preliminary lessons about health care performance evaluation in times of COVID-19 can be drawn. Firstly, new informative needs brought by the pandemic have required to define of a new balance between two of the main, potentially contradictory, characteristics of any evaluation tool: timeliness and accuracy. Monitoring the trend of the infection and the availability of resources to tackle it has required favoring the former over the latter. This has some implications for non-COVID-19 performance evaluation: it became clear that the trade-off between timelines and accuracy strictly refers to the informative and managerial needs the evaluation system intends to satisfy. Secondly, the pandemic has demonstrated the complementarity of real-time monitoring systems and ex-post evaluation systems. They support two different managerial activities: the former supports operation management; and the latter provides evidence for strategic planning. Thirdly, two characteristics seem to be associated to greater flexibility of performance evaluation systems: (a) systems that are not directly linked to potential political or economic implications are likely to encounter less resistance in being modified and innovated; the case of Agenas was exemplary: indeed it was able to set out a new system measuring the resilience in a very short run but it was less prone to include it in the already established performance evaluation system of PNE; (b) systems whose adhesion is voluntary are examples of self-evaluation (such as the IRPES): in this case, acceptance is likely to be easier and potential modifications to the structure of indicators are likely to be more agile. The PNE worked very well but with a rigid protocol to include new indicators or to reshape its structure which requires a longer time of reaction to introduce new items. Fourthly, generally speaking, the pandemic has demonstrated the importance of monitoring and evaluating complex systems—such as health care—by leveraging a range of complimentary tools, that would respond to different information needs, by different institutions, to comply with different managerial needs (operation management vs strategic planning), and by adopting different methodological approaches, ranging from timely monitoring to accurate evaluation.

Hence, despite the new generation of health information systems, real-time-based the development of "traditional" performance evaluation systems has not been hindered.

This study has many limitations. The first one refers to the fact that the authors tried to provide some general considerations about measurements during the pandemic based on the Italian case. These considerations could be supported or criticized by other authors reporting other examples. Another limitation refers to the fact that the qualitative analysis was based on official documents. Certainly, a focus group with experts or key informants of the health systems may provide other insights we didn't report. However, the position of the authors in terms of contact with many stakeholders at the national and regional levels may have offset the lack of additional qualitative interviews.

4 Conclusive Considerations

As already underlined, the pandemic has represented a stress test for performance evaluation systems in health care. In the previous section (Discussions) some characteristics have been hypothesized to be associated with the performance evaluation systems' flexibility (i.e., their intrinsic resilience). This contribution to the Italian case opens at least two main threads of further research.

The first line of research refers to an in-depth analysis of what happened during this emergency period. In particular, evidence produced by health care evaluation systems over the last two years should be investigated, to analyze organizational dynamics during the pandemic and potential associations with different organizational models. In particular, associations between different sets of indicators should be tested, to study the correlations between different dimensions of health care performance (quality, equity, appropriateness, responsiveness, resilience, sustainability…);

The second stream of research would pertain to the further evolution of health care performance evolution. We identify at least three potential innovations deserving careful attention: (1) the evolution of the "resilience" dimension should remain under scrutiny, to verify which of its components should be monitored in non-pandemic times too. In particular, the resilience dimension could evolve into the preparedness dimension as another pillar of the main dimension of performance evaluation systems (together with sustainability, quality, and equity) as well as the relationship between performance evaluation systems and the monitoring systems of the national/regional pandemic flu; (2) the evolution of performance evaluation systems in front of new informative needs, associated to new health care strategic trends should be investigated too. Performance evaluation tools' ability to monitor and evaluate the implementation of the National Recovery and Resilience Plan through the introduction of specific indicators to evaluate the capacity to keep the health care system infrastructure updated; (3) in general, whether comprehensive health care systems, including population health status and process indicators, are more effective than focused ones such as those measuring the capacity to implement digital and technological infrastructures.

References

Adger WN (2006) Vulnerability. Glob Environ Chang 16(3):268–281

Agenas and Mes (2021) Analisi della capacità di resilienza del servizio sanitario nazionale nell'anno 2020. https://www.agenas.gov.it/covid19/web/file/Resilienza_Print_Version.pdf

Agenas (2021a) Programma Nazionale Esiti. Edizione 2020. https://www.agenas.gov.it/images/agenas/In%20primo%20piano/PNE/2020/Agenas_Report_PNE_2020.pdf

Agenas (2021b) Programma Nazionale Esiti. Edizione 2020. AGENAS_-_PNE_2021_-_Stampa.pdf

Barbazza E et al (2022) The experiences of 33 national COVID-19 dashboard teams during the first year of the pandemic in the World Health Organization European Region: a qualitative study. Digital Health 8:1–16

Bititci U et al (2012) Performance measurement: challenges for tomorrow. Int J Manag Rev 14(3):305–27. https://doi.org/10.1111/j.1468-2370.2011.00318.x

Blanchet K, Nam SL, Ramalingam B, Pozo-Martin F (2017) Governance and capacity to manage resilience of health systems: towards a new conceptual framework. Int J Health Policy Manag 6:431

Bosa et al. (2021a) Corona-regionalism? Differences in regional responses to COVID-19 in Italy. Health Policy

Bosa et al. (2021b) Response to COVID-19: was Italy (un)prepared? Health Econ Policy Law 1–13

Chenall RH (2003) Management control systems design within its organizational context: findings from contingency-based research and directions for the future. Acc Organ Soc 28:127–168

Damone A, Vainieri M, Brunetto MR, Bonino F, Nuti S, Ciuti G (2022) Decision-making algorithm and predictive model to assess the impact of infectious disease epidemics on the healthcare system: the COVID-19 case study in Italy. IEEE J Biomed Health Inform 26:8

Expert Group on Health Systems Performance Assessment (2016) So what? Strategies across Europe to assess quality of care. Health and Food Safety. https://doi.org/10.2875/03667

Expert Panel on Effective Ways of Investing in Health (EXPH) (2020) Opinion on the organisation of resilient health and social care following the COVID-19 pandemic. Public hearing 20 Oct 2020

Fattore G (1999) Clarifying the scope of Italian NHS coverage. Is it feasible? Is it desirable? Health Policy 50:123–142

Ferreira A, Otley D (2009) The design and use of performance management systems: an extended framework for analysis. Manag Account Res 20(2009):263–282

Horton R (2020) Offline: COVID-19 is not a pandemic. The Lancet 396(10255):874. https://doi.org/10.1016/S0140-6736(20)32000-6

Ivanković D et al (2021) Features constituting actionable COVID-19 dashboards: descriptive assessment and expert appraisal of 158 public web-based COVID-19 dashboards. J Med Internet Res 23(2):e25682. https://doi.org/10.2196/25682

Ministero della Salute (2021) Monitoraggio dei LEA attraverso la cd. Griglia LEA. Metodologia e Risultati dell'anno 2019. Maggio 2021. https://www.salute.gov.it/imgs/C_17_pubblicazioni_3111_allegato.pdf

Nuti S, Vola F, Bonini A, Vainieri M (2016) Making governance work in the health care sector: evidence from a 'natural experiment' in Italy. Health Econ Policy Law 11(01):17–38. https://doi.org/10.1017/S1744133115000067

Nuti S, Noto G, Vola F, Vainieri M (2018) Let's play the patients music: a new generation of performance measurement systems in healthcare. Manag Decis. https://doi.org/10.1108/MD-09-2017-0907

Nuti S, Grillo Ruggieri T, Noto G, Vainieri M (2021) The challenges of hospitals' planning & control systems: the path toward public value management. Int J Environ Res Public Health 18:2732. https://doi.org/10.3390/ijerph18052732

Nuti S et al (2020) Il Sistema di Valutazione della Performance dei Sistemi Sanitari Regionali. Report 2019. Pacini editore

Nuti S et al (2021a) Il Sistema di Valutazione della Performance dei Sistemi Sanitari Regionali. Report 2020. Pacini editore

Ricciardi W, Tarricone R (2021) The evolution of the Italian National Health Service. Lancet 398:2193–206

Sheldon TA, Wright J (2020) Twin epidemics of covid-19 and non-communicable disease. BMJ m2618. https://doi.org/10.1136/bmj.m2618

Tediosi F, Gabriele S, Longo F (2009) Governing decentralization in health care under tough budget constraint: what can we learn from the Italian experience? Health Policy 90:303–312

Testa et al (2021) Implementation of tele visit healthcare services triggered by the COVID-19 emergency: the Trentino Province experience. J Public Health 1–16. https://doi.org/10.1007/s10389-021-01609-8

Vainieri M, Mantoan D, Nuti S (2022) Does the healthcare system know what to cut under the pandemic emergency pressure? Lessons by the Italian health system. BMJOpen

Vainieri M., Noto G, Ferrè F, Rosella LC (2020) A performance management system in healthcare for all seasons? Int J Environ Res Public Health 17:5590. https://doi.org/10.3390/ijerph17155590i

Vola F, Benedetto V, Vainieri M, Nuti S (2022) The Italian inter regional performance evaluation system. Res Health Serv Reg

The Monitoring Process of Public-Private Partnership (PPP) in the Health Care System. The Case of Albania

Besa Ombashi, Denita Cepiku, and Niccolò Persiani

Abstract The relationship between public sector, private sector, and civil society is considered an important factor in achieving sustainable development and enhances the quality of governance. The aim of this article is to analyze the dynamics of the monitoring process of PPP in the healthcare sector considered that during the transition years, due to a large infrastructure gap in the public sector, inherited from communism, the potential of PPP as a source of alternative funding was easily accepted by governments in Albania, which made numerous efforts to create a suitable environment for their implementation. The article will highlight the need to adopt a long-term strategy in the field of healthcare as well as applicable standards for the monitoring of the implementation procedures. The case study is based on the data collected from the analysis of the contracts signed between the parties, different reports and the documentation collection with regard to the management of this contract are going to be used. During the Pandemic moment, the implementation of these contracts became even more important for a country facing a Global emergency when these contracts were seen as a way of innovation in the management of public services.

Keywords Public-private partnership · Healthcare sector · Monitoring process · Pandemic moment · Long-term strategy

---

B. Ombashi (✉)
Department of Law, University College Bedër, Tirana, Albania
e-mail: bombashi@beder.edu.al

D. Cepiku
Department of Management & Law, University of Rome, Tor Vergata via Columbia 2, 00133 Rome, Italy
e-mail: denita.cepiku@uniroma2.it

N. Persiani
University of Florence, Largo Brambilla, 1, 50129 Florence, Italy
e-mail: niccolo.persiani@unifi.it

N. Persiani et al. (eds.), *Challenges of Healthcare Systems in the Era of COVID-19*, Contributions to Management Science, https://doi.org/10.1007/978-3-031-43114-2_12

1 Introduction

There is increasing interest in using public-private partnership (PPP) to mobilize funds for and enable reforms of health systems. [...] In the healthcare sector, PPP is defined as: [...] means to bring together a set of actors for the common goal of improving the health of a population based on the mutually agreed roles and responsibilities [...] (WHO 1999) The variety of definitions possibly results from the many forms that PPP may take (Warsen et al. 2018).

In Albania, since 2013, the year of the entry into force of the Law no. 125/2013 "*On concessions and public-private partnership*", the number of projects requested by contracting authorities has increased. With the aim of increasing transparency on the implementation of concessions/PPP, strengthening financial discipline, and monitoring fiscal and budgetary risks arising from concession/PPP contracts, by means of the Law No. 50 dated 18.07.2019 "On some additions and changes to Law No. 125/2013 "On concessions and public-private partnership" was amended, some changes were approved which have strengthened the role of to the Ministry of Finance and Economy in monitoring the applicability of the projects Concession/ PPP in terms of financial implications. In this context, before the approval of these changes by the Ministry of Finance and Economy in March 2019, began for the first time the process of monitoring the concession/PPP contracts and reporting by the Authorities Contracting.

With the approval of the amendments to the law "On concessions and public-private partnership", reporting on the progress of the implementation of concession contracts/PPP by the Contracting Authorities is done in implementation and according to the formats defined in the Instruction of Minister of Finance and Economy no. 35, dated 12.12.2019.

Based on the report of the Ministry of Finance and Economy[1] for the year 2020 in the Republic of Albania, there are 226 concession/PPP contracts signed according to the Electronic Register published on the official website of ATRAKO.[2] Based on the periodic reports (on a 3-month basis) carried out during the calendar year 2020 by the Contracting Authorities of the MFE, this report reflects 52 concession/PPP contracts in the Transport, Energy, Urban Development, Economic Development, Fiscal Control, Environment and Health.

The legislation in this field tries to establish a good basis in the field of investments with cooperation among public and private partners. The law based on Article

---

[1] Annual Summary Report "Performance of Concession and Partnership Contracts Public Private"—Ministry of Finance and Economy—2020. https://financa.gov.al/wp-content/uploads/2021/10/Raporti-Vjetor-i-Permbledhur_2020_pdf-1.pdf.

[2] Concession Unit (ATRAKO) is a government institution that has as mission to promote and assist contracting authorities in the review and evaluation of projects concession/public private partnerships, as solicited and unsolicited proposals; drafting bidding documents and following the procedure for granting the concession/public private partnerships through its phases. www.atrako.gov.al.

9 relies on the principles of transparency, non-discrimination, proportionality, efficiency, equality, reciprocity, and legal security. It is closely related with the information, publication, and access of public, obliging the public authority to pursue transparent procedures.

2 The Research Methodology and Study Approach

The case study methodology has been used as a research methodology in this article (Eisenhardt 1989; Yin 2004). The use of this methodology is appropriate when the object of analysis is complex and the aim is to conduct an in-depth analysis of the phenomenon within its reference context (Yin 2012; Berry and Otley 2004). In fact, the case study offers a variety of data collection and analysis techniques that allow a deep understanding of the phenomena investigated (Parker et al. 2012). Furthermore, one of its main strengths lies in its ability to investigate phenomena from a practical point of view, thus filling one of the most debated points in corporate literature, namely the gap between theory and practice (Chiucchi 2014; Ryan et al. 2002).

The monitoring process in Albania has been identified as a significant case study because it started recently, the first report is dated 2019, and because of the aspiration of becoming the first country in the Balkan to be part of the European Union, as well as a country which is particularly related with her border countries such as Kosovo, Montenegro, North Macedonia that are using this instrument in their domestic economies.

The research is also based on secondary information. Secondary research focused on legislation and other government legal acts as well as the official monitoring report. Findings of government and international organizations' reports were also considered, including the government's health sector program, alongside the World Health Organization as well as the annual Progress Report of the European Commission on the relationship between the health sector and PPP.

The findings of this analysis are based on the first PPP in the healthcare sector in Albania. The study approach involved three primary phases: (1) literature review—reviewing current documentation for PPP projects in the healthcare sector and literature about implementation information, (2) synthesis—synthesizing final results and documentation. The literature review collected data on current and domestic approaches to monitoring reports of the four PPPs in healthcare in Albania.

The results of this review provided an understanding of the strengthening of the monitoring process of these contracts as a key factor for their success.

3 Monitoring the Implementation and the Risks of the PPP

The purpose of the monitoring process of the contract is to verify the proper implementation of duties and responsibilities on the part of both the private and public bodies in the partnership. The monitoring can be based on reporting and data from the private partner, to be evaluated by independent experts of the field as well as on the considerations of final users of PPP regarding the works and services as established in the object. The information sources that shall support the monitoring process must be identified and set out in the PPP contract. Due to this purpose, the contract must determine obligations such as: the performance of financial auditing and of periodic technical assessments, setting out the terms and the independent entities that perform those. It is important, that the contract determine some specific standards to be respected, as well as the related competent bodies.

In the contract, the responsibilities of the private partner, the characteristics of works, expected service levels, quality standards, modalities for their implementation, and terms must be regulated. The subsequent effective managing of the contract will strictly depend on the application of procedures, monitoring methods, and schedules as established in the contract. This requires that the contracting authority and the private partner have clear monitoring and reporting modalities. For this reason, the contract must determine the reporting modalities and schedules to be followed by the private partner, as well as procedures and monitoring methods performed by the contracting authority.

Risk monitoring aims to control the risks of a PPP contract by proving that the planning of the allocation of risks determined in the contract is efficiently implemented. Due to the achievement of monitoring the risk levels, undertaking measures for the mitigation of risks, or implementing sanctions when necessary measures shall be taken. The drafting of a risk management plan, listing risks related to the project, and determining which party shall carry such risks can help in achieving this purpose. Some of the contract risks can be exclusively assigned to the private partner, some others to the public partner, whilst some contract risks can be shared between the public and private partner. For each of the identified risks, the information that shall be provided to monitor the actual risk must be determined, as well as the necessary actions to mitigate or avoid its consequences. The PPP contract must clearly determine the risk management plan and the reporting or monitoring method. Risk monitoring aims to ensure the timely reaction and necessary measures to avoid serious consequences due to avoid failure of a PPP project.

4 The Research Methodology About PPP in the Health Sector in Albania

The research is based on secondary data information. Secondary research focused on legislation and other government legal acts especially the official report of the Ministry of Finance and Economy. Findings of government and international organizations' reports were also considered, including the government's health sector program, alongside the World Health Organization, World Bank, and IMF as well as the annual Progress Report of the European Commission on the relationship between the health sector and PPP.

Meanwhile, looking at the topic and the subject addressed in this study, to understand the nature of the research practice, which should be followed, and the results that would be produced at the end of these practices, at the beginning of the research we tried to identify some assumptions, set out in the hypothesis. Of course, the assumptions are difficult to clarify, as they cannot be directly observed without making an analysis of the facts and conditions that lead to their rise.

5 Revisions and Regulations

PPP contracts are considered adequately structured when containing specific provisions which regulate the consequences of some of the most often encountered factors. There are three known typical causes that ruin the financial balance: Force Majeure (natural disasters or civil unrest), *factum principis* (government action), and *ius variandi* (unpredictable changes to the contract's economic conditions as a result of the external factors) (PPP Reference Guide 2017).[3]

The contract should provide the possibility for the parties to renegotiate the contract terms. Changes because of the renegotiation are different from changes applied pursuant to mechanisms preliminarily provided in the contract. In principle, the renegotiation mechanisms must be avoided to the extent possible by contracting authorities, as it changes the initial terms of the contract already agreed upon, risk distorting the market, and may produce consequences for the free competition. For this purpose, the contracting authorities must determine to the extent possible in the contract the above-mentioned mechanisms for the regulation of consequences and the contract amendments. Nonetheless, there are cases when the renegotiation cannot be avoided due to unforeseen situations that happen and when such is in accordance with the public interest and that of the contracting parties.

During the implementation of the contract, disputes may rise between parties with regard to contract duties and responsibilities. To avoid consequences that may cause them and even the early termination of the contract, the PPP contract must contain mechanisms for the disagreement resolution between parties.

[3] https://ppp.worldbank.org/public-private-partnership/sites/ppp.worldbank.org/files/documents/PPP%20Reference%20Guide%20Version%203.pdf.

Usual mechanisms for the dispute resolution are:
The judicial system.
The national or international arbitrage.

Contracting authorities must try to avoid the escalation of disputes which may cause the termination of the contract and project failure. The judicial dispute resolution shall be considered as a final resort, given that it leads to stagnation or creates situations which may present a risk to any of the involved parties.

6 Conclusion and Future Research Recommendations

In 2019, recognizing the importance of PPP monitoring, the government of Albania, with technical assistance from the World Bank's Macroeconomics, Trade and Investment and the Infrastructure Finance, PPPs and Guarantees practices, has therefore designed a new comprehensive PPP monitoring framework (Duarte et al. 2019).

However, the growing PPP portfolio in Albania has given rise to the issue of the potential fiscal risks from PPP contracts. The objective of a strong monitoring and disclosure framework for PPP is, precisely, to address fiscal risks and ensure value-for-money.

The health sector was considered as a case study in the research as the Ministry of Health introduced reforms aimed to improve the public health system, the quality of care provided, and to reduce out-of-pocket healthcare expenses, and the application of PPP in this sector was considered as part of this reforms and their success.

The objective of the monitoring process as provided by the Annual Monitoring Report of Albania the Ministry of Finance[4] regards:

- **Better management of fiscal risks**—a centralized framework gives a bird's-eye view to monitor aggregate PPP budget commitments and contingent liabilities across government contracting authorities, ensuring that new PPPs remain consistent with overall fiscal sustainability.
- **Timely intervention in underperforming projects**—a standardized monitoring framework ensures that contracting authorities systematically review the performance of their PPPs and that they intervene quickly in case of underperformance.
- **Learning from successes and failures**—monitoring enables parties to learn what works and what doesn't across the government portfolio, strengthening the quality of future PPP designs.
- **Increasing government accountability and value-for-money**—government becomes more accountable to ensure that PPPs meet value-for-money targets.
- **Strengthening market confidence**—transparency allows markets to more accurately assess the fiscal sustainability of the government's PPP portfolio, strengthening investor confidence.

[4] https://www.financa.gov.al/wp-content/uploads/2020/09/2019-PFM-Annual-Monitoring-Report.pdf.

Although required by law, value-for-money analysis is still not systematically carried out before the approval of all PPPs. The Ministry of Finance and Economics made attempts to establish regular monitoring and reporting on PPPs. The technical skills and capacity to design and assess concessions and PPPs require further development.

However, since the monitoring process is still in its infancy, the number and complexity of the concession/PPP contracts concluded in the Republic of Albania is high, as well as not every contract has a defined Project Implementation Unit responsible for its monitoring. For the Ministry of Finance and Economy gathering information encountered difficulties and therefore the monitoring reports until now did not reflect all the PPP contracts, for example, in 2021 they conveyed information on 65 concession/PPP contracts out of 228.

In this context, as well as in the implementation of the provisions of point 5 of article 10 of law no. 125/2013 "On Concessions and Public-Private Partnership", amended, the Ministry of Finance and Economy during 2021 has given recommendations to the Contracting Authorities in order to take measures on their part to improve the performance in the provision of services and public works, object of concession contracts, their area of responsibility, as well as for the minimization or elimination of direct and indirect risks affecting the state budget.

Also, each Contracting Authority has been asked to set up monitoring structures for each concession contract even when the specific contract does not define such a structure, in order for the information reported to the Ministry of Finance and Economy to be complete, comprehensive, and in accordance with the legal provisions.

Future research should provide more results on the actual effectiveness, efficiency, and importance of the monitoring process of PPP as a key factor for their success.

References

Allard G, Trabant A (2007) Public-private partnership in Spain: lessons and opportunities. IE Business School Working Paper WP10-07

Cepiku D (2006) L'esternalizzazione nelle amministrazioni pubbliche. Teorie, politiche ed esperienze a livello internazionale. Roma, Aracne

De Vries J, Huijsman R (2011) Supply chain management in health services: an overview. Supply Chain Manag Int J 16(3):159–165

Duarte D, Meco L, Ungerer C (2019) Getting service delivery right in Albania through effective PPP monitoring

Eisenhardt KM (1989) Building theories from case study research. Acad Manag Rev 14(4):532–550

OECD (2011) Government outsourcing. Government at a glance 2011. OECD Publishing, Paris, pp 168–169

OECD (2017) Government outsourcing. Government at a glance 2017. OECD Publishing, Paris, pp 84–85

Osborne SP (2000) Public-private partnerships: theory and practice in international perspective. Routledge, London

Parker RI, Vannest KJ, Davis JL (2014) Non-overlap analysis for single-case research

Roehrich JK, Lewis MA, George G (2014) Are public-private partnerships a healthy option? A systematic literature review

Scapens RW, Ryan B, Theobald M (2002) Research methods and methodology in accounting and finance, 2nd ed. Thompson Learning

Vaillancourt Rosenau P (ed) (2000) Public-private policy partnerships. Cambridge, London

Warsen R, Nederhand J, Klijn EH, Grotenbreg S, Koppenjan J (2018) What makes public-private partnerships work? Survey research into the outcomes and the quality of cooperation in PPPs. Public Manag Rev 20:1165-1185

Yang Y, Wang W, Hou Y (2013) On the development of public-private partnerships in transitional economies: an explanatory framework. Public Adm Rev 73(2):301–310

Yin R (2021) Case study methods, 2nd ed. Sage Publishing, Thousand Oaks

Healthcare Efficiency Assessment in the Southeastern European Countries Using Two-Stage DEA Analysis

Elen Paraskevi Paraschi

Abstract This study aims at evaluating the efficiency of the National Healthcare Systems (NHS) in a number of southeastern European countries (Albania, Bulgaria, Cyprus, Greece, Hungary, North Macedonia, Montenegro, Romania, Serbia, Slovenia, and Slovakia), for the years before and during the covid-19 pandemic. To achieve this goal, a two-stage data envelopment analysis (DEA) model was constructed, comprised of four input variables (health expenditure per capita, number of physicians, number of nurses, number of hospital beds), one intermediate variable (vaccination rates), and two output variables (life expectancy at birth and mortality rates). In the second stage, the DEA results were regressed against socioeconomic variables (Gini index of income inequality, GDP per capita, ratio of population over 65 years old and "EU age"). The data was extracted from a combination of secondary sources (Eurostat, WHO, OECD, The World Bank, Our Word in Data). The DEA results reveal that Cyprus and Albania have the most efficient NHS, while Serbia and Slovakia have the least. The efficiency of the Greek NHS has significantly improved since 2015. Moreover, the regression analysis shows that GDP does not have a noteworthy impact on NHS efficiency, income inequality has a positive, albeit debatable positive impact, increasing aging ratios put substantial pressure on the health systems and EU membership bears important benefits to the NHS. This study sheds light on the comparative assessment and the determinants of the NHS in South-East Europe and provides useful insights for health professionals, economists, and policymakers.

Keywords Healthcare efficiency · DEA analysis · Regression analysis · Southeastern Europe · Greece

E. P. Paraschi (✉)
Department of Business Administration, University of Patras, Patras, Greece
e-mail: eparaschi@upatras.gr

N. Persiani et al. (eds.), *Challenges of Healthcare Systems in the Era of COVID-19*, Contributions to Management Science, https://doi.org/10.1007/978-3-031-43114-2_13

1 Introduction

Health issues gain increasing importance on the global agenda, especially since the covid-19 pandemic onset. Simultaneously, efficiency has become an ultimate goal for both private and public organizations. National health system (NHS) efficiency in particular is of the utmost importance for several reasons (Cylus et al. 2016). The main is that the cost of any healthcare inefficiencies is not only wasted money, but it can be human lives, too. Even in less extreme cases, an inefficient NHS fails to cure patients creating accumulative pressure that generates more inefficiency. This situation generates public frustration and to alleviate it, policymakers often divert resources from other vital sectors, such as education, aggravating social welfare. NHS efficiency is particularly important for southeastern European countries facing financial pressures and concerns over their long-term financial sustainability. A thorough understanding of the NHS efficiency determinants would enable policymakers to make the best possible use of existing resources and provide healthcare funders, such as governments, insurance companies, and individuals, with critical information about how their money is being spent.

This study aims to contribute to a better understanding of the factors affecting NHS efficiency, with a special focus on south-east European (SEE) countries. This area is of particular interest because it is comprised of both developed and developing, EU and non-EU member states, with diverse socioeconomic profiles, which have undergone major financial and organizational transformations during the last two decades, triggered both by the financial crisis (2009–2018) and by the covid-19 pandemic (2020 onwards). To achieve these goals, a two-stage methodology was engaged. First, a DEA model calculates the overall healthcare efficiency of the NHS in Albania, Bulgaria, Cyprus, Greece, Hungary, North Macedonia, Montenegro, Romania, Serbia, Slovenia, and Slovakia, for the years before (2008), during (2015) and after (2019) the financial crisis (and before the pandemic), as well as during the covid-19 pandemic, without and with vaccination (2020 and 2021, respectively). Subsequently, a regression analysis is engaged, aiming at evaluating a number of environmental factors for their contribution to NHS efficiency. The two approaches reveal the (in)efficiencies of the NHSs in the south-east European countries as well as their exogenous determinants and provide useful insights for health professionals, economists, and policymakers.

The structure of the paper is as follows. Section 2 summarizes the situation of the Greek healthcare system. Section 3 describes the study results and Sect. 4 discusses the study conclusions.

2 Literature Review

During the last decades, the SEE countries have engaged in extensive health system transformations, including reforms of primary and secondary healthcare, new governance and funding arrangements, the privatization of healthcare provision, and the introduction of health insurance systems (Bartlett et al. 2012). Especially after the great recession that hit most of the European economies in 2009, additional structural changes took place and efficiency became one of the main concerns of the health sector due to constant pressures on healthcare sources. Amongst these turbulent times, the need for a thorough assessment of the NHS efficiency is indispensable. To this end, Stanculescu and Neculau (2014) conducted a comparative qualitative study on the performance of Public Healthcare Systems in South-East Europe. Among their findings, the researchers conclude that SEE countries lag behind Western European States in terms of living conditions although life expectancy at birth has been increasing since 2000. These nations also display high rates of infant and maternal mortality which may be connected with the existing socioeconomic, ethnic and geographical inequalities in health status. Access to healthcare and social services is much more limited for people with low-income and poor education, for those belonging to minorities (e.g. Roma and migrant populations) and/or who live in rural areas. Additional disparities are generated by the heavy reliance on informal (out-of-pocket) payments for health services, which are substantial in most SEE states.

More recently, OECD published a series of country health profiles (OECD 2021a), providing a succinct overview of health systems in the EU/European Economic Area (EEA), highlighting the unique characteristics and challenges of each country. According to this overview, the countries of southeastern Europe spend less on healthcare than most other EU countries and they have an average NHS effectiveness worse than the EU27. They display high rates of both preventable and treatable mortality.[1] High rates of these two indicators are suggestive of major deficiencies in the health system's ability to provide appropriate and timely treatment to the population and highlight the need for additional spending on preventive care. Moreover, the SEE countries demonstrate generally low life expectancy rates with significant disparities by both gender and socioeconomic status. Two countries however, namely Greece and Cyprus, show a different pattern (OECD 2021a).

Greece was selected as a focal point for the current study because the NHS of this country underwent tremendous reforms during the last fifteen years to become more efficient. Greece followed a bailout program known as Economic Adjustment Program (EAP), for eight years (2010–2018) which stipulated strict austerity measures and structural adjustments in many sectors (Myloneros and Sakellariou 2021). Especially in healthcare, a combination of 'macro' health policy changes

[1] Preventable mortality can be attributed to risk factors including smoking, alcohol consumption and unhealthy diets and can be avoided through public health and primary prevention interventions. Treatable mortality refers to deaths that can be mainly avoided through healthcare interventions.

(including budget caps) and 'micro' structural measures (including gatekeeping, e-prescription and generic drugs) was employed to improve efficiency (Kalavrezou and Jin 2021). Greece completed the Economic Adjustment Program in 2018, however, the shrinkage of healthcare expenditures continued in 2019 (OECD 2021b). The covid-19 pandemic that outbroke in the first months of 2020 led to increased financial support to the NHS, including national and European funding, for emergency medical staff, medical equipment, and the operation of intensive care units (ICUs) (OECD 2021b). The Greek NHS was further strengthened against covid-19, with a vaccination program starting on 27 December 2020 (Greek Government 2022). Nevertheless, the effectiveness of the Greek health system is still threatened, since life expectancy at birth declined by six months in 2020 (OECD 2021b).

Several scholars have assessed the efficiency of the Greek NHS during the economic crisis (Fragkiadakis et al. 2016; Mitropoulos et al. 2018; Flokou et al. 2017; Xenos et al. 2017); however, these studies were limited within national borders and exclusively preoccupied with the public hospital sector. Moreover, technical efficiency focusing primarily on budget control may be inadequate to create an insightful understanding of NHS management. Therefore, a two-stage panel approach was chosen as the most appropriate to examine the NHS efficiency of neighboring countries in different periods. This study focuses on both developed and developing South-East European countries that have undergone significant structural changes during the last two decades. In addition to Greece which underwent significant transformations due to the financial crisis described above, other countries in this region experienced profound economic, political and social changes due to their entrance to the European Union (Cyprus, Hungary, Slovakia and Slovenia joined the EU on 1st January 2004 and Bulgaria and Romania, followed in 2007). The remaining countries of the sample (Albania, the Republic of North Macedonia, Montenegro and Serbia) are EU candidates; therefore, they go through a transition period that also requires structural public administration transformations.

Based on the notion that the NHS of a country may be considered a production system that transforms inputs into outputs (Dhaoui 2019), this study initially uses Data Envelopment Analysis (DEA), which is a popular methodology for assessing technical efficiency in healthcare. Gavurova et al. (2021) adopted an input-oriented Dynamic Network Data Envelopment Analysis (DNDEA) assuming both constant and variable returns to scale (VRS and CRS, respectively), to quantify and compare the efficiency of OECD health systems over three periods (2000, 2008, and 2016). Kozuń-Cieślak (2020) applied three DEA models in 25 OECD countries to examine the relationship between NHS efficiency and economic wealth. She used health expenditure as a percentage of GDP, health expenditure per capita, medical doctors per 1,000 inhabitants, practicing nurses per 1,000 inhabitants, medical equipment per one million inhabitants as inputs and infant mortality per 1,000 live births, as output. Asandului et al. (2014) evaluated the efficiency of the healthcare systems of 30 European countries in 2010, using the number of doctors, the number of hospital beds and public health expenditures as a percentage of GDP as inputs and life expectancy at birth, health adjusted life expectancy and infant mortality rate as outputs in both CRS and VRS DEA models. Ouertani et al. (2018) applied DEA to longitudinal data from Saudi Arabia, using public spending on health as input and life expectancy and 1/infant mortality as outputs.

Based on the above literature, the DEA variables used in this study included four inputs (health expenditure per capita, number of physicians, number of nurses, number of hospital beds), one intermediate variable (vaccination rates), and two outputs (life expectancy at birth and mortality rates).

Thorough evaluation of health efficiency is frequently difficult due to external factors, beyond the control of healthcare management. To overcome this limitation, many studies in this area consider the impact of external (environmental) factors by employing regression analysis on the DEA results. Castaldo et al. (2020) engaged a two-stage methodology to assess the efficiency of health expenditure in 30 OECD countries over the period 2005 to 2015. In the first stage, they applied input-oriented DEA to estimate the technical efficiency using public health expenditure as input and a health performance indicator comprised of infant mortality rate, life expectancy at birth and hospital discharge rates as output. In the second stage, they regressed DEA results against a number of non-discretionary variables, such as the Gross Domestic Product (GDP), the rates of vaccination, weather temperature, red tape (slowness of bureaucracy), tobacco consumption and obesity. Dhaoui (2019) used a two-stage performance analysis, to assess the technical efficiency of eighteen NHSs in the Middle East and North Africa (MENA) region for the years 1997, 2005 and 2014. In the first stage, he used both input- and an output-oriented DEA and in the second stage, he analyzed the health efficiency determinants using a Tobit regression with GDP per capita, health expenditure, adult literacy rate, urbanization level and control of corruption as independent variables. Similarly, Gong et al. (2019) applied input-oriented CRS Network DEA to measure the healthcare efficiency in thirty China provinces from 2009 to 2016. Then, they practiced Tobit regression to analyze the factors affecting overall efficiency, using GDP per capita, number of high education enrollment, government health expenditure, social health expenditure, personal health expenditure, number of public hospitals and number of private hospitals, as independent variables. Zarulli et al. (2021) studied the healthcare system efficiency of 140 countries, using DEA analysis with life expectancy as single output and regression analysis in the second stage with education index; infants lacking immunization against DTP3 and measles; current health expenditure as a percentage of GDP; share of the population using at least basic sanitation services; share of unemployed in the labor force; income inequality measured by the Gini coefficient; and the ratio of 65 or older population to those of working age as dependent variables. Finally, Dincă et al. (2020) examined the healthcare efficiency in 17 EU Member states taking into account the year in which each state joined the EU, separating the sample countries into old member states (before 2004) and new member states (after 2004).

Based on the above literature, the Gini index of income inequality, the GDP per capita, the ratio of population over 65 years old and the "EU age" (i.e. the number of years that a country is a member of the European Union), were selected as independent variables for the regression analysis in the current study.

3 Methodology

3.1 *Data Envelopment Analysis*

DEA is a mathematical linear programming approach used to measure the technical efficiency (TE) of different Decision-Making Units (DMUs), as well as the same DMU over time. In the last case, each DMU is treated as a separate DMU in each period. This procedure enables the comparison of every DMU both to itself over time and to peers allowing us to determine efficiency variations across countries and across time (panel approach).

On these grounds, a DEA for cross-sectional data has been conducted upon five sub-periods: 2008 (before the financial crisis), 2015 (during the financial crisis), 2019 (after the financial crisis, before the pandemic), 2020 (during the pandemic, without covid-19 vaccines) and 2021 (during the pandemic, with covid-19 vaccines). This study aligns with the majority of the DEA studies that use input-oriented models (based on the assumption that the adjustment of inputs cannot significantly increase this output at one time) and both constant and variable returns to scale (CRS and VRS, respectively) assumptions (Cantor and Poh 2018).

The input-oriented model used in this study is described by the following equation (Medarević and Vuković 2021):

$$\text{Min}\,\theta_0, \quad \text{subject to:}$$

$$\sum_{j=1}^{12} \lambda_i x_{si} \leq \theta_0 x_{so} \quad s = 1, 2, \ldots, 5$$

$$\sum_{j=1}^{12} \lambda_i y_{ri} \geq y_{ro} \quad r = 1, 2, 3$$

$$\lambda_i \geq 0 \quad i = 1, 2, \ldots, 12$$

where:

- θ_o is the efficiency score of the NHSs under assessment
- λ_i is a vector of positive constraints, indicating the weight of the restrictions
- x_{si} is the quantity of input s used by the i DMU
- y_{ri} is the output value of the r variable produced by the i DMU.

3.2 *Regression*

In the second stage, the DEA efficiency scores calculated in the first step were used as the dependent variable ($\widehat{\rho}_0^*$), and regressed on potential exogenous (environmental) variables (z_i), according to the following generic equation (Simar and Wilson 2007):

$$\widehat{\rho}_0^* = \alpha + z_i\beta + \xi_i$$

where:

- α is the regression constant
- z_i are the environmental variables
- β is the regression coefficient
- ξ_i is a statistical noise with distribution limited by $\xi_i \leq 1 - a - z_i\beta$ because DEA efficiency scores are less than or equal to unit.

3.3 Data

The data used in this paper were sourced from various sources, as seen in Table 1. The data for most of the DEA and regression variables were extracted from the World Bank (data last updated 27/4/2022) and were supplemented by the latest data for the years 2020–2021 available from the national statistic institute of each country. Data about covid-19 deaths and vaccination rates in 2021 was derived from Our World in Data. As two output indicators (Y1 and Y2) are de-stimulants (they refer to an undesirable output), they were converted into desirable measures by using them as denominators (i.e. Y1* = 1/Y1 and Y2* = 1/Y2), as applied also by Ouertani et al. (2018).

As seen in Table 2, health expenditure as a percentage of GDP (X1) ranges from 9.46 in the EU to 5.42 in Albania, has a tendency to increase over the years and demonstrates a little variation across the countries' sample. The same is true for the number of physicians per 1,000 people (X2), which ranges from 6.22 in Greece to 1.49 in Albania (4.79 is the EU average). The number of nurses and midwives per 1,000 people (X3) displays more variation, ranging from 12.74 in Slovenia to 3.94 in North Macedonia (9.30 is the EU average). The number of beds per 1,000 people (X4) ranges from 7.29 in Bulgaria to 2.8 in Albania (5.25 is the EU average). Vaccine doses per 1,000 people (X5) have been calculated only for the year 2021 (the covid-19 vaccines were made publicly available in December 2020). The number of doses may be more than 1,000 per 1,000 people since multiple doses apply to a single person. The EU average for 2021 was 1,690.00 and the values of the X5 variable ranged from 1,720.00 in Cyprus to 542.00 in Bulgaria. The mortality per 100,000 people caused by covid-19 (Y1) was calculated for the years 2020 and 2021 and ranged from 276.01 in Bulgaria to 31.66 in Cyprus (142.29 is the EU average). Similarly, total mortality of any cause (covid-19 included) per 100 k (Y2), ranged from 1,647.06 in Bulgaria to 628.13 in Cyprus (972.45 is the EU average). Life expectancy (Y3) ranged from 81.22 in Cyprus to 73.84 in Bulgaria (80.38 is the EU average) and generally declined in the two last years (2020 and 2021) due to the covid-19 pandemic.

Regression variables were selected only for the year 2019 both because this was the most recent year with available data for all countries and all variables and because this was the most "normal" year, on the verge between the financial crisis and the

Table 1 Explanation of the variables included in the analyzes

Variable	Description	Role	Data source
X1-Spending	Current health expenditure (% of GDP)	DEA input variable	The world bank, health nutrition and population statistics[a] WHO, the global health observatory[b]
X2-Physicians	Physicians (per 1,000 people)	DEA input variable	
X3-Nurses	Nurses and midwives (per 1,000 people)	DEA input variable	
X4-Beds	Hospital beds (per 1,000 people)	DEA input variable	
X5-Vaccination	Vaccine doses in total (for 2021, per 1000 people)	DEA intermediate variable	Our world in data, coronavirus pandemic (COVID-19)[c]
Y1-Covid_mortality	Deaths due to covid-19 (per 100 k) for the years 2020–2021	DEA output variable Y1* = 1/Y1	Our world in data, coronavirus pandemic (COVID-19) and national statistic institutes
Y2-Total_mortality	Deaths of any cause (covid-19 included) per 100 k	DEA output variable Y2* = 1/Y2	The world bank, health nutrition and population Statistics and national statistic institutes WHO, the global health observatory
Y3-Life_expectacy	Life expectancy at birth, total (years)	DEA output variable	The world bank, health nutrition and population statistics and national statistic institutes WHO, the global health observatory
DEA score	NHS efficiency score derived from DEA	Regression independent variable	Data envelopment analysis (1st stage)
GNI	Gini index	Regression dependent variable	The world bank world development indicators[d] EU-SILC survey[e]
GDP	GDP per capita, PPP (current international $)	Regression dependent variable	

(continued)

Table 1 (continued)

Variable	Description	Role	Data source
Age > 65	Population ages 65 and above (% of total population)	Regression dependent variable	
EU member age	Years elapsed since the country became an EU member	Regression dependent variable	EU country profiles[f]

[a] Available online at: https://databank.worldbank.org/source/health-nutrition-and-population-statistics
[b] Available online at: https://www.who.int/data/gho/data/themes/topics/indicator-groups
[c] Available online at: https://ourworldindata.org/coronavirus#explore-the-global-situation
[d] Available online at: https://databank.worldbank.org/reports.aspx?source=world-development-indicators
[e] Available online at: https://ec.europa.eu/eurostat/databrowser/view/tessi190/default/table
[f] Available online at: https://european-union.europa.eu/principles-countries-history/country-profiles_en

Table 2 Descriptive statistics of the variables included in the analyzes

Variable	Mean	SD	Max	Min
X1-Spending	7.38	1.16	9.46	5.42
X2-Physicians	3.46	1.17	6.22	1.49
X3-Nurses	6.22	2.53	12.74	3.94
X4-Beds	5.09	1.48	7.29	2.80
X5-Vaccination	1,206.33	404.37	1,720.00	542.00
Y1-Covid_mortality	172.99	77.24	276.01	31.55
Y2-Total_mortality	1,170.95	302.00	1,647.06	628.13
Y3-Life expectancy	77.14	3.1	81.22	73.21
GNI	32.3	5.1	40.3	23.2
GDP	28,059.3	9,267.6	42,339.0	13,998.0
Age > 65	17.7%	3.0%	22.0%	14.1%
EU member age	13	12.5	41	0

pandemic. As seen in Table 1, GDP per capita varies significantly across the selected countries, ranging from 42,339€ in Cyprus to 13,998€ in Albania (28,780€ was the EU average). The Gini index (GNI) ranges from 40.3 in Bulgaria to 23.2 in Slovenia (30.6 is the EU average). The Gini index measures the extent to which the distribution of income or consumption among individuals or households within an economy deviates from a perfectly equal distribution. A GNI of 0 represents perfect equality, while an index of 100 implies perfect inequality. The proportion of the total population that is older than 65 years ranges from 21.95% in Greece to 14.05% in Cyprus (20.46% is the EU average). Lastly, the sample contains both non-EU members (Albania, North Macedonia, Montenegro, Serbia) and countries that joined the European Union either a long time ago (Greece has been an EU member country for 41 years, since 1 January 1981) or recently (Romania and Bulgaria are the newest EU members, since 2007).

4 Results

4.1 DEA Results

The DEA efficiency scores range between 0 and 1, where one indicates the unit is relatively efficient, and a value <1 indicates inefficiency. For the years studied, all DEA models used two outputs, namely the total mortality of any cause and the life expectancy. An extra DEA model (2021 covid) was run for the year 2021, including vaccination doses as an intermediate input and covid deaths as output (Table 3).

Both CRS and VRS DEA methodologies were applied giving similar results. Due to space limitations, it was chosen to present and discuss only the CRS results.

As we can see in Table 3 and Fig. 1, Cyprus and Albania constantly rank in the 1st place in NHS efficiency. Greece reached the efficiency frontier from 2019 onwards. North Macedonia ranks high except for a slight decline in 2020. Romania is perhaps the only country with efficiency decreasing over time, except for a temporary increase in 2020. Hungary had an impressive efficiency improvement between 2015 and 2019 but after 2020 efficiency declined sharply, perhaps due to the challenges that the covid-19 pandemic imposed on the NHS. The same pattern applies to Slovakia and Slovenia, to a smaller extent. The reverse pattern is observed for Montenegro, Serbia and the EU average, the efficiencies of which significantly increased during the pandemic. Another rather controversial observation is that the EU average ranks very low until 2020, well below the average efficiency of the sample countries, which is constantly improving.

Additionally, the examination of the 2021-covid model's results reveals that there is a significant efficiency gap between Cyprus (and Albania) that lay on the efficiency frontier and the remaining countries whose efficiencies rank from the minimum of 0.143 (Hungary) to the maximum of 0.417 (Serbia), much lower than the efficiency frontier. This finding indicates that, with the exception of the two countries that constantly record high NHS efficiencies, the other countries fell behind in managing the pandemic, even with the support of the available covid-19 vaccine.

Cluster analysis (Fig. 2) reveals three separate efficiency clusters in the countries under study. Cluster 1 is comprised of the two countries (Albania and Cyprus) located on the efficiency frontier. Cluster 2 contains four countries (Bulgaria, Greece, North Macedonia and Romania) with average efficiency scores between 0.87 and 0.97. Cluster 3 contains five countries (Hungary, Montenegro, Slovakia, Serbia and Slovenia, with the last two displaying the least NHS efficiencies during the years studied).

Table 3 Technical efficiency results of the input-oriented CRS DEA model

Country (DMU)	2008			2015			2019			2020			2021			2021 (covid)		
	TE	Rank	RTS	TE	Rank	RTS	TE	Rank	RTS	TE	Rank	RTS	TE	Rank	RTS	TE	Rank	RTS
ALB	1.000	1	CRS	1.000	1	CRS	1.000	1	CRS	1.000	1	CRS	1.000	1	CRS	0.996	2	IRS
BGR	0.805	4	IRS	0.725	5	IRS	0.881	4	IRS	0.951	4	IRS	1.000	1	CRS	0.382	4	IRS
CYP	1.000	1	CRS	1.000	1	CRS	1.000	1	CRS	1.000	1	CRS	1.000	1	CRS	1.000	1	CRS
GRC	0.740	5	DRS	0.773	4	DRS	1.000	1	CRS	1.000	1	CRS	1.000	1	CRS	0.308	6	IRS
HUN	0.700	7	IRS	0.691	7	IRS	0.894	3	IRS	0.903	5	IRS	0.869	2	IRS	0.143	11	IRS
MKD	0.907	3	IRS	0.930	3	IRS	1.000	1	CRS	0.986	2	IRS	1.000	1	CRS	0.284	7	IRS
MNE	0.693	8	IRS	0.669	8	IRS	0.814	6	IRS	0.835	6	IRS	1.000	1	CRS	0.235	10	IRS
ROU	0.981	2	IRS	0.950	2	IRS	0.905	2	IRS	0.947	3	IRS	0.846	3	IRS	0.360	5	IRS
SRB	0.558	10	IRS	0.536	10	IRS	0.703	7	IRS	0.706	8	IRS	0.805	4	IRS	0.417	3	IRS
SVK	0.725	6	IRS	0.707	6	IRS	0.816	5	IRS	0.809	7	IRS	0.795	5	IRS	0.251	9	IRS
SVN	0.679	9	DRS	0.650	9	DRS	0.657	8	DRS	0.673	9	DRS	0.637	6	DRS	0.257	8	IRS
EU average	0.583		DRS	0.533		DRS	0.564		DRS	0.599		DRS	0.779		DRS	0.268		IRS
Sample average	0.799		IRS	0.785		IRS	0.855		IRS	0.879		IRS	0.892		IRS	0.421		IRS
SD	0.151			0.159			0.122			0.120			0.124			0.285		
Min	0.558			0.536			0.657			0.673			0.637			0.143		
Max	1,000			1,000			1,000			1,000			1,000			1,000		
Efficient DMUs	CYP, ALB			CYP, ALB			CYP, ALB, GRC, MKD			CYP, ALB, GRC			CYP, ALB, GRC, MKD, MNE, BGR			CYP, (ALB)		

Notes TE = Technical efficiency
RTS = Returns of scale
CRS = Constant returns of scale
IRS = Increasing returns of scale
DRS = Decreasing returns of scale

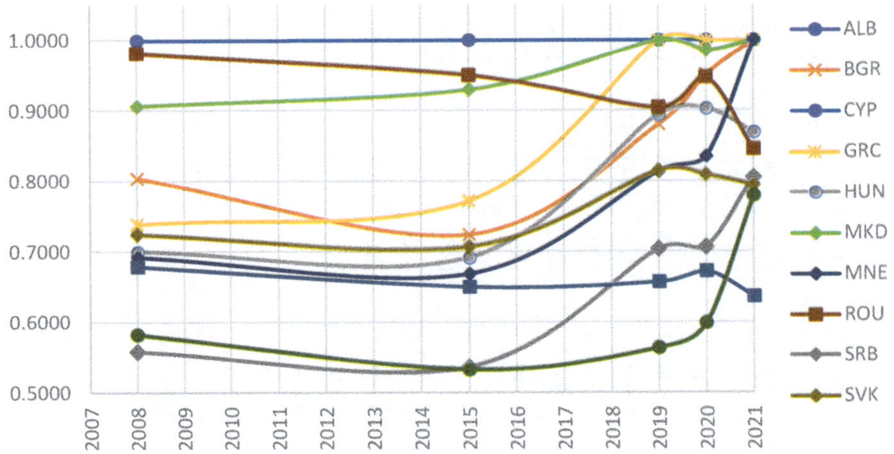

Fig. 1 NHS technical efficiency across time

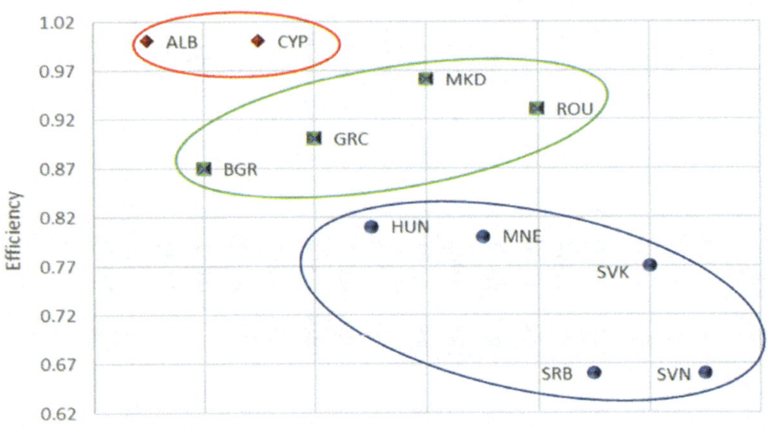

Fig. 2 Cluster analysis based on the average DEA CRS model scores

The above results call for a closer examination of the observed differences. Regression analysis was engaged to test for external factors that may affect NHS efficiency.

4.2 *Regression Results*

The regression results suggest that our model has a good explanatory value and it is statistically significant ($R^2 = 0.797$, $p < 0.05$). According to the regression results (Table 4), GDP does not have a significant impact on NHS efficiency. On the contrary,

Table 4 The regression results ($N = 12$)

Variable	β coefficient	Sig.
GDP per capita	−6.387e−6	0.144
GNI	0.012	0.059
Age over 65	−0.045	0.006
EU age	0.013	0.008
Constant	1.307	0.004
R^2	0.797	0.029

GNI has a relatively significant positive impact. This was also obvious from the DEA results, since Bulgaria which has the highest Gini index in the sample scored better than Slovenia, which has the lowest Gini index and the lowest efficiency score, too. Furthermore, human age over 65 has a significant negative impact, while the EU age (the time elapsed since a country joined the EU) has a significant positive impact on NHS efficiency.

5 Discussion and Conclusions

This study evaluated the NHS efficiency in eleven SEE countries, engaging a two-stage analysis. In the first stage, the technical efficiency of the healthcare systems was calculated, using a Data Envelopment Analysis. In the second stage, the DEA scores were regressed against socioeconomic variables to examine their impact on NHS efficiency.

According to the DEA results, Cyprus and Albania are the two countries with the highest NHS efficiency over the years. The Cypriot population enjoys good health overall, with one of the highest life expectancies in the EU (OECD 2019). The Cypriot healthcare system has undergone several major transformations since the induction of the Republic of Cyprus into the European Union in 2004 intensified by the bailout agreement with the International Monetary Fund, the European Commission and the European Central Bank (known as the Troika) which prevented Cyprus bankruptcy in 2011 (Petrou 2021). Apart from the structural changes, the progressive rise in life expectancy reflects the urbanization of the Cypriot population's lifestyle, the improvement of the diagnostic approach, and easier access to health services (Agathokleous et al. 2016).

Albania has struggled with sustained periods of economic and political isolation within Europe as a former Communist group of countries, leading to great challenges to reforming the country's economic and social establishments, including healthcare. Despite these obstacles, the Albanian government has conducted many reform cycles over the last three decades. Albania made economic progress during this time, reducing national poverty and gaining upper-middle-income status (Saric et al. 2021). In 2015, the World Bank announced €32.1 million in financing for the Health System

Improvement Project in Albania. The project would support improving the efficiency of care in selected hospitals in Albania, improving the management of information in the health system, and increasing financial access to health services (World Bank 2015). A recent study (Saric et al. 2021) observed a significant improvement in the quality of primary healthcare in Albania, between 2015 and 2018.

Greece scored the biggest efficiency improvement between 2015 and 2019, something that has also been measured by other scholars (Gavurova et al. 2021) and can be partially explained by the major transformations that Greek NHS has undergone since 2010 when the country entered the Economic Adjustment Programs. Another factor that may play a positive role is that Greece is an old EU member (since 1981), therefore the country has a good knowledge of the EU supporting mechanisms and may leverage them to its benefit. However, a point of concern is the high percentage of elderly people that may jeopardize the efficiency progress made by the Greek NHS.

On the other hand, among the countries with the lowest efficiency, we can see Serbia and Slovenia. Serbia has made significant gains in terms of life expectancy and basic health indicators but remains far below the EU average, and significant differences are visible across the country's districts and population groups. There is also a large variation in productivity within and across types of hospitals (World Bank 2017; Medarević and Vuković 2021). Serbia's healthcare system is relatively costly. The total health expenditure as a share of gross domestic product (GDP) gradually increased from 6.5% in the mid-1990s to around 10% in 2010, almost twice the health spending of Albania. Moreover, private spending on health services (out-of-pocket money) remains high, amounting to 42.4% of total health expenditure in 2017 (Bjegovic-Mikanovic et al. 2019). Nevertheless, even though the average NHS efficiency in Serbia is low, it has significantly improved since 2015.

Healthcare reforms in Slovenia have been delayed or failed in recent years as a result of rejected proposals to eliminate complementary health insurance and health financing. This difficulty in reaching a consensus is especially concerning given the fiscal sustainability challenges that Slovenia faces if no policy changes are implemented (OECD 2017). Though population health has improved in recent decades, health disparities due to gender, social and economic factors, and geography continue to pose significant challenges. Outdated facilities are another issue that must be addressed to ensure the long-term sustainability and resiliency of the Slovenian NHS (Albreht et al. 2016).

Rather controversially, the EU average efficiency is much lower than the sample's average score, which may further support that NHS efficiency is not a direct outcome of health expenditure since EU has the highest health spending and Albania has the lowest. Besides, Slovenia constantly ranks low in efficiency although it has one of the highest scores in healthcare public spending, something that may be the result of decreasing returns of scale, as already reported by Asandului et al. (2014), meaning that adding more inputs may have an adverse result on the outputs. This also was the case for Greece until 2015, when health spending was significantly shrunk due to structural measures, allowing for constant RTS from then on.

Overall, the DEA results align with previous studies. Asandului et al. (2014) also found that in 2010, Cyprus was on the efficiency frontier and Greece scored higher than Hungary. Medarević and Vuković (2021) who applied DEA in Serbian hospitals from 2015 to 2019, found that they operated at a low-efficiency level, compared to most European peers. However, when comparing the findings, we must bear in mind that the year of the study, the peers compared, and the mix of inputs and outputs selected have an impact on the DEA results (Cantor and Poh 2018).

In the regression analysis, GDP is found not to have a significant impact, indicating that the NHS efficiency cannot be attributed to a single factor, even though this is a significant financial feature, such as the national health expenditure or GDP per capita. This finding is consistent with Gong et al. (2019) who also found that the effect of GDP per capita on the efficiency of the healthcare system in China provinces is not statistically significant. Dhaoui (2019) has also observed that low-income countries can be a reference in terms of health efficiency. Moreover, Asandului et al. (2014) reported that Romania and Bulgaria were among the most efficient NHS, although these countries' general economic performances are poor. Kozuń-Cieślak (2020) who examined the Bismarckian and Beveridgean-style healthcare systems in 25 OECD countries to identify the relationship between the efficiency of the country's NHS and its economic wealth, found that more developed economies are technically less efficient, supporting the view that technical efficiency is only one of many factors influencing the superiority of the healthcare system and patient satisfaction. Similarly, Ouertani et al. (2018) claim that increasing public spending does not necessarily result in improving healthcare efficiency, since an NHS is a complex system and other factors (i.e. primary healthcare quality) may interfere with the final results.

GNI has a positive impact which is relatively significant. This finding is rather controversial, given that in most of the studies examining the relationship between income inequality and health levels, it is observed that the population health levels are lower in societies with greater income inequality (Wilkinson and Pickett 2006). However, some scholars have produced evidence that the Gini index has no significant effect on health outcomes (Lorgelly and Lindley 2008; Mackenbach 2002). Other authors claim that the evidence linking income inequality with health levels is inconsistent and insufficient (Lynch et al. 2004). Deaton and Paxson (2004) concluded that inequity itself is not a direct determinant of health levels, but possible correlations between the Gini index and health efficiency may refer to broader notions of inequality and inequity that are most likely important for health. Finally, since income inequalities are reduced in developed economies that enjoy a longer life expectancy and have a great proportion of the elderly population, this observation can be an indicator of the complex interrelations between the socioeconomic determinants having an impact on the NHS outcomes. Lastly, Cornia and Court (2001) came to the conclusion that a Gini coefficient value between 0.25 and 0.40 has a growth-promoting effect. Given that the countries of our sample display a GNI between 23.2 and 40.3, it is possible that this GNI range enables health efficiency growth, too.

Population aging has an adverse impact on NHS efficiency. Medarević and Vuković (2021) have also observed that the efficiency of the Serbian hospitals was negatively associated with the proportion of elderly in the hospital catchment area.

This finding is unsurprising since Dincă et al. (2020) mention that healthcare costs increase exponentially for elderly people. Additionally, after the age of 65, people often have more complicated and long-term healthcare needs due to functional deterioration, a decline in mental abilities, physical illness, and psychosocial needs, that demand a great amount of health resources (Kim et al. 2018). This is of particular importance not only for Greece (which has the highest proportion of the elderly population in the sample) but also for the entire Europe, which is an 'aging society', and, given the expected extension of life expectancy, will be a 'post-aged society' in the near future (Zlotkin 2017). The effects of the expected 'silver tsunami' due to population aging are well documented, underlining the fiscal and political difficulties that many countries' health and social protection systems are projected to encounter in the next decades. Age > 65.

EU age has a significant positive impact on NHS efficiency. This finding is in line with Dincă et al. (2020) who also observed that the old EU members displayed high-efficiency scores, their general sustainable economic performance being proof that they obtained good results with respect to healthcare efficiency. It is possible therefore that a country that belongs to the EU family can benefit from financial support from the European Structural and Investment Funds and the European Regional Development Fund to move its NHS to a higher level. Lomba (2019) reports that EU membership brings significant benefits to the EU citizens, economies and health policy, through the following mechanisms: economies of scale (joint action, procurement and funding), free movement of persons (patient access to healthcare in different EU member states and harmonized patient rights), reduction of cross-border threats (synchronized responses to pandemics/epidemics), promotion of best practices (extensive databases and diffusion of standards), networking (of scientists and national authorities), benchmarking for decision-making, unlocking pharmaceutical and treatment innovation potential and implementing health EU legislation ensuring a safe and well-functioning internal market and the protection of public health.

Overall, the results of this study are useful to governments, regulators, healthcare providers and funders, and the general public. Policymakers aim to achieve both technical efficiency, i.e. maximizing the outputs for the amount of given inputs and allocative efficiency, i.e. directing the limited resources towards the most productive sectors and using the optimal mix of inputs to achieve the productivity goals. Healthcare funders including governments, insurance organizations, households and the general public are interested in knowing which systems, providers and treatments contribute the largest health gains in relation to the level of resources they devour. Our results indicate that more efficient use of resources can help countries to improve their life expectancy even without increasing health expenditure.

This study also has some limitations. The DEA results should be treated with caution, because different countries, different input/output mix, and different years could produce different outcomes. Moreover, both DEA and regression results are sensitive to the data used, which is often unavailable especially when examining current phenomena. In this case, the use of proxies is unavoidable, therefore a re-examination of the same situation in a few years may produce dissimilar results.

Future research can attempt a more detailed examination of the NHS efficiency, by extending the list of DEA inputs and outputs, examining additional socioeconomic factors in the regression analysis, including data from the private healthcare sector and using a larger sample of countries. Furthermore, NHS efficiencies could be assessed with alternative methodologies, either non-parametric (e.g., FDH) and/or parametric (e.g., SFA) or, using a mix of quantitative and qualitative methods, to gain a more comprehensive understanding of the multifaceted factors that affect healthcare systems' performance.

References

Agathokleous MN et al (2016) Estimating life expectancy of the population in Cyprus with the use of life tables. Hippokratia 20(2):99

Albreht T et al (2016) Slovenia: health system review. Health Syst Transit 23(1):1–183

Asandului L et al (2014) The efficiency of healthcare systems in Europe: a data envelopment analysis approach. Procedia Econ Finance 10:261–268

Bartlett W, Bozikov J, Rechel B (eds) (2012) Health reforms in south-east Europe. Springer

Bjegovic-Mikanovic V et al (2019) Serbia: health system review. Health Syst Transit 21(3):i-211

Cantor VJM, Poh KL (2018) Integrated analysis of healthcare efficiency: a systematic review. J Med Syst 42(1):1–23

Castaldo A et al (2020) Determinants of health sector efficiency: evidence from a two-step analysis on 30 OECD countries. Econ Bull 40(2):1651–1666

Cornia GA, Court J (2001) Inequality, growth and poverty in the era of liberalization and globalization. In: Policy Brief 4 of the UNU world institute for development economics research (UNU/WIDER), The United Nations University, Helsinki

Cylus J, Papanicolas I, Smith PC, World Health Organization (2016) Health system efficiency: how to make measurement matter for policy and management. World Health Organization, Regional Office for Europe

Deaton A, Paxson C (2004) Mortality, income, and income inequality over time in Britain and the United States. In: Perspectives on the economics of aging, pp 247–286

Dhaoui I (2019) Healthcare system efficiency and its determinants: a two-stage data envelopment analysis (DEA) from MENA countries. Economic Research Forum (ERF), Giza, Egypt

Dincă G et al (2020) The efficiency of the healthcare systems in EU countries–a DEA analysis. Acta Oeconomica 70(1):19–36

Flokou A et al (2017) A window-DEA based efficiency evaluation of the public hospital sector in Greece during the 5-year economic crisis. PLoS ONE 12(5):e0177946

Fragkiadakis G et al (2016) Operational and economic efficiency analysis of public hospitals in Greece. Ann Oper Res 247(2):787–806

Gavurova B et al (2021) Health system efficiency in OECD countries: dynamic network DEA approach. Heal Econ Rev 11(1):1–25

Gong G et al (2019) Has the efficiency of china's healthcare system improved after healthcare reform? A network data envelopment analysis and tobit regression approach. Int J Environ Res Public Health 16(23):4847

Greek Government (2022) COVID-19 vaccination statistics. https://www.data.gov.gr/datasets/mdg_emvolio/. Accessed 2 May 2022

Kalavrezou N, Jin H (2021) Healthcare reform in Greece: progress and reform priorities. IMF Working Papers 2021(189)

Kim YS et al (2018) Unmet healthcare needs of elderly people in Korea. BMC Geriatr 18(1):1–9

Kozuń-Cieślak G (2020) Is the efficiency of the healthcare system linked to the country's economic performance? Beveridgeans versus Bismarckians. Acta Oeconomica 70(1):1–17

Lomba N (2019) The benefit of EU action in health policy: the record to date: European added value in action. European Added Value Unit. PE 631.729

Lorgelly PK, Lindley J (2008) What is the relationship between income inequality and health? Evidence from the BHPS? Health Econ 17(2):249–265

Lynch J et al (2004) Is income inequality a determinant of population health? Part 1. A systematic review. Milbank Q 82(1):5–99

Mackenbach JP (2002) Income inequality and population health: evidence favouring a negative correlation between income inequality and life expectancy has disappeared. BMJ 324(7328):1–2

Medarević A, Vuković D (2021) Efficiency and productivity of public hospitals in Serbia Using DEA-Malmquist model and tobit regression model, 2015–2019. Int J Environ Res Public Health 18(23):12475

Mitropoulos P et al (2018) The impact of economic crisis on the Greek hospitals' productivity. Int J Health Plann Manage 33(1):171–184

Myloneros T, Sakellariou D (2021) The effectiveness of primary health care reforms in Greece towards achieving universal health coverage: a scoping review. BMC Health Serv Res 21(1):1–12

OECD/European Observatory on Health Systems and Policies (2017) Slovenia: Country Health Profile 2017, State of Health in the EU, OECD Publishing, Paris/European Observatory on Health Systems and Policies, Brussels

OECD/European Observatory on Health Systems and Policies (2019) Cyprus: Country Health Profile 2019, State of Health in the EU, OECD Publishing, Paris/European Observatory on Health Systems and Policies, Brussels

OECD/European Observatory on Health Systems and Policies (2021a) Country Health Profiles 2021. https://www.oecd.org/health/country-health-profiles-eu.htm

OECD/European Observatory on Health Systems and Policies (2021b) Greece: Country Health Profile 2021, State of Health in the EU, OECD Publishing, Paris/European Observatory on Health Systems and Policies, Brussels

Ouertani MN et al (2018) Assessing government spending efficiency and explaining inefficiency scores: DEA-bootstrap analysis in the case of Saudi Arabia. Cogent Econ Finance 6(1):1493666

Petrou P (2021) The 2019 introduction of the new national healthcare system in Cyprus. Health Policy 125(3):284–289

Saric J et al (2021) Assessing the quality of care at primary health care level in two pilot regions of Albania. Front Public Health 9

Simar L, Wilson P (2007) Estimation and inference in two-stage, semi-parametric models of production processes. J Econom 136(1):31–64

Stanculescu MS, Neculau G (2014) The performance of public health-care systems in South-East Europe: a comparative qualitative study. Friedrich-Ebert-Stiftung, Belgrade

Wilkinson RG, Pickett KE (2006) Income inequality and population health: a review and explanation of the evidence. Soc Sci Med 62(7):1768–1784

Word Bank (2015) Press release: world bank to help improve quality, access, and efficiency of Albania's health care system. https://www.worldbank.org/en/news/press-release/2015/02/27/world-bank-to-help-improve-quality-access-and-efficiency-of-albanias-health-care-system

World Bank (2017) Delivering health services efficiently for Serbian's. World Bank, Washington, DC

Xenos P et al (2017) Efficiency and productivity assessment of public hospitals in Greece during the crisis period 2009–2012. Cost Eff Resource Alloc 15(1):1–12

Zarulli V et al (2021) Health care system efficiency and life expectancy: a 140-country study. PLoS ONE 16(7):e0253450

Zlotkin (2017) World population prospects: the 2017 revision. United Nations. https://www.un.org/development/desa/publications/world-population-prospects-the-2017-revision.html

Operations

Reorganization of the Community Care Model Based on Evolving Needs and Solutions: The Tuscan Case, Transforming Pandemic into Opportunity

Chiara Barchielli and Paolo Zoppi

Abstract A healthcare system based on a rigid division into care settings and poor integration between health and social services does not provide effective answers to the health demand expressed by the population and generates disparities between territories in the provision of services. This emerged powerfully in Italy, one of the first countries that experienced COVID-19 cases. Emergency solutions from the Italian Government have been successful in avoiding many hospitalizations through the establishment of the Special Continuity Care Units (USCA), instituted to support General Practitioners and Primary Care Pediatricians in preventing their COVID-19 infected patients from being hospitalized. USL Toscana Centro, one of the three Local Health Authorities (LHA) in Tuscany experimented with a complementary model, the Hospital-Territory intervention group (GIROT), benefiting from the pioneer experience of the family and community-based nursing model (FCN). This case study illustrates and discusses the replicability and scalability of this model, in urban areas as well as in peripheral areas aiming at a more resilient and egalitarian health provision, enforcing the community-based delivery of care, by outlining the characteristics of the Tuscan community care reorganization according to NRRP's Mission 6.

Keywords Family and community-based care · Nursing organizational model · Public healthcare · Post-Covid-19

JEL Classification Codes I10 · I14 · I19

C. Barchielli (✉)
Institute of Management and EMBEDS Department, Sant'Anna School of Advanced Studies, Pisa, Italia
e-mail: chiara.barchielli@santannapisa.it

P. Zoppi
Usl Toscana Centro, Piazza Di Santa Maria Nuova 1, Firenze, Italy
e-mail: paolo.zoppi@uslcentro.toscana.it

N. Persiani et al. (eds.), *Challenges of Healthcare Systems in the Era of COVID-19*, Contributions to Management Science, https://doi.org/10.1007/978-3-031-43114-2_14

1 Introduction

A healthcare system based on a rigid division into care settings and poor integration between health and social services does not provide effective answers to the health demand expressed by the population, especially the elderly, fragile, or multichroic people. It generates disparities between territories in the provision of services. While hospitals are always innovating their procedures, devices, and technologies, especially in high-tech intensive settings (Barchielli et al. 2021), primary and community care have always been left aside. As Porter underlines (Porter et al. 2013), this pivotal aspect of healthcare has a history of undervaluation, doesn't matter which national healthcare system is considered. When thinking about its importance, at least three factors qualify it as the backbone of healthcare: (i) it orients people towards the multitude of available services, (ii) it deals with the concept of illness, chronicity, multiplicity of needs, (iii) it bases itself in the community, to which it transfers self-management techniques, empowering the people who express those needs (Shi, 2012).

The World Health Organization (WHO, 2020) qualifies people not merely as "patients" but as service co-creators, making them part of a system that through the exchange and circulation of competences and experiences (Vargo and Lusch 2004) makes the healthcare system more valuable for them while making it such for the community at large, innovating it to the point of making this evolution a non-negotiable goal (Berry 2019). The system has to provide an integrated care which represents the projection into reality of a system that transformed itself to be integrated, multidisciplinary, and person-centered supplier of services (Fisk et al. 2020). All the upsurging transformations and evolutions through which healthcare systems around the world were undergoing were abruptly stopped by the pandemic outbreak of Covid-19. As Zakoij et al. (Zakoji and Sundararaman, 2021) pointed out, the service disarray was tempered in those countries where a decentralization of healthcare provision was in place and the patient centeredness was an inspiring organizational principle.

Italy was one of the first countries that experienced the explosion of COVID-19 cases. The case here presented is the one of Tuscany, one of its twenty Regions. From 2018, Tuscany started a transition towards the direction of operationaldecentralization or the strengthening of the community care with the aim of bringing the healthcare system closer to the population (Regional Decree n.597/2018, Family and Community Nurse institution).

If the pandemic on the one hand diverted the attention from the ongoing organizational process, on the other hand created in the decision-makers the urge for reinforcing what was already in place and moving towards in the same direction. The outbreak occurred when one of the three Local Health Authorities (LHA) in Tuscany was experimenting the organizational model of the Family and Community Nurse (FNC) from 2018. The FNC was designed to implement a "personalized local care" while representing a health resource for people in the geographical portion of the territory assigned (about 3500). The closeness to the community was the key that allowed the FNC a deep knowledge of its health and epidemiologic profile and a privileged point of view from where the identification of health needs–even not yet expressed- was possible. The value of the service the FNC provided and still does, lies in its continuity through time and different healthcare settings, the first of which is the patient's house. Benefiting from this experience, the massive confusion and emergency generated by the Covid-19 outbreak was community care oriented and handled from the very beginning with the creation of the Rapid Hospital-Community intervention group (GIROT, Gruppo di Intervento Rapido Ospedale-Territorio), formed by a FNC and a physician. Its first purpose was to prevent the outpouring of nursing homes' patients in hospital emergency rooms and in general to avert the race to the hospital, providing homebased care instead. GIROT's work has avoided many hospitalizations and has made the emergency rooms less congested, because the team reached the patients inside their homes, with the support of basic point-of-care treatment (POCT) like saturators and portable ultrasound machines. GIROT complemented the Italian Government's emergency solutions to avoid hospitalization, i.e., the establishment of the Special Continuity Care Units (USCA, Unità Speciali di Continuità Assistenziale), instituted to support General Practitioners and Primary Care Pediatricians in preventing their COVID-19 infected patients from being hospitalized. This experience provided evidence of the importance of a community-based healthcare organization and has reinvigorated the will to proceed towards its strengthening. In fact, this innovation has been maintained and has become an integral part of the wider territorial reorganization which will be outlined below. The entire system had to be redesigned: extensive and pervasive reforms must be undertaken when primary or community care must be strengthened (Peiris et al. 2011), otherwise, an innovation is unlikely to happen in practice if system robustness is not addressed. As it has been pointed out (Harvey et al. 2020), systems also need the infrastructure to deliver the care people need in a community-based way.

In this paper, we will outline the reorganization of the Community care model in Tuscany, based on the evidence collected through the pandemic that oriented the change towards an "evolving needs and solutions" approach, and its compliance with the Next Generation European Union Plan (NGEU). Furthermore, we will provide evidence of how this reorganization led to actual best practices. In fact, the pandemic-tested solutions became part of the Regional Law (Regional Decree n. 257, adopted during the year 2022), contributing to the management of the so-called "new normality". Particularly, we will focus on the novel "Tuscan health, social and territorial model" which has treasured the pandemic experience and has harmonized apparently irreconcilable solutions like GIROT and USCA. The latter is now fully functioning as UCA (Unità di Continuità Assistenziale), a care continuity unit, with the intention of not losing what has been learned during the last three years and capitalizing on the experiences that have returned the best outcomes.

2 The Community Care Model Within The NRRP

Next Generation EU is a European one-time program (Fuest, 2021) created to financially support the member states of the Union to help them recover from the adverse effects that the pandemic caused in their economies and to foster advancement in fields like technological innovation, sustainability, etc. Italy is one of the main beneficiaries of the program, which it will follow through the National Recovery and Resilience Plan (NRRP, or PNRR: Piano Nazionale di Ripresa e Resilienza). The NRRP is addressing matters such as digitalization, ecologic transition, healthcare (Mission 6), etc. The latter has to be organized in a way that ensures equal access to care, which is currently lacking especially due to the lack of continuity and integration among healthcare settings, i.e., hospital care and community care (Filippini and Vinceti, 2021). More precisely, the NRRP indicates the following as major issues to address: (i) territorial disparities in the provision of prevention and assistance services, (ii) a divide among hospitals, communities, and social services, (iii) inefficiencies in the provision of social benefits, (iv) insufficient exploitation of technological solutions in healthcare processes. The Ministerial Decree 77/2022 is the Italian law that must implement a substantial part of Mission 6 of the NRRP, that is the reform and reorganization of the territorial health and social care. It has adopted the models and standards for the development of community care in the National Health Service. This means that every Region has obligations to achieve in terms of outcome. This is probably the biggest reform of the Italian NHS since its establishment in 1978.

3 The Community Care 2.0 Project in Tuscany

Here we outline the characteristics of the Tuscan reorganization according to NRRP's Mission 6, "Community Care 2.0", or home delivery strategy. The reorganization project has two components: Progressive Patient Care (PCC) and Proximity Networks (PN).

Progressive Patient Care (PPC) was first defined as the organization of the components of the healthcare system (e.g., hospitals, staff, community care, etc.) around the patient's needs (Abdellah and Strachan, 1959), focused on the promotion of health and on the prevention of illness, directed to the population, that is divided into homogeneous groups based on their "degree of illness and dependency (Raven, 1962). PPC is responding to the different identified degrees in a proactive way. Instead of waiting for the need to show, the healthcare system tries to identify it, better if *in nuce*, in the community. A recent systematic review (Colamesta et al. 2018) shows how the healthcare system that have undergone a PPC reorganization attest "an increase in level of satisfaction and nursing care, a reduction in average length of stay, costs and tensions between nurses and an improvement in nurse-physician communication". Proximity Networks (PN) describe a widespread healthcare system organization presence on the territory, where the General Practitioner (GP) holds the

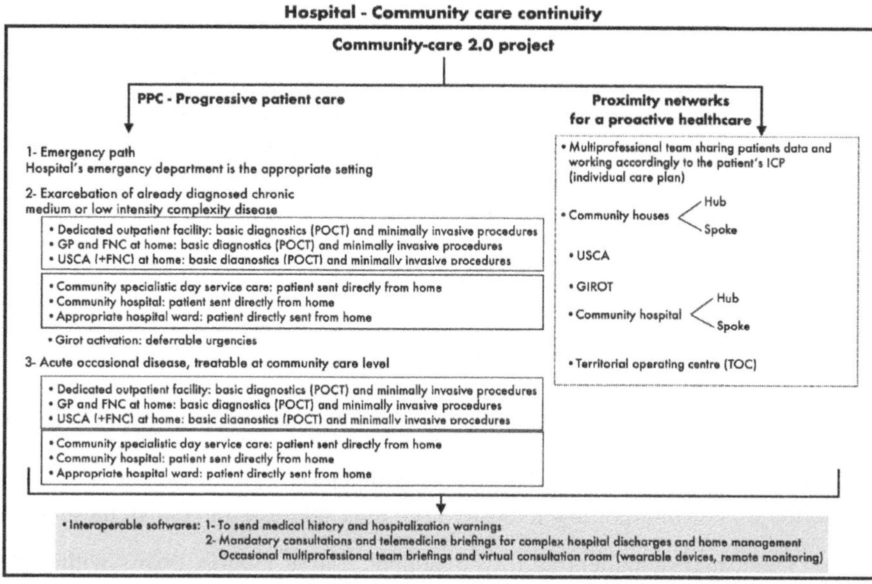

Fig. 1 Community care 2.0

charge of the assisted person, who can be reached (i) in the "first place of care" (i.e., the patient's home) also through technological solutions like telemedicine, (ii) and in intermediate settings based in the community, such as the "Community Houses" (Case della Comunità) and Community Hospitals (Ospedali di Comunità). In Fig. 1, a reorganization scheme is depicted.

This is an action-oriented approach that was forced in its conceptualization by the pandemic and by the NRRP. Whereas the latter both Mission 6 ("Health", whose aim is to digitalize the healthcare system in order to ensure equal access to care) and some components of Mission 5 ("Inclusion and Cohesion", whose aim is to facilitate labor market participation and foster social inclusion) are addressed: (i) Mission 5, part 2: Social infrastructures and Third Sector (a group of private entities that act in different areas, from assistance to people with disabilities to the protection of the environment, from health and social care services to cultural animation): strengthen the role of local social services as a tool of resilience, aiming at the definition and implementation of personalized models for the care of families, minors, adolescents, the elderly and people with disabilities, (ii) Mission 5, part 3: Social measures to be undertaken to foster community cohesion: strengthening of the national strategy for "internal areas", those significantly distant from the centers that offer essential services (education, health and mobility) and rich in important environmental and cultural resources. The quality levels of healthcare must be enhanced in these areas, by strengthening the presence of the community-based organized NHS, to mitigate disparities in opportunities for access to services. (iii) Mission 6, part 1: Proximity networks, infrastructure, and telemedicine for Community Care. This element addresses the need to align healthcare services to the population's needs, also in view of the criticalities that emerged during the pandemic period, as well as the development of telemedicine solutions in support of home care. (iv) Mission 6, part 4: NHS innovation, research, and digitization. Public health that can be effective must value the investments made in the "health system" in the form of dedicated human, structural, instrumental, and digital resources.

The PPC approach, as mentioned before, is primarily the grouping of people based on their medical and nursing needs. For this reason, the system must respond in the appropriate way to be sustainable and maximally effective: three response levels are foreseen in the reorganization.

- First level: The emergency is an inescapable element, hence the possibility of responding with an emergency response must be always kept. The hospital and the Emergency Department (ED) are the appropriate settings in which to provide the necessary assistance.
- Second level: The exacerbation of already diagnosed chronic conditions, which determines a medium or low intensity need to be addressed in one of these ways:

  (i) Dedicated outpatient facility treatment, where POCTs (visits with ultrasound, spirometer, saturator, ultrasound, Holter ECG, and pressor) are available and meant to diagnose the entity of the exacerbation to be addressed and treated without referring to the ED. POCTs increase the likelihood of an immediate treatment, hence a quicker resolution of the problem by cutting the hospital waiting times.

  (ii) GP and FNC at patient's home: people will be assessed and assisted at home, as the first place of care. The patient will receive a multidisciplinary assistance and care. The FCN model provides for the existence of a list of specialists (in mechanical ventilation, pressure ulcers, etc.) that can be activated to the need by the FNC whenever it is to solve a complex need of which he has no experience. The reference specialists work in the hospital and provide time slots to assist the patient at home.

  (iii) USCA, with FNC, at home: the Special Continuity Care Units (USCA, Unità Speciali di Continuità Assistenziale), were instituted in March 2020 by the Italian Government to support General Practitioners and Primary Care Paediatricians in preventing their COVID-19 infected patients from being hospitalized and to "triage" the Covid-19 cases hospitalizing exclusively severe cases. The proximity to the population they embodied, and the competence developed in recognizing, managing, and treating Covid-19 made the NHS decide to keep this tool and integrate it into the system, as it is still not possible to know when we will be able to control the virus, since too little information is yet available to hypothesize the natural history of the disease. It is preferable to maintain the competence the system developed.

  (iv) Deferrable urgencies: GIROT activation. The GIROT model is based on a chronic disease management care delivery model that meets the patient outside the hospital, before the pathologies worsen by stopping the escalation of disease exacerbation, thus ensuring adequate and differentiated interventions fit for the level of risk. It provides high-intensity care at home in chronic patients with the availability of POCTs as multi-wave ultrasound, ECG with traced teletransmission, blood gas analyzer, and the possibility of infusing hospital drugs and perform simple invasive maneuvers as well as blood transfusions.

- Third level: The occurrence of an occasional disease that can be addressed at Community Care level in the following settings:
  (i) Dedicated outpatient facility, GP and FNC at home, USCA (with FNC) at home as foreseen for the previous scenario
  (ii) Community specialistic day service care, for the targeted management of diseases such as diabetes, heart failure etc.
  (iii) Community Hospital: this is an intermediate care setting (Melis et al. 2004) that provides healthcare interventions to people that are not acute enough to be sent to the acute care but at the same moment they cannot be home as the care they are provided there is not enough to solve their problems or address their needs. The GPs oversee their patients, as they have a thorough knowledge of their health situation.

The Proximity Networks are built with the aim to realize a proactive healthcare, as opposed to the "waiting healthcare" embodied by hospital. There are six components to it: USCA, GIROT, Community hospital, of which we have previously spoken, and three more that are illustrated below:

(i) Multi-professional teams sharing patient's data and working accordingly to the patient's individual care plans: the customization of care to be provided is becoming more and more important for two main reasons i.e., the necessity of giving people exactly what they need while exploiting at best the healthcare system's resources, using them when are required and not offered to everyone.
(ii) Community houses (hub and spoke): they can be defined as strategic points of promotion of primary health care, according to a model of global management and bio-psychosocial approach: through community healthcare teams made of physicians and FNC or community care nurses they address population's need. Tuscany will set up eighty Community houses and will communicate to the residents that those facilities represent the first place to visit or to refer to in case of need. GPs, Pediatricians, nurses, and FNC will be based in the Community houses that will be the first diagnostic stage as POCTs will be available.
(iii) TOC, Territorial operating center: it is the pivotal element of the community care 2.0 organization as it coordinates all the subjects that take part in the provision of care to the patient. It coordinates and monitors the patient's transitions through different settings, always ensuring a comprehensive care.

The Community Care 2.0 cannot happen if the different software is in use if they do not evolve towards a logic of interoperability: the presented architecture primarily needs to share information and access it whenever needed. Digital solution will provide virtual rooms in which multidisciplinary teams and healthcare operators in general will meet for mandatory briefings regarding complex hospital discharges and will also be the place to visit when consulting patient's vitals remotely (downloading of data from wearable devices, remote monitoring in complex chronic conditions). Teleconsultation and telemedicine were powerfully boosted during the pandemic as people were subjected to long lockdowns (Filippini and Vinceti, 2021).

4 The Peculiarities of the USL Toscana Centro's Community Care Model

The house is the Community Care's place of choice. The patients who benefit from it are young and old, precisely because "the patient" in a figurative sense is the family and the community at large. A large share of patients is over-65, as it is reported in "Passi d'Argento" (Silver steps), a national epidemiological surveillance system which monitors the health status of the 65-year-old and over population. The system tells us that 25.8% of the over-65's population resides in peripheral areas, which are more structurally vulnerable as they do not offer the vast range of healthcare services that are available in the cities. The sick, in the elderly Tuscan population, represent 84% of the total and 13% of them are not self-sufficient (PASSI, 2021). In this epidemiological context, the NRRP and the Tuscan NHS recognize and plan to address the imperative need to develop homebased care and expand the offer of services by bringing home the specific professionalism of healthcare operators who normally work in the different NHS facilities. In Fig. 2, the project of the homecare-based team is depicted. All the healthcare operators that can take part in the care of the patient have the primary aim of addressing the needs expressed or assessed and improve the patient's quality of life.

In Fig. 2 the home-as-primary-place-of-care approach is depicted. The patients, the families, and the communities, primarily refer to the FNC assigned to their area of residence, which is at the center of the network. FCNs and all the other healthcare professionals will work together as a team in all the settings outlined above, bringing their specific competence. The rationale behind this new organization has to do with the need to make the NHS more flexible, and above all more resilient to the external events. The pandemic was a clear reminder of the limits of the current organization that was found to be too rigid, hence easily prone to paralysis. The FNC has a set list of healthcare professionals that work in the area's healthcare facilities which allocate specific working time slots to provide advice to the FNCs. When the FNC needs a specialist's advice or needs another set of professional skills to bring to patient's home, he or she activates the network with a request call and makes an appointment with the required professional. This is the way in which people's needs are met without bringing them to the hospital. They no longer need to build themselves a path made of multiple settings' visits, the FNC will. And, doing so, will keep people away from the hospitals.

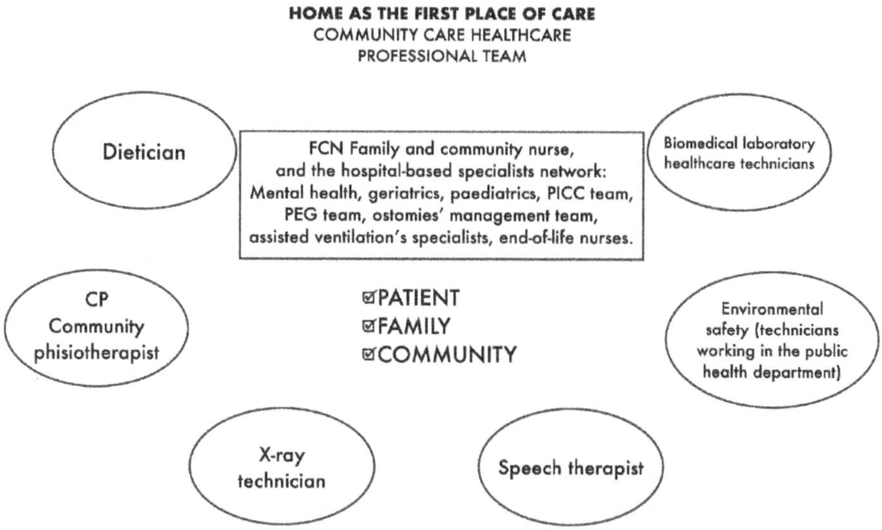

Fig. 2 The multi-professional team can benefit from specific competences, all available for home care

The experiences of the FCN and the GIROT have been the proof that a flexible and oriented way of working to meet people outside the hospital is the most effective solution, even if in extremely difficult times. The FNC model provides that the nurse has a network of expert colleagues who can call when needed to meet the specific needs of the assisted patients. The Community Care 2.0 model wants to expand this logic, bringing other health professionals close to the population. These professionals are:

(i) The dietician: A good nutritional status and good nutritional habits are the basis for a good state of health and for a prompt recovery from a period of illness. The formulation of an appropriate and safe dietary-nutritional care path is a specific competence of the dietician: the Community Care 2.0 aims at delivering this competence with continuity, through planned home meetings, in the social and healthcare structures (i.e., from the hospital to the Community houses, etc.). This proximity can also be "digital": the dietician can carry out tele-monitoring consultancies as well. During the meetings, patient's and caregivers' self-awareness, self-control, self-management, and self-efficacy are enhanced.

(ii) The physiotherapist: The importance of the physiotherapy treatments is well known in addressing acute and chronic impairments, and literature affirms the importance of the Physiotherapist within the multidisciplinary team in the various areas of primary care (McColl et al., 2009). As Fritz et al. (2012) report, the timely treatment of the patient "is associated with a reduced number of requests for advanced imaging, additional specialist visits, surgical interventions, with a general reduction in health costs". In the context of chronic and degenerative diseases, the physiotherapy treatment is crucial to reduce disabling effects. The Community Physiotherapist model aims to ensure adequate and differentiated interventions according to the specific needs expressed by patients and pursues the principles of prevention, education, and health promotion.

(iii) The X-ray technician: Home Radiology refers to the radiological examinations performed at the patient's home, Nursing homes or intermediate care facilities. This solution is used when it is burdensome to carry out the examination at the hospital, due to the patient's condition. Moreover, it reduces the discomfort of elderly, frail people, and people with disabilities.

(iv) The speech therapist: This healthcare professional finds their place in the community professionals' network as the performer of important tasks, like supporting the Family Pediatrician in the detection of signs and early predictive indices disorders that a child might show, in the educational interventions for the prevention of socio-relational discomfort, in the treatment of dysphagic patients, etc. Having this know-how at the patient's home allows to reduce complications such as malnutrition, dehydration, and respiratory infections and the planning of follow-ups promotes the wellbeing of patients and their families.

(v) The environmental safety technicians: Their contribution has been and will continue to be particularly important, especially for what the activities of contact tracing and healthcare surveillance are concerned.

(vi) The biomedical laboratory technicians: These healthcare professionals implement a decentralized diagnosis process with the use of POCTs, which is also particularly relevant in follow-up visits.

5 Discussion and Conclusions

Scarce prior research is present on emergency reorganization of an entire national healthcare system during a global pandemic, hence building new evidence through a lesson-learnt-sharing process is crucial. The experience of USLTC and Tuscany Region at large, are indicative of how the community care organizations and the primary care are nothing less than pivotal for the general resilience of the healthcare system and for the increase of access equity and health security (Singh and Topp, 2021). In this paper, we outlined the case of the reorganization of the Community care model in Tuscany, and in the USLTC in particular. The organizational models and the solutions provided were considered to be best practices, hence transformed into a regional standard by force of the Regional Decree 257, adopted in 2022, in compliance with the National Decree 77 previously mentioned. The USCA introduced at national level during the pandemic turned into UCA: Unità di Continuità Assistenziale, or Continuity Care Unit, dropping the wording "S" as "Special", indicating the attribution of something episodic to something belonging to a system. UCA qualifies as a mobile team that manages individuals or communities who are in particularly complex clinical conditions, and which involve a proven operational difficulty. Albeit apparently redundant, the GIROT introduced at regional level is also a part of the community care Tuscan system: it provides complex services for chronic and fragile patients at home, mainly featuring FNCs and geriatricians, due to the patients' cases followed. The overall strengthening process of the territorial system governance benefited greatly from the experience of the USLTC.

The limits of the proposed model reside in the fact that it is a specific territorial experience, which is unlikely to capture the nuances of the whole healthcare system or the complexity of its needs in an adequate manner. Different territories, especially peripheral and less dense in population may need to adapt it, if not operationally change it. The elements that support the possible scalability of the model or of this model's components have their reasons d'être in the evidence that proves that primary care and community care models foster prevention and support disease self-management, and not only the quality of care improves, but it improves along with the "cost and the efficiency of care" (Harvey et al. 2020). When replicated-this model or parts of it- is able to increase the level of resilience of the health system as follows: (i) supporting the fight against Covid-19 and helping in facing new potential threats making the healthcare system more flexible and resilient avoiding hospitalizations (ii) realizing substantial money savings from the avoided hospitalization and long term positive economic system effects by boosting education and prevention, (iii) providing personalized clinical offer through a system of specialist called upon need, (iv) increasing healthcare and political accountability. When talking about patient/family/community centeredness, the multidisciplinary redesign of the healthcare team has to be undergone (Sangiorgi et al. 2019) to be positive that the availability side (NHS) is compliant with the demand side that expresses more and more complex needs. The core of the innovations contained in the reorganization is the promotion of de-hospitalization as the guiding principle of all health policy lines included in the NRRP, national and regional health regulations, and scientific evidence. Transferring the diagnostic tools and the competences of the different healthcare professionals rather than the patient, can be one of the answers to the need to provide increasingly flexible, innovative, and patient-friendly healthcare service and to use the NHS resources more wisely.

Acknowledgements The Authors would like to thank Marco Pantini for his graphical contribution to the paper.

References

Abdellah FG, Strachan EJ (1959) Progressive patient care. Am J Nurs JSTOR, 649–655

Barchielli C et al (2021) Nurses and the acceptance of innovations in technology-intensive contexts: the need for tailored management strategies. BMC Health Serv Res 21(1):1–11. Springer

Berry LL (2019) Service innovation is urgent in healthcare. AMS Rev 9(1–2):78–92. Springer

Colamesta V et al (2018) Intermediate care units in progressive patient care model: a systematic literature review. Prex SpA
Filippini T, Vinceti SR (2021) Italian national recovery and resilience plan: a healthcare renaissance after the COVID-19 crisis?
Fisk RP et al (2020) Elevating the human experience (HX) through service research collaborations: introducing ServCollab. J Serv Manag. Emerald Publishing Limited
Fritz N et al (2012) Physiotherapy in huntington's disease: guidance for practice. Hygeia 47(1):15–22
Fuest C (2021) The NGEU economic recovery fund. In: CESifo forum. München: ifo Institut-Leibniz-Institut für Wirtschaftsforschung an der …, pp 3–8
Harvey JB et al (2020) Understanding how health systems facilitate primary care redesign. Health Serv Res 55:1144–1154. Wiley Online Library
McColl MA et al (2009) Models for integrating rehabilitation and primary care: a scoping study. Arch Phys Med Rehabil 90(9):1523–1531. Elsevier
Melis RJF et al (2004) What is intermediate care?. Bmj, 360–361. British Medical Journal Publishing Group
PASSI GTN (2021) PASSI e PASSI d'Argento e la pandemia COVID-19. Versione del 9
Peiris CL, Taylor NF, Shields N (2011) Extra physical therapy reduces patient length of stay and improves functional outcomes and quality of life in people with acute or subacute conditions: a systematic review. Arch Phys Med Rehabil 92(9), 1490–1500. Elsevier Inc. https://doi.org/10.1016/j.apmr.2011.04.005
Porter ME, Pabo EA, Lee TH (2013) Redesigning primary care: a strategic vision to improve value by organizing around patients' needs. Health Aff 32(3):516–525
Raven RW (1962) Progressive patient care. Br Med J. 1(5270):43. BMJ Publishing Group
Sangiorgi D et al (2019) A human-centred multidisciplinary, and transformative approach to service science: a service design perspective. In: Handbook of service science, Volume II. Springer, pp 147–181
Shi L (2012) The impact of primary care: a focused review. Scientifica. Hindawi
Singh A, Topp SM (2021) The significance of primary health care for building back better: lessons from COVID-19. WHO South-East Asia J Public Health 10(3):3. Medknow Publications
Vargo SL, Lusch RF (2004) Evolving to a new dominant logic for marketing. J Mark 68(1):1–17. Sage Publications Sage CA, Los Angeles, CA
WHO (2020) WHO global strategy on health, environment and climate change: the transformation needed to improve lives and wellbeing sustainably through healthy environments. World Health Organization
Zakoji M, Sundararaman T (2021) Emerging good practices and lessons learnt to maintain essential health services during the COVID-19 pandemic. WHO South-East Asia J Public Health 10(3):26. Medknow Publications

Using Telemedicine in Organizing Health Emergency. An Analysis of Country-Based Experiences During the COVID-19

Alberto Romolini, Eleonora Veglianti, and Yaya Li

Abstract **Purpose**: Since Coronavirus 2019 (COVID-19) was first announced in December 2019, a global emergency has impacted the society and the economy of different countries with the largest global recession in eight decades. Moreover, the health emergency has established the need for social distancing to protect patients and medical practitioners from the infection. In this context, telemedicine represents a powerful instrument for adopting new initiative for the treatment of patients. Indeed, telemedicine permits fast diagnosis and medical services using digital instruments and preserving the social distance in a health emergency period. For this reason, telemedicine was adopted during COVID-19 emergency in different countries using telecommunication technology, either asynchronously or synchronously and via audio–video systems. Consequently, the objective of this paper is to investigate the use of telemedicine during COVID-19 emergency analyzing the experience of different countries. **Design/methodology/approach**: The research provides a review of the recent studies and experiences on this topic summarizing the most common applications of telemedicine for the management of public health emergencies. **Research implications and limitations**: The research provides a picture about the different approaches in the use of telemedicine applied during the COVID-19 emergency. The comparative analysis represents a fundamental approach for health managers for developing telemedicine for facing the current and new health emergencies. This research has also the limitation to consider the European and the Chinese experiences; in the future, this analysis could be enlarged considering other countries such as the USA, Japan, etc. **Originality**: This research has an exploratory

A. Romolini (✉)
Faculty of Economics, International Telematic University UNINETTUNO, Corso Vittorio Emanuele II, 39, 00186 Rome, Italy
e-mail: a.romolini@uninettunouniversity.net

E. Veglianti
FGES University Catholique of Lille, 60 BD Vauban, 59800 Lille, France
e-mail: eleonora.veglianti@univ-catholille.fr

Y. Li
School of Finance and Economics, Jiangsu University, Jiangsu 212003, PR China
e-mail: yizhi19881107@126.com

N. Persiani et al. (eds.), *Challenges of Healthcare Systems in the Era of COVID-19*, Contributions to Management Science, https://doi.org/10.1007/978-3-031-43114-2_15

nature as, to the best of our knowledge, no previous studies focused on comparing telemedicine with this approach. Our aim is to produce original research that produces new knowledge through observations and analysis.

Keywords Telemedicine · Emergency · COVID-19 · Country-based

JEL Classifications Codes O1 · O2 · O3

1 Introduction

The COVID-19 emergency opens new discussions and questions regarding the role of telemedicine in several countries. Thus, digitalization in healthcare was progressing slowly (Steinhauser et al. 2020), COVID-19 emergency results as an accelerator for telemedicine application in many countries in the fight against the pandemic (Steinhauser 2021).

More specifically, in both developed and less economically developed countries, the healthcare system is facing important challenges in terms of accessibility, quality, and cost-effectiveness. In such scenario, technologies in general, and Information and Communication Technology (ICT) in particular, are creating new settings for healthcare services as they are often perceived as a possibility to improve the quality of and access to care while containing cost (Fichman et al 2011). In other words, ICT is providing a more appropriate and equal access to various services in the healthcare field such as prevention, and diagnosis as well as in terms of more adequate therapies (Palozzi et al., 2017; Rossignoli et al., 2014).

Considering this transformation in the healthcare system due to the digital sphere and due to the widespread of the COVID-19 pandemic, recently, numerous governments and countries in the world are rethinking the healthcare organizations (Hasoon et al. 2022). This means that, at the institutional and political level, the reconfiguration of the services delivered in the healthcare is an issue of growing importance to better manage the pandemic disastrous emergency.

Hence, the usage of technological solutions to enhance the access and the quality of healthcare services is capturing the attention of increasing numbers of policymakers to improve the public health (Saigí-Rubió et al. 2022). For example, to reach a more efficient healthcare service portfolio, the World Health Organization (WHO) highlights the need to adopt new business models that should consider the role of technological tools as well as people participation (WHO 2021). Indeed, the Italian Ministry of Health (Italian Ministry of Health 2012) considered from about ten years the telemedicine as one of the most relevant elements for the reorganization of health services. This implies higher attention to the single citizen and facilitates the accessibility to a bunch of services such as cardiological disease prevention.

Telemedicine represents the provision of healthcare at a distance in an accessible way, cost-effective medical system, providing high-quality care and reducing overall morbidity and mortality (Armaignac et al. 2018). In the pandemic situation, many countries were not prepared to face a lockdown, especially in managing chronic diseases. A larger number of healthcare entities worldwide suffered in delivering their services due to the weak availability and spread of large-scale telemedicine solutions which have represented a crucial element during the pandemic event with an increase of applications (Mouratidis and Papagiannakis 2021; Suran 2022).

The COVID-19 could be analyzed as an important test that should be a driver to foster a new approach in the healthcare in future. Thus, the healthcare should fit with the technological transformation and with new relationship among patients and professionals. It is argued that due to the COVID-19 telemedicine has become an effective and powerful feature in the public health structure as it responds to the need of improving the overall care in an emergency. Moreover, telemedicine represents a powerful solution for those people affected by chronic conditions and at the same time by the COVID-19 disease (Casariego-Vales et al. 2021).

Therefore, this paper wants to shed a light on the telemedicine applications during the COVID-19 emergency analyzing the experience of different countries. As discussed above, technological innovation has a predominant role also in terms of cost-effectiveness. In fact, telemedicine applications can have a significant influence on the costs in the long-term perspective.

The rest of the paper is structured as follows. First, the theoretical background of the study is presented along with a review of relevant literature. Next, the research methodology is detailed. Finally, we provide a summary of the key findings as well as the discussion and conclusion section.

2 Literature Review

Telemedicine represents the way of delivering healthcare services remotely using ICT tools like telephone, video calls, chatbots, and e-portals. The World Health Organization defines telemedicine as the delivery of healthcare services where distance is a critical factor by using ICT (WHO 1997).

Also, if telemedicine has ancient origins, this practice was increasing especially in the last 2–3 decades with the improvement of ICT applications. Considering its role, we can observe that telemedicine could be very helpful in case of natural disasters and emergencies or in remote locations with inaccessible ways of transportation. In this sense, one of the beneficiaries of telemedicine applications could be people living in remote locations or rural areas of developing countries (Alelyani et al. 2021).

For its power of supporting people without a physical presence, telemedicine has become fundamental in healthcare service during COVID-19, especially for patients living a lockdown conditions. In this period telemedicine was used by different types of patients especially by families of pediatric patients who wants to take their children far from hospitals. Ortega et al. (2020) show that the use of telemedicine in primary pediatric care increased drastically during the lock-time period. In this sense, the pandemic seems an opportunity to improve telemedicine practices considering that, after the emergency, it could represent a normal approach in healthcare services creating a real blended health system (Bashshur et al. 2020). Moreover, the technological improvement realized during the emergency could help to disseminate telemedicine also in rural and remote areas.

Previous studies have discussed some benefits of telemedicine considering different factors like the opportunity for patients to reduce travel costs and save time and, in a broader view, the possibility to reduce the connected environmental pollution (Grossman et al. 2020). However, there is again a necessity to better understand the success factors, the future opportunities, and barriers regarding the full implementation of this practice in a global perspective (Kim and Lee 2014).

Telemedicine has in fact some challenges that healthcare managers need to consider (Degerli and Ozkan-Yildirim 2021). The first is the relationship between patient and doctor. In the first-time of adoption, users give more confidence to the in-person visit with a doctor rather than a telemedicine interaction. In this case, telemedicine should augment the in-person visit confidence and not replace it. We can also observe some possible resistance to the use of technology linked to perceived risks, age of users, and social influence. The policy seems to play a fundamental role for removing the principal barriers to telemedicine implementation (Scott Kruse et al. 2018).

The second challenge is linked to the capability of users in using technology interfaces. Telemedicine portals need to be user friendly designed and ensure high levels of data privacy protection. For these reasons, it's crucial to ensure equity in the access and use of internet and ICT and to build an efficient digital infrastructure with high standards and training for doctors and nurses (Mahajan et al. 2020, Moazzami et al. 2020).

For instance, Alelyani et al. (2021) have analyzed the IT instruments for telemedicine; considering the previous studies in this field they discovered a classification of IT instruments in artificial intelligence, human–computer interaction, and security. The combination of artificial intelligence with virtual reality could improve the diagnosis accuracy, give more efficiency to operational costs, and increase the interaction between patient and doctor (Rutledge and Wood, 2020). At the same time, applications as chatbots could allow patients to improve the benefits of telemedicine combined with video calls.

3 Methodology

The present research follows a qualitative approach comparing two different case studies related to diverse international areas such as Europe (EU) and China. This approach was selected to allow the exploration and understanding of a complex issue such as telemedicine in a global pandemic emergency. In this way, the paper reveals complexity by its richness and holism (Miles et al. 2014). This method provides an in-depth analysis of the social and behavioral problems in question. The study considers a broad level of analysis, both providing insights on the theoretical and empirical side (Bryman and Bell 2011).

The rationale for the selection of the case study is based on the aim to compare two different contexts engaged in the pandemic response using telemedicine applications. The EU represents an area where telemedicine tools are highly debated in the literature (Saigí-Rubió et al. 2022) and managed in many countries from many years. From this point of view, the EU could be interpreted as a best practice in this field. At the same time, China represents an emerging country where the adoption of IT technology is very fast and where the rural areas could benefit from the introduction of this type of healthcare services.

The purpose is to analyze in-depth the information within a specific context; as Yin (1984: 23) suggested, the use of a qualitative research method is "*an empirical inquiry that investigates a contemporary phenomenon within its real-life context; when the boundaries between phenomenon and context are not clearly evident; and in which multiple sources of evidence are used*".

To closely study data, we decided to conduct an analysis comparing Europe and China, based on the literature review of reference and secondary information. Moreover, the authors can read the scientific literature in several languages such as Chinese as well as they can share their personal experiences in those contexts. Therefore, in addition to the relevant literature, to better understand the contexts under investigation several sources of information were collected. Given the contexts and the uniqueness of the COVID-19 pandemic, secondary data and tacit knowledge of the authors represent the main sources of this study.

The information collection was repeated several times to reach a clearer framework that leads from a broader to a more detailed level of analysis. The analysis considered both at the theoretical and empirical spheres of the phenomenon studied (Bryman and Bell 2011). Following the relevant literature and the aim of this paper, we adopt a descriptive approach to analyze the phenomenon in a narrative form (McDonough and McDonough 1997). The latter provides an examination of data conducted within the context of its use that is within the situation in which the activity takes place (Eriksson and Kovalainen 2008).

4 Emerging Results in the EU

During the pandemic disease, telemedicine has seen a lot of applications in different countries within the EU and its application increased drastically. This phenomenon was connected to the necessity of reducing physical and human interaction (Ortega et al. 2020), especially between patients and doctors. In this sense, telemedicine has given the opportunity to reduce the level of contact among people and prevent the COVID-19 diffusion and contamination (Baudier et al. 2021; Rockwell and Gilroy 2020). Finally, telemedicine has the goal to continue providing care to patients with a remote medical support also if they are infected by COVID-19 or not.

However, the pandemic emergency was not the first-time adoption of this practice in this geographic area. Indeed, telemedicine was applied outside of emergency situations since more than 20 years: for example, in the year 2000, the North Atlantic

Treaty Alliance (NATO) (a military organization including most part of the European countries) developed a Multinational Telemedicine System for military members (Doarn et al. 2018). Other international experiences are instead connected with emergency situations outside the EU territory in developed countries as the hurricanes Harvey and Irma in the USA or some similar disasters in Australia (Smith et al. 2020).

If we consider the situation outside of the emergency, the uptake of telemedicine is generally slow and fragmented with a use of 1% in the USA and Australia (Smith and Gray 2009; Wade et al. 2014). The situation is similar also in Europe. In EU, telemedicine could provide new opportunities for supporting patients with disability problems, financial restraints, or work commitments. In this sense, it could be useful also for general purpose and not only for rural or other areas far from transportation services (Alami et al. 2017).

Moreover, in the last years, a large part of barriers to the telemedicine implementation has been overcame in the EU especially if we consider the reduction in the cost of audio and video devices, the increasing access to the fast internet connection, and the people's confidence with IT tools (Garattini et al. 2017). Despite this situation, the diffusion of telemedicine adoption in Europe in different forms of clinical practice remains again low.

5 First Applications and Emerging Results in China

Following the aim of this paper, we present a broad level of activity to better understand telemedicine in different contexts—especially developed and less developed areas—in facing the COVID-19 health emergency. As stated in the methodological section, the present research has a multifaceted perspective dealing with telemedicine. China is one of the main actors in the COVID-19 case, with Wuhan as the city in which everything started. The choice of studying China is driven by two main reasons.

First, it results in the outbreak of this pandemic and, thus, it is important to have insights on this context to better investigate the role of telemedicine in this unique health situation. Then, the authors have deep knowledge of the context under examination and a direct experience. This aids the translation issues and possible biases, the accessibility to original information and documents in Chinese as well as the personal experience knowledge. The latter is a fundamental feature, especially to study telemedicine services during the pandemic because it has a relevant impact on people's lives. In other words, tacit knowledge of a specific context provides more details and specificities to comprehend the local implications. All these elements help the overall understanding of the health system during this pandemic event in China.

From our analysis, since the 1980s, telemedicine services in China have undergone initial development. In the last decades, driven by the national policy interest in innovative medical services, the development of telemedicine services in China improved, and it has been more widely used in underdeveloped and rural areas.

Given this, China adopted different ways to spread telemedicine. For example, there are one-to-one telemedicine services or one-to-many, many-to-many telemedicine service systems. This creates the possibility to provide this kind of services also to the more distant areas with a top-down approach from the national level, to province, then to city (county), to township, and finally, to village level especially during the COVID-19 pandemic experience (Guan et al. 2020). In such situation, health service activities have gradually formed a B2B telemedicine service model between hospitals, a B2C model in which hospitals directly face the patient, and a B–B–B–C model in which hospitals are third-party platforms associated with patients (Guan et al. 2020).

However, telemedicine was not a relevant topic of interest only during the pandemic. Telemedicine results are crucial even before the COVID-19 crisis, especially among the aging population. For example, as some Chinese authors suggested, in an aging society the execution of technical innovation in which telemedicine is a crucial part is a matter that should be considered in the agenda of scientific research centers, technological companies as well as of the government (Huang et al. 2016). In such scenario, some of the most important services to develop are remote nursing and smart home technologies (Huang et al. 2016). Therefore, as other scholars argued, attention to telemedicine is before the pandemic, and research institutions represent the major cooperative cluster (Gu et al. 2020).

In fact, China experienced another dangerous epidemic situation before the COVID-19 one. Specifically, in 2003, during the SARS diffusion, many provinces in China opened the so-called SARS Telemedicine Consultation System, with experts providing suggestions to face the SARS difficulties. In this case, indeed, experts had remote lectures, or used real-time videos to answer and communicate to the population. (Guan et al. 2020). In other words, through communication technologies, the citizens in China have the chance to be in touch with doctors and health experts to avoid isolation due to the health crisis and to receive care and information to be prepared during the SARS critical situation.

After a while, China had the boom of the COVID-19 pandemic that increased the discussion about telemedicine in response to this unique health case. A few number of state managed applications emerged to better manage this public issue. The reason behind these applications is due to the fact that new innovative tools in telemedicine helped healthcare and disease control and prevention in the Chinese context (Zhu et al. 2020).

As He et al. (2021) suggested four aspects should be considered in China to better answer to the COVID-19 situation: information technology development, medical insurance payment, industry supervision, and direction, as well as relevant policy creation. In China, telemedicine—combining hardware, digital medicine, image capture, and disease diagnosis—operates in the reduction of distance issues attempting to create quality services (Wang et al. 2020).

In other words, the outbreak of COVID-19 highlights that the process of medical resource allocation was more difficult; thus, the country needs alternative managerial approaches to maintain a balanced allocation of resources. In such scenario, telemedicine appears to be a relevant strategy to care about COVID-19 patients (Wang et al. 2020).

Moreover, in the Chinese context, with the outbreak of the new COVID-19 emergency, the government plays a crucial role. In fact, the National Health Commission required the active development of telemedicine services to manage remote consultation, especially, in the case of severe and critical diseases. In addition, telemedicine spreads multidisciplinary expert consultations as well as prevention and treatment guidance. Therefore, the COVID-19 emergency increases the role of telemedicine to efficiently manage the public health in a critical situation. This highlights how diversified telemedicine services should be seen as a supplement to traditional medical services during the COVID-19 crisis management (Guan et al. 2020).

6 A Comparison of Telemedicine Applications During the Pandemic

Although the increasing use of IT in healthcare, telemedicine has been encountered in Europe and China with some challenges for a full application, especially in primary care. The first application problems were connected to the low knowledge of IT from patients, especially for aged ones and people living in rural villages with lower level of education. Nowadays, in the EU these problems seem reduced especially if we consider the recent diffusion of IT instruments in the last years. In this sense, it is important also to guarantee a general access to high-speed internet connections and IT tools as to develop a real equality of access to telemedicine services (Garattini et al. 2021). Moreover, telemedicine will benefit from IT and general educational programs for people with low grades of education especially in low- and middle-income countries.

However, in comparison to China, the EU has not experienced before the pandemic COVID-19 some short period of fast growth in telemedicine connected to health emergencies. The experience about the use of telemedicine in supporting global emergencies could be derived in China from previous pandemic events in this area, as MERS or SARS, that strongly impact the country. However, the diffusion of telemedicine appears in a growing stage in the EU where, starting from a relevant expertise, various countries are realizing new organizational IT solutions.

In addition, the territorial dimension of China, different from Europe in terms of extended rural areas far from the principal communication hubs, represents a peculiar aspect where the usage of telemedicine could represent a way to spread a global healthcare assistance for the population living in this area. Indeed, in China, the attention to telemedicine resulted high as well as the government interest to provide better healthcare services not only during the pandemic but also for offering better healthcare services in all the country. Another feature specific of China is the recent development of several applications that improve the telemedicine field. This is due to the collaboration that private companies have at the institutional level as well as to the possibility to invest strongly in this area.

Another emerging telemedicine challenge in the EU is linked to the security of electronic medical records. Indeed, telemedicine produces and uses a huge amount of electronic data that needs to be protected as to respect the principles of confidentiality and privacy. From this point of view, the situation is different compared to China, where the problems are seen in a different perspective, with a relevant role played by the Chinese government as the general owner of personal data belonging to patients using telemedicine services.

Moreover, a fundamental challenge in applying telemedicine, afflicting the EU, China, and other countries, is linked to the financial effects of this form of service in comparison with the traditional healthcare activities. Indeed, telemedicine could not be able to compensate for the loss of the tariff reimbursed for traditional visits and consultations. It could be a fundamental problem for hospitals and professional operations in primary care services (Garattini et al. 2020) and, more in general, for financing the national healthcare system.

As mentioned before, compared to Europe, China presents more experiences about pandemic situations. It seems somehow more prepared. Moreover, China shows an up-down approach mainly driven by government policies and political decisions that suggest telemedicine has a crucial element in the healthcare system.

7 Conclusion

This paper provides preliminary results on the telemedicine state of the art in different countries during the pandemic disease with a focus on the experiences of the EU countries and China. It highlights that the overall public health institutions in the countries analyzed are interested in the development of telemedicine applications. The latter has a crucial role in providing health services during pandemic and emergency situations.

More in detail, the paper provides examples of common and divergent experiences between the countries studied which are also characterized by different experiences in using telemedicine during healthcare emergencies as China already experimented with critical health diseases in the recent past. However, the paper clarifies that telemedicine could not be useful only in healthcare emergencies as the Covid-19. In general, the more urgent challenges in the telemedicine development appear the education in the use of ICT instruments for aged people and patients with low educational levels especially in emerging countries, the security and protection of personal medical data, the effects on the financial performance on traditional healthcare entities and services.

However, some of the most interesting applications for policymakers belong to the healthcare organization. Implications in terms of public healthcare strategic approaches can be provided, also considering the political decisions in the current and in future situations. More specifically, if policymakers are highly interested in improving patient care quality and cost reduction, the development and implementation of telemedicine represents a way to provide health services, especially for people living in rural areas or for patients with mobility problems. This point outs an urgent necessity for developing healthcare services in several areas of a country, especially in low- and middle-income states. In other words, telemedicine favors health services throughout the territory or in the community that should be widespread at different levels to easily reach each citizen. It also shows the importance of increasing the coordination and the integration of these services to promote the public health in each possible condition.

Therefore, COVID-19 opens a new debate that implies a review of obsolete features in the health sector and it requires a rethinking of many elements such as new organizational models to enhance the overall health services. Thus, given this scenario, in several contexts, telemedicine answers to this important and crucial need. In line with the above, professionals and academics, telemedicine gives the opportunity to explore and embrace new paradigms to continue to question about the achievement of a higher quality patient care services.

This creates relevant implications for further scholarly research alike as well as for practitioners. Future studies should investigate telemedicine in other economies both developed and underdeveloped cases to present additional evidence to support its implementation. Despite the relevance of the topic, the paper fails in developing a theoretical understanding of the telemedicine phenomenon and in generating implications for politicians. However, it can present significant hints and insights for practitioners and academics who want to consider telemedicine in the contexts examined.

References

Alami H, Gagnon MP, Wootton R, Fortin JP, Zanaboni P (2017) Exploring factors associated with the uneven utilization of telemedicine in Norway: a mixed methods study. BMC Med Inform Decis Mak 17(1):180

Alelyani T, Shaikh A, Sulaiman AA, Asiri Y, Alshahrani H, Almakdi S (2021) Research challenges and opportunities towards a holistic view of telemedicine systems: a systematic review. In: Marques G, Kumar Bhoi A, de la Torre Díez I, Garcia-Zapirain B (eds) Enhanced telemedicine and e-Health. Studies in Fuzziness and Soft Computing, vol 410. Springer, Cham. https://doi.org/10.1007/978-3-030-70111-6_1

Armaignac DL, Saxena A, Rubens M, Valle CA, Williams LM, Veledar E., Gidel LT (2018) Impact of telemedicine on mortality, length of stay, and cost among patients in progressive care units: experience from a large healthcare system. Crit Care Med 46(5):728–735

Bashshur R, Doarn CR, Frenk JM, Kvedar JC, Woolliscroft JO (2020) Telemedicine and the COVID-19 pandemic, lessons for the future. Telemed E-Health 26:571–573

Baudier P, Kondrateva G, Ammi C, Chang V, Schiavone F (2021) Patients' perceptions of teleconsultation during COVID-19: a cross-national study. Technol Forecast Soc Chang 163:120510

Bryman A, Bell E (2011) Business research methods. Oxford University Press, Oxford

Casariego-Vales E, Blanco-López R, Rosón-Calvo B, Suárez-Gil R, Santos-Guerra F, Dobao-Feijoo M (2021) On Behalf Of The Telea-Covid Lugo Comanagement Team. Efficacy of telemedicine and telemonitoring in at-home monitoring of patients with COVID-19. J Clin Med 10(13):2893

Degerli M, Ozkan-Yildirim S (2021) Telemedicine in the current new normal: opportunities and barriers. In: Marques G, Kumar Bhoi A, de la Torre Díez I, Garcia-Zapirain B (eds) Enhanced Telemedicine and e-Health. Studies in fuzziness and soft computing, 410. Springer, Cham

Doarn CR, Latifi R, Poropatich RK et al (2018) Development and validation of telemedicine for disaster response: the North Atlantic Treaty Organization multinational system. Telemed E-Health 24:657–668

Eriksson P, Kovalainen A (2008) Qualitative methods in business research. SAGE Beverly Hills, California

Fichman RG, Kohli R, Krishnan R (2011) The role of information systems in healthcare: current research and future trends. Inf Syst Res 22(3):419–428

Garattini L, Baldinella Martini M, Zanetti M (2021) More room for telemedicine after COVID-19: lessons for primary care? Eur J Health Econ 22:183–186

Garattini L, Baldinella Martini M, Zanetti M (2020) Improving primary care in Europe beyond Covid-19: from telemedicine to organizational reforms. Intern Emerg Med 16:255–258

Grossman Z, Chodick G, Reingold SM, Chapnick G, Ashkenazi S (2020) The future of telemedicine visits after COVID-19: perceptions of primary care pediatricians. Isr J Health Policy Res 9

Gu H, Feng Z, Wu D, Yang NC (2020) Research status and trends of telemedicine in china——quantitative analysis based on citespace. J Inf Resour Manag 10(4):119–129. 顾海,奉子岚,吴迪,杨妮超.我国远程医疗研究现状及趋势-基于CiteSpace的文献量化分析[J].信息资源管理学报, 2020, 10(04):119–129

Guan XH, Lan H, Huang ZD, Chen Y, Zhang T, Huang XB, Du YT, Xu XY (2020) Practice and reflection on telemedicine to help prevent and control the novel coronavirus pneumonia epidemic. Pract J Med & Pharm 37(10): 958–960. 管细红,兰昊,黄智德,陈禹,张彤,黄行波,杜耀婷,徐晓英.远程医疗助力新型冠状病毒肺炎疫情防控的实践与思考[J].实用医药杂志,2020,37(10):958–960

Hasoon J, Urits I, Viswanath O, Kaye AD (2022) Pain Management and Telemedicine: A Look at the COVID Experience and Beyond. Health Psychol Res 10(3):38012–38012

He D, Shi Y, Gu YC, Wu H, Sun MM, Lou ZX, Jin CL (2021) The development of Internet diagnosis and treatment in China under the novel coronavirus pneumonia epidemic. Chin Health Resour 24(1):79–84. 何达,石瑛,顾一纯,吴宏,孙明明,楼哲汛,金春林.新型冠状病毒肺炎疫情下我国互联网诊疗的发展[J].中国卫生资源,2021,24(01):79–84

Huang LC, Liu YM, Miao H, Wu FF, Chang LL (2016) Identification of frontier in telemedicine based on gerontechnology innovation. J Intell. 35(2):63–68+138. (黄鲁成,刘玉敏,苗红,吴菲菲,常兰兰.面向老年福祉技术创新的远程医疗领域前沿识别[J].情报杂志,2016,35(02):63–68+138)

Italian Ministry of Health (2012) Telemedicina. Linee di indirizzo nazionali, C_17_pubblicazioni_2129_allegato.pdf (salute.gov.it)

Kim TH, Lee HH (2014) Is telemedicine a worldwide trend? Arch Gynecol Obstet 289:925–926

Mahajan V, Singh T, Azad C (2020) Using telemedicine during the COVID-19 pandemic. Indian Pediatr 57:658–661

McDonough J, McDonough S (1997) Research Methods for English Language Teachers. Arnold, London

Miles MB, Huberman AM, Saldana J (2014) Qualitative data analysis: a methods sourcebook. SAGE Beverly Hills, California

Moazzami B, Razavi-Khorasani N, Dooghaie Moghadam A, Farokhi E, Rezaei N (2020) COVID-19 and telemedicine: immediate action required for maintaining healthcare providers wellbeing. J Clin Virol 126

Mouratidis K, Papagiannakis A. (2021) COVID-19, internet, and mobility: the rise of telework, telehealth, e-learning, and e-shopping. Sustainability Cities and Society, Nov;74, 103182

Ortega G, Rodriguez JA, Maurer LR, Witt EE, Perez N, Reich A, Bates DW, Telemedicine (2020) COVID-19, and disparities: policy implications. Health Policy Technol 9:368–371

Palozzi G, Binci D, Appolloni A (2017) E-health and co-production: Critical drivers for chronic diseases management. Service business model innovation in healthcare and hospital management. Springer, Cham, pp 269–296

Rockwell KL, Gilroy AS (2020) Incorporating telemedicine as part of COVID-19 outbreak response systems. Am J Manag Care 26:147–148

Rossignoli C, Zardini A, Benettollo P (2014) The process of digitalisation in radiology as a lever for organisational change: the case of the academic integrated hospital of Verona, In: Phillips-Wren G, Carlsson S, Respício A, Brézillon P (eds) DSS 2.0 – Supporting decision making with new technologies, vol 261. IOS Press, London, pp 24–35

Rutledge G, Wood JC (2020) Virtual health and artificial intelligence: Using technology to improve healthcare delivery. In: Human-machine shared contexts. Elsevier, pp 169–175

Saigí-Rubió F, Israel Júnior Borges dN, Robles N, Ivanovska K, Katz C, Azzopardi-Muscat N, Ortiz DN (2022) The current status of telemedicine technology use across the world health organization european region: an overview of systematic reviews. J Med Internet Res 24(10):e4087

Scott Kruse C, Karem P, Shifflett K, Vegi L, Ravi K, Brooks M (2018) Evaluating barriers to adopting telemedicine worldwide: a systematic review. J Telemed Telecare 24:4–12

Smith AC, Thomas E, Snoswell CL, Haydon H, Mehrotra A, Clemesen J, Caffery LJ (2020) Telehealth for global emergencies: implications for coronavirus disease 2019 (COVID-19). J Telemed Telecare. 10.1177%2F1357633X20916567

Smith AC, Gray LC (2009) Telemedicine across the ages. Med J Aust 190:15–19

Steinhauser S, Doblinger C, Hüsig S (2020) The relative role of digital complementary assets and regulation in discontinuous telemedicine innovation in European Hospitals. J Manag Inf Syst 37(4):1155–1183

Steinhauser S (2021) COVID-19 as a driver for digital transformation in healthcare. In Glauner P, et al (eds) Digitalization in healthcare, future of business and finance. Springer, https://doi.org/10.1007/978-3-030-65896-0

Suran M (2022) Increased use of medicare telehealth during the pandemic. JAMA 327(4):313

Wade V, Soar J, Gray L (2014) Uptake of telehealth services funded by Medicare in Australia. Aust Health Rev 38:528–532

Wang Y, Li B, Liu L (2020) Telemedicine experience in China: our response to the pandemic and current challenges. Front Public Health 8:549669. https://doi.org/10.3389/fpubh.2020.549669

WHO (World Health Organization) (2021) Global strategy on digital health 2020–2025. Geneva.

WHO Group Consultation on Health Telematics (1997) A health telematics policy in support of WHO's Health-for-all strategy for global health development: report of the WHO Group Consultation on Health Telematics, Switzerland, Geneva

Yin RK (1984) Case study research: design and methods. SAGE Beverly Hills, California

Zhu H, Wu K, Wu QH, Hao YH, Li C, Shan LH, Liu H, Qi XY (2020). Application and innovation of telemedicine in response to major public health emergencies. Chin J Public Health 36(12): 1724–1728. 朱虹,吴柯,吴群红,郝艳华,李翠,单凌寒,刘欢,齐新业.重大突发公共卫生事件中远程医疗服务应用与创新[J].中国公共卫生, 2020, 36(12):1724–1728

The Impact of Proper Surgery Planning on Operating Room Efficiency. An Italian Case Study in 2021

Giacomo Carli, Stanislav Russo, Lorenzo Michelin, Emanuele Adorno, Peter Perger, Beatrice Ricci, Erik Boetto, Viola Damen, Anselmo Campagna, and Matteo Buccioli

Abstract The study aims to investigate whether correct organizational procedures associated with correct operating room planning and scheduling led to fewer canceled patients and improved OR performance indicators. The following performance and efficiency metrics were monitored: Start Time Tardiness, Turnover Time, Overtime, Under Utilization, and Case Cancellation Rate. We conducted a retrospective case

---

G. Carli (✉)
Department of Economics, University of Bologna, 40126 Bologna, Italy
e-mail: Giacomo.carli5@studio.unibo.it

S. Russo · L. Michelin · B. Ricci · V. Damen · A. Campagna · M. Buccioli
IRCCS Rizzoli Orthopedic Institute, 40136 Bologna, Italy
e-mail: Stanislav.russo@studio.unibo.it

L. Michelin
e-mail: Michelin.lorenzo@gmail.com

B. Ricci
e-mail: beatricericci@gmail.com

V. Damen
e-mail: viola.damen@ior.it

A. Campagna
e-mail: anselmo.campagna@ior.it

M. Buccioli
e-mail: matteo.buccioli@gmail.com

E. Adorno · E. Boetto
Department of Biomedical and Neuromotor Sciences, School of Hygiene and Preventive Medicine, University of Bologna, 40126 Bologna, Italy
e-mail: emanueleadorno@gmail.com

E. Boetto
e-mail: erik.boetto@gmail.com

P. Perger
UMIT Tirol – Private University for Health Sciences, Medical Informatics and Technology, 6060 Hall in Tirol, Austria
e-mail: peter.perger@gmail.com

N. Persiani et al. (eds.), *Challenges of Healthcare Systems in the Era of COVID-19*, Contributions to Management Science, https://doi.org/10.1007/978-3-031-43114-2_16

study at the Orthopedic Institute Rizzoli of Bologna, a specialized orthopedic surgery hospital. The analysis considered 674 operations performed between October and November 2021, including cases from all operating units. In order to evaluate the correct planning of operations, we divided the slots retrospectively based on correct scheduling: those with more than 50% of correctly scheduled surgeries and those that fell short of this percentage. The results of performed t-tests indicated a statistically significant difference for Turnover Time and Start Time Tardiness. For the group of operations that followed the complete organizational scheduling procedure, the t-tests showed an average reduction of 8.35 min ($-19.5\%, p < 0.05$) for Turnover Time per single operation and 13.12 min ($-17.8\%, p < 0.01$) shorter Start Time Tardiness. No significant differences were observed for Under Utilization, Overtime, and Case Cancelation Rate. In conclusion, we found completeness in surgical scheduling had a positive effect on operating room waste time, with reductions of over 17% in Turnover Time and Start Time Tardiness. These results highlight the importance of proper surgical programming for hospital managers and the areas with more room for improvement.

Keywords Operating room efficiency · Surgery planning

JEL Classification Codes I18 · I20 · M10

1 Introduction

Growing demand for surgical services, correlated with the phenomenon of an aging population (Etzioni et al. 2003) and the rise of capital-intensive technological innovations requires substantial cost-saving measures inside hospitals (Schwierz 2016; Italian Guidelines for the Governance of the Planned Surgical Patient Pathway 2020). The Covid-19 Pandemic placed further stress on Health Systems due to disruptions to routine hospital services, further highlighting the urgent need for good practices in order to boost efficiency and productivity (CovidSurg Collaborative 2020). Within this framework, Operating rooms (ORs) represent both the core unit of hospital surgical production and the most critical cost centers of Healthcare Systems, accounting for 35 to 40% of total costs and generating 60–70% of revenues (Healey et al. 2015).

Thus, ORs require stringent monitoring, as their efficiency has important implications for cost savings, patient satisfaction, and medical team morale (Rothstein and Raval 2018). In particular, surgery planning and scheduling have the potential to improve efficiency, while inefficient scheduling has a detrimental effect on healthcare providers, resulting in the suboptimal use of resources, lower returns on investment and longer waiting lists for patients (Erdogan and Denton 2011). In context, "optimal efficiency is achieved by the ability to deliver the highest-quality care with the minimal use of time, money, and space" (Healey et al. 2015, p. 1). Therefore "improving efficiency means shorter case durations, rational scheduling of various types of surgery, and minimizing nonoperative time" (Marjamaa et al. 2008, p. 596). Focus on Healthcare System productivity and output is crucial in times of budget constraints.

The theoretical framework is rooted in the teachings of Operation Room Management, which aims to provide appropriate tools for monitoring and optimizing processes (Marjamaa et al. 2008). This discipline, combined with the surgical pathway guidelines in place in Italy (Guidelines for the Governance of the Planned Surgical Patient Pathway 2020), defines systematic controls on the performance levels of different surgical phases through various indicators and rules for proper surgical planning. The OR optimization process consists of three phases: preoperative, operative, and postoperative (Rothstein and Raval 2018). OR planning can be divided into three different decision levels (Zhu et al. 2019). The strategic level consists of capacity planning, capacity allocation, and case mix choices, spanning several months to 1 year or longer. Secondly, the tactical level allocates OR time to surgical specialties according to specific requirements, and determines workload distribution. Finally, the Operational level involves short-term decision-making, matching, and the scheduling of resources and patients. This analysis will focus on the Operational level, examining the use of proper scheduling by evaluating its potential effects on productivity and reporting on two scheduling tools currently in use at the Rizzoli Institute, with five performance indicators commonly applied in Operating Room Management.

A considerable volume of literature has been published on operating room planning and surgical case scheduling. Like most previous papers, our work focused on elective patients (Cardoen et al. 2010). Elective surgery scheduling involves assigning an operation date, a starting time, and an OR for elective surgeries selected from the hospital waiting list (Marques et al. 2015). It is impossible to plan for emergency patients since they require urgent treatment, which is why they are less commonly involved in research studies on this topic. Current OR theory indicates that the problem of optimization arises due to the number of participants involved (OR managers, surgeons, OR staff, patients) and the level of uncertainty (duration uncertainty, arrival uncertainty, resource uncertainty, and care requirement uncertainty). Mathematical models such as the bin-packing model, flow-shop model, and stochastic and multi-criteria models have been formalized to solve surgery planning problems, yet "despite the great deal of theoretical work that has been published, none seems to have a profound effect on the real-world practice of OR management" (Zhu et al. 2019, p. 794). Therefore, this concept appears to have been inadequately considered by earlier research but is relevant in practice, despite not always being ensured. Zhu et al. (2019, p. 758) clearly stated in their literature review that "the performance of operating theatres is largely influenced by the planning and scheduling policies used in practice"; however, existing scientific literature focuses on the optimization of surgery sequencing and lacks a tangible demonstration of the connection between proper scheduling and OR performance. Despite different approaches to maximizing OR efficiency, no evidence in literature indicates the importance of correct, complete, and accurate performance of all organizational procedures associated with operating room planning and scheduling by all operators involved. Routine is fundamental in

OR planning (and hence OR efficiency), but within the hectic reality of hospitals, its implementation by operators is not always possible. Single operators do not always have a "whole hospital system" perspective and sometimes organizational procedures linked to OR planning and scheduling are considered trivial administrative tasks. However, the accurate execution of these procedures by all staff members involved is crucial for OR planning, scheduling, and overall OR management. All individual patient processes require planning to ensure: the availability of the right person at the right time on the ward, transportation to surgical facilities, preparation of correct surgical instruments in the correct OR, and so on. Inadequate planning and scheduling of this process results in a drastic decrease in efficiency. With this study, we want to fill the existing literature gap by assessing whether proper surgery scheduling is associated with better OR performance indicators, by measuring the differences between correctly and incorrectly scheduled slots at a surgical hospital. The conclusions would provide hospital managers with invaluable insight on the importance of procedures associated with correct operating room planning and scheduling by all staff members involved. Correct scheduling is a fundamental prerequisite for the implementation of other improvement strategies.

2 Methods

This is a cross-sectional retrospective case study structured according to Yin's (2013) theoretical considerations on case study design. The single-case study rationale is to critically support the general theory about correct operating room scheduling and OR performance. Data were retrospectively collected from the IRCCS Rizzoli Orthopedic Institute (IOR), a highly specialized public hospital and research center in orthopedics and traumatology. The IOR is part of the Emilia Romagna Regional Health Service. It performs tasks of high clinical-organizational expertise, pursues research and training of internationally recognized prestige, and made the 2022 Newsweek Magazine ranking of the top five Orthopedic Institutes in the world. This Hospital was chosen due to the quality and availability of data, and due to its rigorous adherence to national and regional Resolutions. No. 272 of 03/13/2017, Emilia Romagna is a landmark regulation that paved the way for further national legislation on waiting list governance, and the standardization of pre-operative and perioperative management pathways for hospital productivity enhancement. The legal framework stipulates close monitoring of average room utilization times per surgery, further incentivizing the full utilization of operating rooms with the formulation of weekly schedules based on objective and significant data.

Moreover, thanks to its multidisciplinary expert team, IOR has played a key role in drafting and implementing national good practice guidelines in the past year. The IOR has twelve distinct and highly specialized Operating Units. In particular, the medical areas of intervention are orthopedic oncology, spinal surgery, pediatric orthopedics, prostheses revision and replacement, surgical therapy of severe infectious bone disease, foot surgery, and upper limb surgery. The institute has a horseshoe-shaped operating block of 10 operating rooms in which medium-to-high complexity orthopedic surgeries take place. Regular operating room days are scheduled from Monday to Friday and are divided into two slots. Each slot lasts 380 min: the morning session takes place from 7 a.m. to 1:20 p.m., while the afternoon session starts at 1:20 p.m. and finishes at 7:40 p.m. As stated in the introduction, we focused our research on elective surgery only, since the IOR does not accept urgent cases, indeed emergencies are treated in other hospitals in the Bologna Metropolitan Area. The description of operative phases (pre, peri, post) in National Guidelines includes a specific section for surgery scheduling, stressing the importance of planning and the rules for the proper preparation of production factors (room space, clinical and technical specialists, materials, and instruments). It establishes two distinct levels of planning: the Weekly Operating Note (WON) and Daily Operating Note (DON). The WON must be completed on the Thursday of the week before operations. The Programming Group checks it in terms of integrity and compliance with internal directions. Macro errors or inconsistencies are adjusted at the weekly meeting every Thursday at the Medical Direction Office. The weekly scheduling proposal is prepared for patients from the Waiting List identified as eligible for surgery at the pre-admission check. It should be prepared in compliance with assigned operating room utilization times, hospitalization, and bed availability. After validation, the proposed Operating Note becomes definitive and is the essential tool for the proper execution of the organizational path toward operating room activities.

The DON derives directly from the WON and must be prepared and sent no later than 12 p.m. on the day before operations. It must contain and confirm data from the corresponding WON. Any subsequent modification must be reported to the anesthesiology and nursing coordinators. For the purpose of our study, patients had to be present in both WON and DON within the terms in order to be considered correctly scheduled.

The WON is the first tool used for scheduling patients and must include the following elements:

- patient's personal data,
- surgery duration,
- type of surgery,
- laterality (if needed),
- allergies report,
- request for transfer to the Intensive Care Unit (ICU) or Recovery Room (RR),
- request for room electro-medical devices/equipment that differs from the standard setting (e.g., specific surgical bed, fluoroscope),
- indication of the instrumentation and implantable material to be used; must contain all necessary elements for correct and complete identification of material to be prepared and taken into the OR,
- first operator,
- type of anesthesia,
- patient position,
- prediction of airway risk,

- possible infection/colonization of multi-resistant micro-organisms.

In addition to the list above, the DON also requires a more specific indication of instrumentation for surgery. Correct identification of material that must be prepared and taken into the operating room is crucial.

The IOR internal procedures provide the following practices for the slot's scheduling:

- Patients who have already been postponed should generally be scheduled at the beginning of the session to avoid further suspensions;
- the most demanding cases in terms of total planned time (preparation, surgical time, and operating room exit) should usually be made at the beginning of the session;
- unpostponable cases cannot be placed at the slot's end;
- cases with air-borne infections should be included at the end of the session;
- latex-allergic patients must be placed in the latex-free OR or at the beginning of the session in ordinary ORs;
- The first three patients on the operating note should maintain their list position to ensure the supply of the planned materials.

The Operations Group is responsible for enforcing the rules and implementing the necessary corrective actions when needed.

2.1 Study Design

The observation period started on the 26th of October 2021 and ended on the 26th of November 2021.

The following procedure was used for analysis:

1. Review of the 4 WONs and 31 DONs;
2. Analysis of performed surgeries and comparison with scheduled ones;
3. Computation of the percentage of scheduled operations in both WON and DON (correctly planned surgeries) for each daily slot;
4. Formation of two groups based on the percentage of correctly scheduled patients per slot. From the experience of the Institute's Programming Group, we used 50% as the cut-off value. Slots with more than half of operations that follow the entire planning process are thus placed in the "correctly scheduled ORs" group and all others in the "incorrectly scheduled ORs" group. Omitted patients or interventions present in only one of the two scheduling tools and submissions beyond the prescribed deadlines are considered incorrect for the purposes of this analysis.
5 Finally, we performed a T-test and Mann–Whitney test on both groups according to data distribution (McElduff et al. 2010). Tested performance indicators are:

Table 1 Performance indicators definitions

Performance Indicator	Formula	Definition	Meaning
Start time tardiness	STT = StartChirOp – StartSlot	Difference between the actual start of the first surgical operation of the day and the programmed time	Start delay of the first intervention
Turnover time	TT = InORp2 – OutORp1	Difference between the next patient's entrance into the OR and the exit of the previous patient	Timeframe for the preparation of the OR, the sum of cleaning, and the setup time
Overtime	OT = OutOR – EndSlot	Difference between the exit of the last patient from the OR and the programmed slot end time	Additional time used to finish the last patient's surgery
Under utilization	UU = EndSlot – OutOR	Difference between the programmed slot end and the actual last patient exit	Timeframe of not utilized Operating room due to an early exit of the last patient
Case cancellation rate	N. of cases canceled/ N. of total cases	The ratio of canceled patients and the total number of cases performed	It describes the rate of programmed patients who did not undergo surgery

Start Time Tardiness (STT), Turnover Time (TT), Overtime (OT), Under Utilization (UU), and Case Cancellation Rate (CCR), as defined by Macario (2006). Definitions are in Table 1.

Data was obtained from the institutional operating records platform. Some observations have been excluded from the analysis due to measurement errors, such as excessive or omitted timings. Private practice surgery, day Hospital, or outpatient surgeries were not included in the analysis.

3 Results

674 surgeries were performed in the observed period (Table 2).

- 42% (282) followed the complete scheduling process;
- 41% (280) were in one of the scheduling tools only;
- 17% (112) were not in the programming tools at all, or were scheduled beyond the deadline.

Table 2 Surgeries summary

Surgeries performed				
Total	Patients in both WON and DON	Patients only in DON	Patients only in WON	Patients not scheduled or scheduled beyond the deadline
674	282	274	6	112
100%	42%	41%	1%	17%

With the chosen breakdown (cut-off at 50%), the 172 slots have been split into two groups: 95 slots went into the "incorrectly scheduled" group and 77 "correctly scheduled" one.

A total of 47 postponed scheduled patients were recorded in the observed month.

Table 3 shows completion rates for fields in the WON. These data are part of the hospital's weekly note efficiency report, presented and discussed at the Planning Group every Thursday at 1 p.m. at the medical direction office with unit coordinators. The scores in the last column are low because this field is only filled in if OPT or Allen Bed are required.

The results of the *t*-test performed (Table 4) showed a statistically significant difference in Turnover Time and Start Time Tardiness. Indeed, for the "Correctly scheduled," group, the *t*-test showed an average reduction of 8.35 min (−19.5%, $p < 0.05$) for Turnover Time per single operation and a 13.12 min (−17.8%, $p < 0.01$) shorter Start Time Tardiness. We performed a Mann–Whitney test due to the asymmetric distribution of other variables. No statistical differences between both groups emerged from this non-parametric test (Table 5).

Our results are mostly aligned with the general assumption that more accurate planning leads to better OR performance. Results indicate a significant impact of correct scheduling on STT and TT, while UU, OT, and CCR do not significantly differ.

4 Discussion and Limitations

The Study indicates a clear improvement of TT and STT in the "correctly programmed" slot group. This may be due to the early morning calling of the first patient, more thorough case study, and surgery preparation with the availability of instrumentation, radiological equipment, and support staff. Reducing these times is crucial, as "prolonged operating room turnover time remains an area of frustration for surgeons, anesthesiologists, perioperative staff and administrators. Long operating room wait times also erode patient satisfaction" (Cerfolio et al. 2019, p. 1004). Moreover, saved time implies an increase in room efficiency, with an equal amount of resources involved. Childers and Maggard-Gibbons (2018) reported that on average,

Table 3 Weekly note completeness report, period of observation 26th October 2021–26th November 2021

Completion percentage for each field of the weekly operating notes											
Operation unit	Scheduled surgeries	Surgery duration (%)	Type of surgery (%)	Laterality (%)	First operator (%)	Position (%)	Materials (%)	ASA (%)	Intubation (%)	Recovery room (%)	Fluoroscope (%)	OPT or ALLEN bed (%)
Unit 1	22	100	100	100	0	0	95	55	55	14	73	14
Unit 2	69	100	100	100	99	100	61	41	38	12	46	0
Unit 3	57	100	100	100	98	100	98	89	94	68	35	0
Unit 4	16	100	100	88	0	6	88	56	44	31	19	0
Unit 5	19	100	100	100	0	89	47	37	44	0	47	0
Unit 6	119	100	100	100	99	3	68	7	37	0	56	0
Unit 7	11	100	100	91	36	100	91	27	7	0	100	100
Unit 8	9	100	100	100	89	89	89	44	27	11	100	100
Unit 9	12	100	100	100	100	75	58	33	33	25	33	0
Unit 10	3	100	100	100	100	100	0	0	0	0	0	0
Total/ mean	**337**	**100**	**100**	**99**	**80**	**56**	**74**	**37**	**35**	**18**	**51**	**7**

Table 4 *t*-Test results

Characteristic	Not correctly scheduled ORs, N = 95[a]	Correctly scheduled ORs, N = 77[a]	*p*-Value[b]
Start time tardiness (minutes)	74.13 (24.30)	60.95 (25.53)	0.001
Mean turnover time (minutes)	44.09 (25.55)	35.50 (20.52)	0.019

[a]Mean (SD)
[b]Welch Two Sample *t*-test

Table 5 Mann–Whitney test results

Characteristic	Not correctly scheduled ORs, N = 95[a]	Correctly scheduled ORs, N = 77[a]	*p*-Value[b]
Under utilization (minutes)	11.01 (38.83)	7.66 (17.77)	0.8
Overtime (minutes)	25.59 (41.57)	25.31 (31.18)	0.6
Canceled case rate (per day and OR)	0.08 (0.21)	0.19 (0.29)	0.2

[a] Mean (SD)
[b] Wilcoxon rank sum test

1 min of a running OR costs 36 dollars, so 13 min less TT for every operation means thousands of dollars saved every day for the Hospital.

We compared our results to the standardized scoring system presented by Macario (2006). In his paper, Macario assigns points to ORs according to their performance, defined in eight metrics, differentiating between low, medium, and high performers. Our "correctly scheduled" group has a TT of 35.30 min, thus falling in the medium class (40 min < TT < 25 min), while the "not correctly programmed" group belongs to the worst class (TT > 40 min). Similarly, the value of STT (60.57 min) brings the first group near to the upper limit of the medium class (60 min < STT < 45 min). The high values for STT could be explained by the high complexity of operations performed at the IOR requiring long anaesthesiological induction times.

UU e OT are not statistically significant, nor is the Canceled Case Rate. Despite the high P value, this indicator appears to yield a counterintuitive result: the number of postponed patients is higher for the Correctly scheduled group. A reasonable explanation for this is that it is impossible to monitor and capture unscheduled cancelled patients. This problem should be taken into consideration in further analysis. The lack of completeness of the WON and the fact that only 42% of patients undergoing surgery followed the complete scheduling process can lead to problems with surgical procedures, increasing the risk of unused theatre time allocated for operations, resulting in poor performance, delays, change of patient order, change of instruments, or patients postponed due to lack of theatre time, as well as problems in perioperative process management. Errors and/or delays in weekly and daily scheduling penalize the synergistic efforts of healthcare staff as they strive to provide correct surgical organization and an optimal care experience for patients admitted to the IOR.

Several limitations must be taken into account. We can assume problems related to a lack of good scheduling belong to macro-areas of reference:

- Postponed patients generate problems with bed occupancy and room availability for newly scheduled incoming patients;
- Patients that are changed in the order list, or ineffectively scheduled generate increased TT and delays for the equipment preparations. According to Gottschalk et al. (2016), factors that affect TT include variables outside the OR, such as equipment failure/sterilization, and we expect these elements to improve with correct planning;
- Patients are not adequately studied before surgery: failure to forecast intubation and allergy problems.

It is important to note that the majority (53%) of total patients were not included in the WON. From this information, we deduct three possible causes of inefficiency in patient scheduling: operators delay WON generation as: (I) they consider it to be of low relevance, (II) organizational problems arise (lack of medium-term programming), or (III) technical issues arise (e.g., difficulties in programming types of patients). Each reason leads to different possible solutions. For example, the first case has managerial implications and can be solved through an internal review and the alignment of goals between hospital shareholders. The second condition requires additional training for operators, whereas the third is the most challenging to overcome. Indeed, it is important to note that some of the units included in the study manage case mixes of particular complexity, in which health conditions vary considerably, even in a short period, such as with oncologic patients. The scheduling of these interventions is subjected to greater organizational stresses precisely because of the rapid changeability of the patient's disease course. This leads to difficulties in long-term planning and the need for pre-admission checks close to the actual surgery to minimize the chances of the patient's clinical situation deteriorating.

As a further limitation, it should be noted that the observation period is only one month long. An extension would enable the study of variables with specific unit coverage, resulting in greater uniformity of surgery types.

5 Conclusion

As we have seen in our case study, proper adherence to scheduling led to better OR performance, at least in terms of start-time tardiness and turnover time. There is a lack of scientific evidence on the link between OR planning, scheduling, and resulting performance, and on which performance indicators are influenced. Such information is invaluable for OR managers striving to achieve correct planning by all operators involved, through the identification of affected performance areas.

Increased efficiency limits waste and promotes savings in terms of time and economic resources. A lack of scheduling can generate organizational, accessory, efficiency, patient, and employee well-being issues that affect the performance of operating theatres, hospital budgets, and surgical production. Therefore, hospital managers should focus on implementing good practices in the scheduling of patient procedures.

References

Book

Yin RK (2013) Case study research and application: design and methods, 6th edn. Sage Publications

Journal

Agnoletti et al (2013) Operating room data management: improving efficiency and safety in a surgical block. BMC Surg 13:7

Cardoen et al (2010) Operating room planning and scheduling: a literature review. Eur J Oper Res 201(3):921–932

Cerfolio et al (2019) Improving operating room turnover time in a New York City academic hospital via Lean. Ann Thorac Surg 107(4):1011–1016

Childers CP, Maggard-Gibbons M (2018) Understanding costs of care in the operating room. JAMA Surg 153(4):e176233

Collar RM et al (2012) Lean management in academic surgery. J Am Coll Surg 214(6):928–936

COVIDSurg Collaborative, (2020) Elective surgery cancellations due to the COVID-19 pandemic: global predictive modelling to inform surgical recovery plans. Br J Surg 107(11):1440–1449

Dexter F et al (2003) Use of operating room information system data to predict the impact of reducing turnovertimes on staffing costs. Anesth Analg 97(4):1119–1126

Erdogan SA, Denton BT (2011) Surgery planning and scheduling. In: Wiley encyclopedia of operations research and management science. Wiley, Hoboken, NJ

Etzioni DA et al (2003) The aging population and its impact on the surgery workforce. Annu Surg 238(2):170–177

Fong AJ, Smith M, Langerman A (2016) Efficiency improvement in the operating room. J Surg Res 204(2):371–383

Gómez-Ríos MA et al (2019) Keys to optimize the operating room efficiency. Revista Española De Anestesiología y Reanimación (english Edition) 66(2):104–112

Gottschalk, Michael B et al (2016) Factors affecting hand surgeon operating room turnover time, hand (New York, N.Y.) 11(4):489–494

Healey T et al (2015) A improving operating room efficiency, Part 1: general managerial and preoperative strategies. JBJS Rev 3(10) e3:1–10

Macario A (2006) Are your hospital operating rooms "efficient"? A scoring system with eight performance indicators. Anesthesiology 105:237–240

Macario A (2010) What does one minute of operating room time cost? J Clin Anesth 22(4):233–236

Marjamaa et al (2008) Operating room management: why, how and by whom? Acta Anaesthesiol Scand 52:596–600

Marques I et al (2015) A bicriteria heuristic for an elective surgery scheduling problem. Health Care Manag Sci 18(3):251–266

McElduff F et al (2010) When t-test or Wilcoxon-Mann-Whitney test won't do. Adv Physiol Educ 34(3):128–133

Peltokorpi A (2011) How do strategic decisions and operative practices affect operating room productivity? Health Care Manag Sci 14(4):370–382

Perger P et al (2014) Operating Room Efficiency Improving through Data Management. In: Roa Romero L (eds) XIII Mediterranean conference on medical and biological engineering and computing 2013. IFMBE Proceedings, vol 41. Springer, Cham

Rothstein DH, Raval MV (2018) Operating room efficiency. Semin Pediatr Surg 27(2):79–85

Tyler DC, Pasquariello CA, Chen CH (2003) Determining optimum operating room utilization. Anesth Analg 96(4):1114–1121

Ubiali A et al (2021) Operating Room Efficiency measurement made simple by a single metric. Ann Ig 33(1):100–102

Zhu et al (2019) Operating room planning and surgical case scheduling: a review of literature. J Comb Optim 37:757–805

Conference paper or contributed volume

Italian National Guidelines, Guidelines for the Governance of the Planned Surgical Patient Pathway, 2020, State-Regions Agreement No. 100 /CSR of July 9

James J, Cochran Louis A, Cox Pinar, Keskinocak Jeffrey P, Kharoufeh JC, Smith SA, Erdogan Brian T. Denton Wiley Encyclopedia of Operations Research and Management Science Surgery Planning and Scheduling Wiley

Regional Decree n.272 13/03/2017, Emilia Romagna

Schwierz C (2016) Cost-containment policies in hospital expenditure in the European union, directorate general economic and financial affairs (DG ECFIN), European Commission (European Economy—Discussion Papers 2015)

Privacy and Security in Digital Health in the Western Balkans During the COVID-19 Pandemic

Vesna Lukovic

Abstract The COVID-19 pandemic led to mobility restrictions and lockdowns and disrupted traditional face-to-face patient–physician care. As a result, digital health tools became an immediate necessity. The aim of this paper was to look into the state of digitalization from the perspective of a patient in 2020, the first year of the pandemic. By taking into account the context of the Western Balkans, the aim of the study is to explore the online behavior of people in regard to privacy and security issues related to the online delivery of certain health-related data, such as COVID-19 certificates. The methodology of the research is quantitative, based on statistical analysis of data from the databases at the Eurostat, the statistical office of the European Union. Data was generated from the annual Eurostat's survey on the use of information and communication technologies in households and by individuals. The finding of this research is that the use of digital technologies in the Western Balkans has been growing, but more should be done with respect to digital health at the public level. Another finding is that the general population should improve their digital skills in order to protect their health records and other health-related data online.

Keywords COVID-19 pandemic · Digital technology · Health · Western Balkans

JEL Classifications Codes I19 · K39 · O31 · O32

1 Introduction

In 1937, at the time of the Great Depression, John Mynard Keynes wrote that people's knowledge of the future was fluctuating, vague, and uncertain (Keynes 1937). In the world of 2020, the COVID-19 pandemic clearly brought a new level of uncertainty to the every-day life. Governments around the world tried to map the virus and its transmission while searching for a vaccine to end the pandemic and data-driven

V. Lukovic (✉)
Thessaloniki, Greece
e-mail: lukove@yahoo.com

N. Persiani et al. (eds.), *Challenges of Healthcare Systems in the Era of COVID-19*, Contributions to Management Science, https://doi.org/10.1007/978-3-031-43114-2_17

technology was given a central role in contact-tracing of people (Pila 2020). The pandemic clearly exposed the need for additional push for digitalization, electronic management of patients' data, and digital transformation of healthcare (Baudier et al 2023). This is consistent with the findings that digitally supported health management system can improve the overall performance of healthcare during pandemics (Javaid and Khan 2021).

The term *digital health* typically refers to the use of digital technologies to improve health (World Health Organization 2022). There are many advantages of digitalization of health services (Bhavnani et al. 2016; Svendsen et al. 2021; Buul et al. 2020), its impact on quality of the healthcare (Ossebaard and Gemert-Pijnen 2016) and implementation approaches (Eysenbach 2002; Heinsch et al 2021). Digital health technologies can lead to major improvements in the efficiency of the health systems, including in the administration of the system as a whole (World Health Organization 2022). Still, before the pandemic, some authors found that the high-quality evidence on the benefits of eHealth interventions was somewhat lacking (Elbert et al 2014). Other authors emphasized that the acceptance of telemedicine by potential users depends on the theory-guided and user-centered design approaches (Harst et al. 2019). Nevertheless, the impact of digitalization of health services has been growing and is expected to be even more important in the future, especially in diagnostic, preventive care, treatment, and rehabilitation (European Commission 2019a, b). Some authors found that the COVID-19 pandemic highlighted the importance of telehealth, specifically the use of Internet of Things (Shamsabadi et al. 2021). Digitalization in the health sector in the Western Balkans has been underdeveloped. That was confirmed by the European Commission in its annual reports on the progress of candidates and potential candidates to become EU members (European Commission 2019a, b). There isn't a large body of research about the security and privacy in the digital sphere in the Western Balkans. This paper aims to shed some light in this respect. While access to internet has increased in the Western Balkans, the sophistication of technology with respect to digital health is still low. This is partly because health systems in the Western Balkans are only modestly digitalized. In addition, people might not be aware of dangers with respect to the privacy and security of their medical records and other health-related data delivered over the internet. Budak et al (2014) explored individuals' concerns related to privacy, data protection, and surveillance in Bosnia and Herzegovina, Serbia, and North Macedonia in 2012 with an aim to categorize individuals into different groups according to their privacy concerns, concerns about data protection and surveillance.

This paper does not aim to categorize people according to these concerns. The focus of this paper is on people's use of digital technology in 2020, the first year of the COVID-19 pandemic. The aim of the paper is to look into the state of digitalization from the perspective of a patient during the year of 2020, the first year of the pandemic. The aim is also to provide a comparative look at the indicators in the Western Balkans vis-à-vis EU at the point of the COVID-19 pandemic outbreak.

The paper is divided into the following sections. Section 2 defines key terms and explains data sources and research methodology. Section 3 frames the use of digital technology in the Western Balkans, providing insights into specific issues, while

Sect. 4 depicts the role of the European Union (hereinafter: EU) and World Health Organization (hereinafter: WHO) in the Western Balkans in regard to digitalization of the healthcare, particularly during the COVID-19 pandemic. Section 5 is a discussion on security and privacy in the Western Balkans while Sect. 6 discusses challenges and issues with respect to older patients and their use of digital technology. Section 7 elaborates on the key findings of the study.

2 Definitions, Data and Research Methodology

2.1 Definitions

EU Digital COVID Certificate is a digital proof that a person has either been vaccinated against COVID-19, recovered from COVID-19, or received a negative test result. This certificate is not particularly relevant in 2022, but it was crucial in the early stages of the pandemic when vaccines became available and people were getting vaccinated. The certificate gave people the freedom of movement compared to restrictions at the start of the pandemic. The certificate was in the national language and English language, in digital and/or paper format with QR code, and valid in all EU countries (European Commission 2021a).

With respect to the EU Digital COVID Certificate, *mobile applications* were designed so that the EU verifier applications could read Western Balkans' COVID-19 certificates in the EU Digital COVID Certificate (EUDCC) system. Western Balkans' certificates were connected to the EUDCC and therefore they were "recognized" in the EU member states. *Mobile application (app)* is a computer program (or software application) designed to run on a mobile device (a smartphone or tablet computer) rather than on desktop or laptop computers. In the COVID-19 health crisis, specific mobile applications have been seen as more effective than other processes that could have been used, although some emphasized the absence of evidence of these specific mobile applications' efficacy and the proportionality of the measures adopted (Council of Europe 2020).

The above concept of digital certificate is associated to the term *digital health* that typically refers to healthcare practices supported by electronic processes and communications that include services and information technology such as electronic medical records, electronic prescriptions, electronic ordering systems, telemedicine, and consumer health informatics (European Commission 2019a, b). The term *digital healthcare* therefore covers many terms, including telemedicine, electronic health (eHealth), telehealth, and mobile devices mobile health (m-health). *Telemedicine* is about healthcare services that are delivered to a patient by healthcare providers, from a geographical distance by using information and communication technology. On the other hand, *telehealth* covers the use of Internet of Things (IoT) to enable quantified self and self-management of health data (Harst et al. 2019). From the healthcare perspective, IoT can be considered as any device that can collect health-related data from individuals, including computing devices, mobile phones, smart bands and wearables, digital medications, implantable surgical devices, or other portable devices, which can measure health data and connect to the internet (Javaid and Khan 2021). All of the above is connected to the term *innovation* in health systems that refers to the organizational innovation on one hand and biomedical and technological innovation on the other (European Observatory on Health Systems and Policies 2021).

2.2 Data and Research Methodology

Data used for this research is derived from surveys carried out by national authorities of the EU and the Western Balkans. These surveys are based on the Eurostat and its annual model survey on the use of information and communication technologies in households and by individuals. Survey data were collected through face-to-face and telephone interviews or online questionnaires by relevant statistical authorities in the EU member states and the Western Balkans. After collecting data from these surveys, these data were then transmitted from national statistical authorities to the Eurostat where they were verified from a logical and consistency point of view at the level of variables, breakdowns, and time series checks (Eurostat 2021).

Since the use of digital technology in health covers a wide range of health and care services[1] that are delivered through information and communication technologies (ICT), relevant ICT indicators available in the databases at the Eurostat have been selected for this research. The data extracted from Eurostat were ICT indicators such as access to information and communication technologies (ICT) by individuals and/or households, the use of internet for different purposes (e.g. searching for health information online), internet of things (IoT), ICT security and trust and ICT competence and skills. In this research these data were sorted, analyzed, and compared in regard to the average of the EU vis-à-vis the Western Balkans.

Research methodology in this paper is quantitative and based on statistical analysis. The statistical analysis of these data provides an insight into certain aspects related to digitalization in health, such as trust, security, and privacy of health data delivered over the internet, particularly in the form of digital COVID-19 certificates required for most basic economic and social activities at the time.

The research was undertaken in the last quarter of 2021 when the relevant data for 2020 was available in the Eurostat's databases.

[1] They cover health data analytics, health information systems, electronic health records, remote consultation and monitoring services (e.g. telehealth, telemedicine).

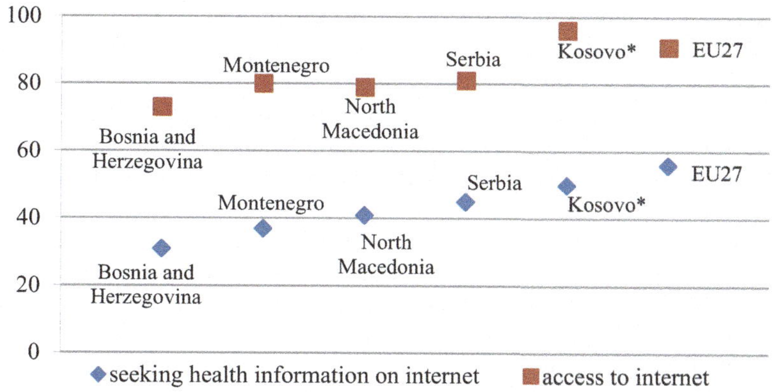

Fig. 1 Percentage (%) of households seeking health information online in 2020.[2] *Source* Author's compilation of data from the Eurostat (2021)

3 Digital Technology and Health in Western Balkans

Transforming health services towards more digitalization is a complex process (European Commission 2019a, b). In the early stage of the COVID-19 pandemic, the health authorities in the Western Balkans focused mainly on the management of the pandemic and on the provision of key health services, monitoring, case investigation, contact-tracing, communication, surveillance, and vaccine rollout (European Commission Reports 2021). The pandemic confirmed again that the Western Balkans suffer from the lack of resources on all levels of digital health. One of the reasons in this respect is underinvestment in healthcare infrastructure and services, accompanied by the constant outflow of the professional workforce, including medical staff, particularly specialists (European Commission Reports 2021).

In the EU, the COVID-19 pandemic has led to a strong acceleration of the uptake of digital health technologies to strengthen public health systems (Petracca et al. 2020) and it also influenced a public demand for easy-to-access health information as people have been looking for health information and advice on the internet. Extraordinary public measures and various fake news and conspiracy theories in 2020 pushed people to seek answers on the internet. More than a third of the Western Balkans and more than 50% of households in the EU searched for health information online in 2020 (Fig. 1).

It is not only that the governments and authorities in Western Balkans have been slow in technology uptake compared to the EU, households and individuals have been slow, too. Bosnia and Herzegovina recorded the lowest share (31%) of households seeking health information online and the country also had the lowest share of households with access to internet (73%), compared to the average of the EU (91%) in 2020 (Fig. 1). The percentage of those individuals who used internet for other

[2] Data for Albania was not available as of December 2021.

health services via a website or application instead of having to go to the hospital or visit a doctor reached 14% in Kosovo, one percentage point higher than the average of the EU (Table 1).

In 2019, a year before the COVID-19 outbreak, the use of portable devices and smartphones to access internet rose in the Western Balkans by more than 2 percentage points compared to 2018. The use of a laptop, notebook, or tablet computers increased even more in the same period (Table 2).

With respect to how to protect personal health data records in online environment, people should know how to deal with personal and sensitive information, for instance how to encrypt mobile access, data transfer, and storage on their smartphones and how to have a good identity and user access system. This is relevant not only in regard to the COVID-19 pandemic but in general as well, because the healthcare sector, which typically processes large amounts of personal data, has been increasingly using information technologies, such as smartphone applications (apps) and other devices, for information collection and treatment plans (Mulder 2019).

Countries of the Western Balkans lag behind the EU average with respect to those digital skills that are above basic digital skills (Fig. 2). In 2019, a year before the COVID-19 outbreak, Albania was at the lower end with only 7%, while Serbia was at the higher end with 20% of individuals who had above basic overall digital skills. However, that was still 10 percentage points below the average of the EU (Fig. 2).

The share of individuals who used IoT technology (internet-connected devices) for self-management, i.e. monitoring blood pressure, sugar level, or body weight, has been generally lower in the Western Balkans compared to the most advanced EU member states. In 2020, the highest share of individuals who used IoT in the EU was in Denmark, above 10%. On the other hand, most of the Western Balkans were at the lower end of that scale (Fig. 3).

Table 1 Percentage of individuals (%), seeking health information online in 2020

	Internet use: seeking health information	Internet use: for other health services via a website or app instead of having to go to the hospital or visit a doctor	Internet use: accessing personal health records online
EU27	56	13	10
Montenegro	37	6	7
North Macedonia	41	3	5
Albania	n/a	n/a	n/a
Serbia	46	2	3
Bosnia and Herzegovina	31	1	1
Kosovo*	50	14	12

Source Author's compilation of data from the Eurostat (2021)

Table 2 Percentage of individuals (%) with portable devices prior to pandemic

	2018		2019	
	Individuals used a laptop, notebook, netbook, or tablet computer to access the internet away from home or work	Individuals used a mobile phone (or smartphone) to access the internet	Individuals used a laptop, notebook, netbook, or tablet computer to access the internet away from home or work	Individuals used a mobile phone (or smartphone) to access the internet
EU27	27	65	39	71
Montenegro	46	68	45	70
North Macedonia	13	59	30	71
Albania	5	54	18	68
Serbia	7	57	9	62
Bosnia and Herzegovina	18	55	12	56
Kosovo*	15	75	24	79

Source Author's compilation of data from the Eurostat (2021)

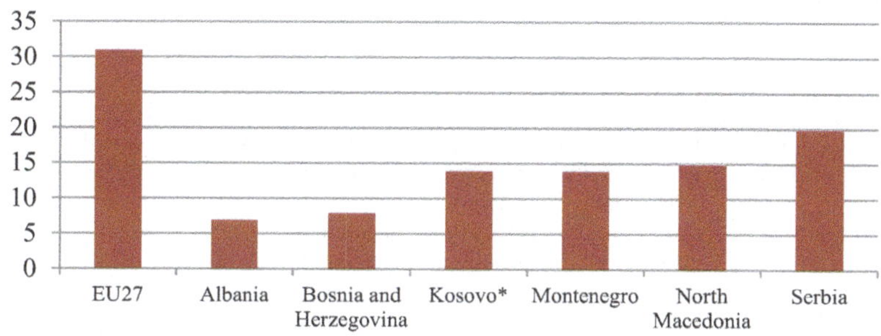

Fig. 2 Percentage (%) of individuals with above basic digital skills in 2019.[3] *Source* Author's compilation of data from the Eurostat (2021)

There are many reasons why people don't use IoT devices. The share of those who cited the lack of skills to use those devices was 8% in Bosnia and Hercegovina, the same as the EU average (Table 3). That share was the smallest in Serbia and Kosovo. Montenegro and North Macedonia recorded the highest share of individuals who answered in the survey that they do not use IoT because costs were too high, reaching 18% and 8%, respectively. The share of individuals who did not use IoT because of the lack of the compatibility with other devices or systems were 5% in Serbia and 6% in Montenegro, at the level of the average EU.

[3] At the time of writing this paper the last update of data at the Eurostat was on 25 May 2021. Data on Montenegro for 2019 is a proxy set at the same level as in 2018.

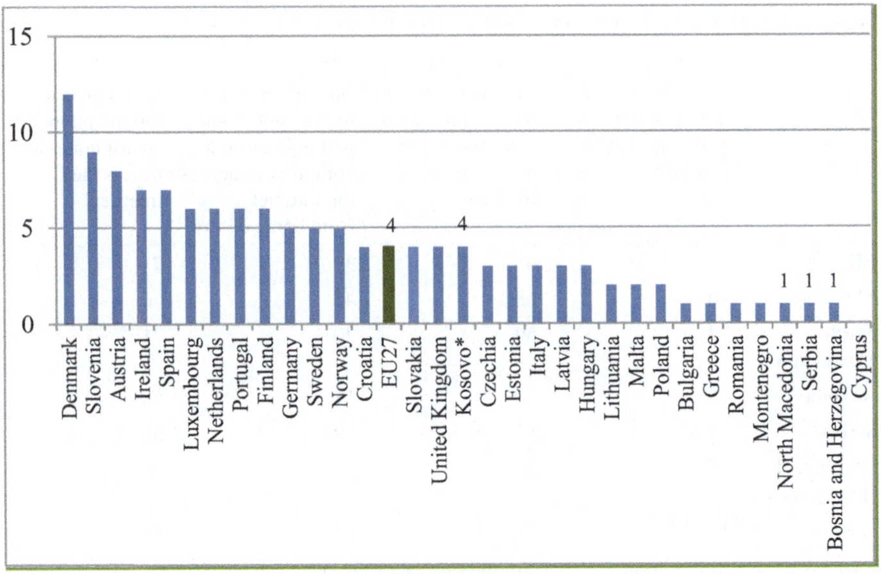

Fig. 3 Internet of Things (IoT)—for monitoring blood pressure, sugar level, body weight or other health and medical care, 2020. *Source* Author's compilation of data from the Eurostat (2021)

Table 3 Main reasons for not using IoT, percentage (%) of individuals, 2020

	Costs too high	Lack of compatibility with other devices or systems	Lack of skills to use those devices or systems	Concerns about the privacy and protection of personal data generated by those devices or systems	Concerns about security	Concerns about safety or health
EU27	11	5	8	11	10	4
Montenegro	18	6	6	4	3	5
North Macedonia	8	2	4	0	0	1
Serbia	5	5	2	0	1	1
Bosnia and Herzegovina	3	1	8	3	4	2
Kosovo*	11	2	2	0	0	0

Source Author's compilation of data from the Eurostat (2021)

Concerns about security were considerably lower in the Western Balkans compared to the average EU where it stood at 10% in 2020 (Table 3). The same is also true for the concerns about the privacy and protection of personal data generated by those devices or systems (Table 3).

4 EU, WHO, and Western Balkans During Pandemic

The implementation of digital tools in healthcare had been increasing before the pandemic, although the increase was rather slow (European Observatory of Health Systems and Policies 2021a). The WHO launched a new network in 2021 in order to support digital transformation of health systems in the Western Balkans (WHO 2021). The WHO found that despite highlighting the importance of investing in data and digital health to reform health systems, the uptake and trust in digital health by the people in the Western Balkans were low and uneven (WHO 2021). More digital health products with a higher level of intelligence capability should be applied in the management of pandemics and health-related crises in the Western Balkans. The WHO/Europe Western Balkans Digital Health Network that was established in 2021, aims to support the implementation of digital health priorities, identified by the WHO Western Balkans Roadmap for Health 2021–2025 (WHO 2021). This network aims to find ways to accelerate the digitalization of national health systems and the development of equitable digital health services in the Western Balkans (focusing on the delivery of primary healthcare) while also promoting the sharing of knowledge and identification of best practices across borders (WHO 2021).

One of the key health-related issues for people from Western Balkans in 2020 was traveling across borders. An important achievement in this respect was integrating the national COVID-19 certificates into the EU system. For instance, Serbia integrated its national COVID-19 certificate with the EU Digital certificate and on 15 November 2021, the European Commission adopted the decision that Serbia would be connected to the EU's system. As a result Serbia's COVID certificates were accepted under the same conditions as the EU Digital COVID Certificate (European Commission 2021a, b) when crossing borders with the EU. The same EU equivalence decisions were adopted for Montenegro, Albania, and North Macedonia. As of 31 December 2021 Kosovo* and Bosna and Herzegovina were not yet included in that system (European Commission 2021a).

These decisions by the European Commission were based on technical tests performed by the EU which demonstrated that COVID-19 vaccination, test, and recovery certificates of the above mentioned countries were in accordance with the EU system and trust frameworks established by the Regulation (EU) 2021/953, and therefore allowed for the verification of the authenticity, validity, and integrity of the certificates. As a result, certificates of these Western Balkan countries were connected to the EU's digital COVID certificate system. What did this mean in practice? In practice, it meant that a national from the Western Balkans could, when entering the EU, present the national digital COVID certificate that is recognized by the EU. Moreover, since many countries in the EU restricted the use of public places, shops, restaurants, and similar by requiring a COVID certificate, if a traveler from the Western Balkans entered a shop or a restaurant in EU, her/his digital COVID certificate was given a green light as it was included in the EU's system of digital COVID certificates.

This is in line with a broader idea to create a so-called *European Health Data Space* and to promote health data research and exchange of information on new preventive strategies, as well as medicines, medical devices, treatments, and outcomes (European Commission 2022a, b). With respect to digital health in the Western Balkans, the Government of Serbia in 2021 formed a coordination body for healthcare system digitalization to establish a joint group involving the public and private sectors in this area, with an aim of a strategic approach to eHealth development (NALED 2021). The task of this body was to work on creating the National Program for the Development of eHealth with an action plan, introducing modern technological solutions in this area.

In Montenegro, AmCham wrote a policy paper on digitalization of healthcare in Montenegro (AmCham Montenegro 2021a, b). The Government of Montenegro announced its national digital COVID-19 certificate as of July 30, 2021.

In North Macedonia, also in July 2021, the Government announced that "the National ICT Strategy 2021–2025 will put the Republic of North Macedonia at the top in the field of digitalization in the region" (North Macedonia 2021).

With respect to digitalization in Albania, the country set up a digital agency and started a digitization of electronic health records. The digitization of citizens' medical records was already an on-going project (European Commission 2019a). In regard to digital transformation in the public sector in Bosnia and Herzegovina, in August 2020 the United Nations Development Program prepared a project titled "Digital Transformation in the Public Sector in Bosnia and Herzegovina (2020–2024)" with an aim to "support authorities in Bosnia and Herzegovina in their journey towards the country's digital future by promoting new capabilities and leveraging technology and innovation for more effective and inclusive governance and public service delivery" (UNDP 2020, p. 2).

As of the end of 2021, Albania, North Macedonia, Montenegro, and Serbia are EU candidate countries, while Bosnia and Herzegovina and Kosovo*[4] are potential candidate members. They have all concluded Association and Stabilization Agreements with the EU, and therefore they should gradually align their legislation with the EU legislation, including in regard to consumer and health protection. The latest reports from the European Commission (2021a, b) stated that there had been some progress in this respect.

In Montenegro, the Integrated Health Information System covers state-owned medical institutions, pharmacies, and privately owned dentist offices. The national legislation on healthcare is partly aligned with the EU acquis, however, patients' rights in cross-border healthcare still need to be addressed (Report Montenegro 2021a, b). Montenegro continued to make use of the EU Joint Procurement Agreement on medical counter-measures to which it is a signatory. The country joined the European COVID-19 Surveillance Network, reporting COVID-19 data to the European Surveillance System managed by the European Center for Disease Prevention and Control.

Serbia's legislation on healthcare is partly aligned with the EU acquis. At the time of writing this research, the centralized electronic health record system that has been

[4] Throughout this paper Kosovo is understood within the meaning of the United Nations. Resolution 1244 (UN Resolution 1999).

funded by the EU was still not used and the compliance with the EU health indicators has not yet been ensured, according to the latest European Commission's report on Serbia (Report Serbia 2021). Serbia joined the European COVID-19 Surveillance Network reporting COVID-19 data.

In North Macedonia, there was no progress to finalize the draft Law on Security of Networks and Information Systems, prepared in 2019 (North Macedonia Report 2021). North Macedonia became a member of the Joint Procurement Agreement on medical counter-measures as an observer in the EU Health Security Committee, which provides access to the EU Early Warning and Response System. Further commitment is needed still in order to align the national rules with the EU legal order (North Macedonia Report 2021).

In Albania, the Ministry of Health and Social Protection is currently implementing and operating an electronic system for collecting and reporting health information of medical records based on European Core Health Indicators. However, in 2020 the system was still not operational (Albania Report 2021). Albania joined the European COVID-19 Surveillance Network managed by the European Center for Disease Prevention and Control (ECDC).

In Kosovo, its public health authorities focused mainly on the management of the pandemic. In 2020 Kosovo's public health information system was still not functional (Kosovo Report 2021). Around one fifth of the population has very limited access to healthcare in Kosovo.

Bosnia and Hercegovina's participation in technical activities of the European Center for Disease Control and Prevention remained limited. Bosnia and Herzegovina needed to strengthen coordination between the entities and the state level in the field of communicable disease surveillance and response. The EU provided EUR 7.76 million in assistance to support public health (Bosnia and Herzegovina Report 2021).

5 Security and Privacy

Healthcare authorities collect data about their patients and store them on network servers to make them accessible all the time (Seh et al. 2020). As the health information environment becomes more complex and medical technology develops further, the vulnerability to error increases (Hesse and Shneiderman 2007). Online access to data implies potential harm related to confidentiality, security, and privacy of health records (Jusob et al. 2022) as institutional interest focused mainly on the public and regulatory frameworks in this respect (Sahama et al. 2013). The privacy of health records on smartphones could be threatened by mobile phone applications, especially if these applications were not only about tracing people with COVID-19, but for other purposes, as well (Council of Europe 2020). In regard to COVID-19 certificates and their delivery via internet, there is a potential possibility that end-users would be harmed because of privacy and security questions.

Data for 2019, just before the COVID-19 outbreak at the end of the year, show that the percentage of individuals with security concerns that limited or prevented

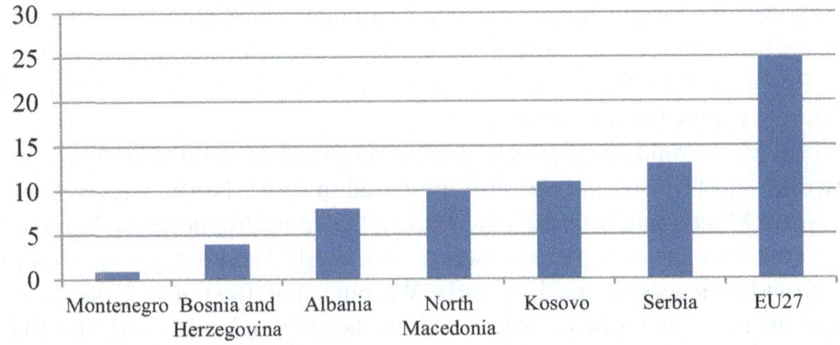

Fig. 4 Percentage (%) of individuals with online security concerns in 2019. *Source* Author's compilation of data from the Eurostat (2022)

providing of personal information to social or professional networking services was considerably lower in the Western Balkans compared to the average of the EU (Fig. 4).

In the beginning of 2020, governments in the Western Balkans, similarly as other governments in Europe, tried to trace the spread of the virus with the use of traffic and location data from mobile phones and apps and individual data from mobile network operators. However, there was a growing concern on governments' breaching people's digital rights and freedoms, particularly concerning personal data privacy and security, misinformation, and attacks on journalists in the Western Balkans (Krivokapic et al. 2020). The culture of privacy at the public level in the Western Balkans is low as some governments-in their attack on political opposition-have leaked and might leak health records of any critic or accuser online (Zivanovic 2019). In addition to lax attitude of the state authorities, general population does not seem much concerned about privacy, either.

In general, data privacy and security are especially critical in the healthcare systems. With respect to data protection in the EU, the General Data Protection Regulation (GDPR) from 2016 is a harmonized EU's legal framework and in the Western Balkans, there has been some modeling of the national legislation in line with the GDPR (Krivokapic et al. 2020).

In 2020, almost 10% more individuals used a smartphone in the Western Balkans compared to 2018 (Table 4). However, the share of individuals who lost information, pictures, documents, or other kinds of data on their smartphones as a result of a virus or other hostile type of programs in 2020 was generally higher in the Western Balkans than in the EU (Table 4). The highest share of those was in Kosovo and North Macedonia (9%), while the average of the EU stood at 4%. On average, individuals in the EU were more inclined to restrict or refuse access to personal data when using, installing, or downloading an application from the internet on their smartphone (Table 4).

Compared to the average of the EU, people in the Western Balkans have lower levels of higher digital skills which might be an obstacle for them to know how and why they should restrict or refuse access to data on their smartphones. However,

Table 4 Privacy and security on smartphone in 2020 compared to 2018

	Percentage (%) of individuals use a smartphone for private purposes		Percentage (%) of individuals who already lost information, pictures, documents, or other kind of data on the smartphone as a result of a virus or other hostile type of programs		Percentage (%) of individuals who at least once restricted or refused access to personal data, when using or installing an app on the smartphone	
	2018	2020	2018	2020	2018	2020
EU27	73	81	4	4	43	52
Montenegro	67	70	5	8	25	39
North Macedonia	61	71	9	10	28	34
Albania	54	n/a	7	n/a	19	n/a
Serbia	58	69	5	4	19	17
Bosnia and Herzegovina	55	68	5	5	20	34
Kosovo*	80	87	11	9	17	37

Source Author's compilation of data from the Eurostat (2022)

the awareness of privacy and safety on internet is rising. By way of example, in 2018, Serbia (19%) and Kosovo (17%) recorded the lowest percentage of those who restricted or refused access to personal data at least once when downloading an application on their smartphone in 2018. Data for 2020 compared to 2018 show a higher number of individuals who restricted or refused access to personal data at least once when using or installing an application on the smartphone (Table 4).

It is a fact that data has become more mobile, digitized, and distributed in the last decade (European Commission, 2022a, b). The use of smart phones and other smart devices has facilitated privacy breaches due to security failures, software vulnerabilities, and human error (Seh et al. 2020). From an end-user point of view, privacy and security options on people's smartphones are based on access control possibilities such as passwords and PIN numbers (FTC 2022). However, to help limit access to health information, people should encrypt their stored information on their computers, tablets, or smartphones so that health information cannot be read or understood by others except for those using a system that can decrypt that data with a "key" (Microsoft 2023).

In 2020, 44% of internet users restricted or refused access to their geographical location in the EU (Fig. 5). That share was below 40% in the Western Balkans, with the lowest share (20%) in North Macedonia. Almost half (49%) of internet users in the EU refused to allow the use of personal data for advertising. The average in the Western Balkans (Fig. 6) was lower, with the highest share in Montenegro (30%) in this respect. The situation is similar in regard to the percentage of individuals who limited access to their profile or content on social networking sites or shared

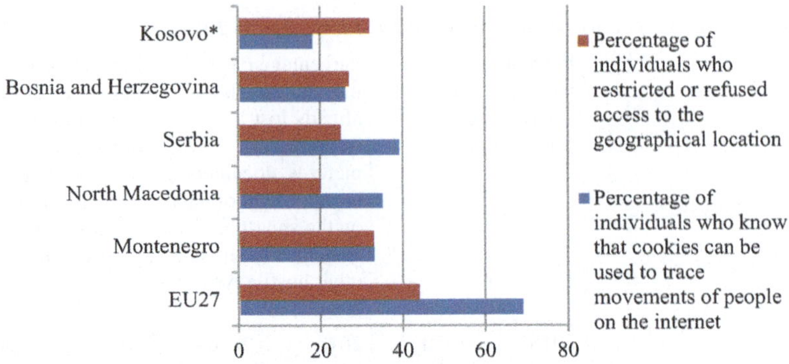

Fig. 5 Access to personal data on the internet in 2020: geographical location, knowledge about cookies.[5] *Source* Author's compilation of data from the Eurostat (2021)

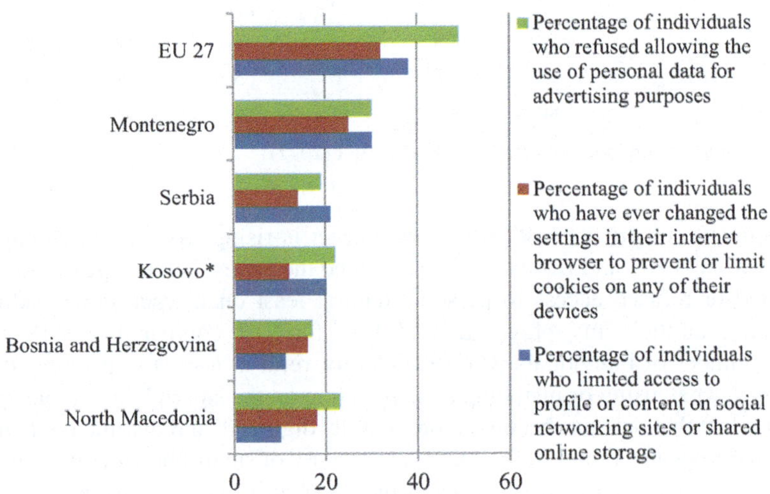

Fig. 6 Access to personal data on the internet for advertising purposes, limiting access to profile or content on social networks in 2020. *Source* Author's compilation of data from the Eurostat (2022)

online storage (EU 38%, Montenegro 30%). The percentage of individuals who have changed the settings in their internet browser to prevent or limit cookies on any of their devices was 32% in the EU and 25% in Montenegro. When a person visits a website, that website immediately displays a message offering the visitor to accept or refuse cookies. *Cookie* is a small text file that a website (which a person is visiting) stores on this person's computer or mobile device when they visit the website (European Commission 2022a). Cookies can be used to establish anonymized statistics about the person's browsing experience and may keep track of a person's visit of the website.

[5] Data for Albania was not available.

The fact that people in the Western Balkans are generally less careful or concerned about privacy and security on the internet (Figs. 5 and 6) appears to be consistent with the findings of Budak et al (2014) who stated that people in Bosnia and Herzegovina, Serbia, North Macedonia, and Croatia seemed used to providing personal information without questioning, which could be a "cultural residual of the past socialist, i.e., collective mindset "(p. 8).

In 2020, slightly less than three quarters (69%) of the individuals in the EU who used the internet for private purposes, were aware that cookies could be used to trace movements of people on the internet. In the Western Balkans that share was much lower. It reached 33% in Montenegro, 35% in North Macedonia, 39% in Serbia, 27% in Bosnia and Herzegovina, and only 18% in Kosovo (Fig. 5).

When people access any online service or website using social networks' login information (e.g. Facebook, Instagram, Twitter) or download applications that ask phone owners' permissions for accessing media, files, etc. on their smartphones, this can be a security risk that can reveal all personal data stored on their smartphones, including health records. By way of example, if a person wants to access some specific information or download an application from any website on the internet, that person might be asked by that website to open an account on that website. Alternatively, instead of registering and opening an account there, that website may offer an option to "log in with Facebook". If a person, instead of creating an account on this website, decides to log in with his/her Facebook login information, the company behind that website or application will get some information about this person from this Facebook login. Information available on this website includes all public information on a person's Facebook profile, full name, profile picture, gender, networks, and access to his/her list of friends.

Using online applications and social networks, such as Facebook, can cause harm similar to the Cambridge Analytica scandal. In 2018 it was revealed that millions of Facebook users' personal information was used by a third-party for various purposes during the 2016 US Presidential elections (BBC 2021). Although Facebook apologized and allowed users to check "banned apps", some emphasized that Facebook's users' data was compromised because "Facebook didn't care" (BBC 2021).

Privacy and security concerns can be exacerbated when national health authorities officially use social media and networks such as Facebook. In the Western Balkans for instance, the health facility in Montenegro's capital, Podgorica, has its Facebook page (Dom zdravlja Podgorica 2022) where a Facebook member can communicate with this health facility by sending them messages via Messenger. To provide health-related information via social networks (e.g. Messenger on Facebook), is akin to giving others access to your health records, and not only that; other personal data might be revealed to third-parties as well.

Only 7% of individuals in the EU, who limit access to personal data on internet, use software that limits tracking their activities on internet. That share is even lower in the Western Balkans (Fig. 7). The lowest share in this respect was recorded in Serbia and Bosnia and Herzegovina where it stood at 6% in 2020 (Fig. 7). While 40% of individuals in the EU read privacy policy statements before providing personal data, that share is lower in the Western Balkans. The exception is Kosovo, where 42%

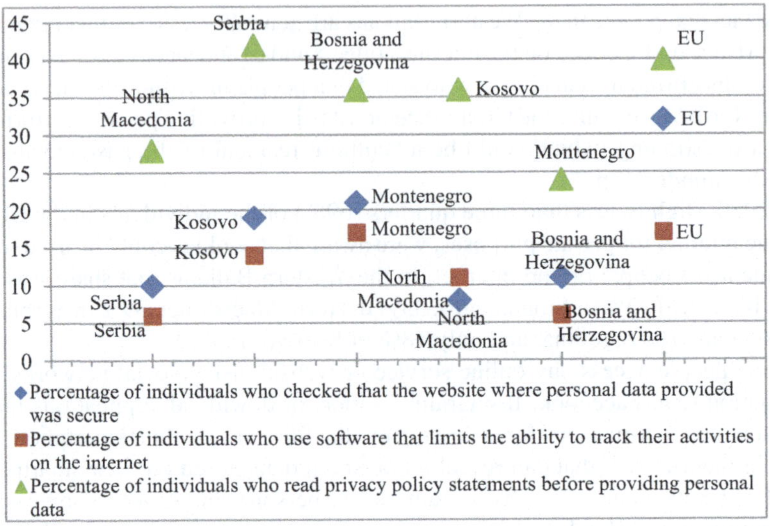

Fig. 7 Access to personal data on the internet: other issues in 2020. *Source* Author's compilation of data from the Eurostat (2022)

of individuals who limited access to personal data on internet, read privacy policy statements before providing personal data (Fig. 7). In 2020, 32% of individuals in the EU who checked that the website where they provided their personal data was secure, while that share in the Western Balkans was lower, with the lowest in North Macedonia at 11% (Fig. 7).

The increasing power of various online social networks, social media, and online platforms has led to the systemic erosion of the right to privacy in the digital space (Amnesty International, 2021). As large technology companies become more powerful, there are even more concerns about the use of data-driven technologies. In the Western Balkans, there is a high share of individuals who have not used any electronic identification procedure for accessing online services (Fig. 8). If people are unaware of how social networks work and that their personal data can be accessed by a third party, they might unintentionally expose health records when they login into any website, including social networks, which individuals in the Western Balkans seem to be less aware of, compared to the average of the EU (Fig. 8).

There is a higher share of those individuals who do not know that it is possible to restrict or refuse access to personal data in the Western Balkans compared to the average of the EU27 (Table 5).

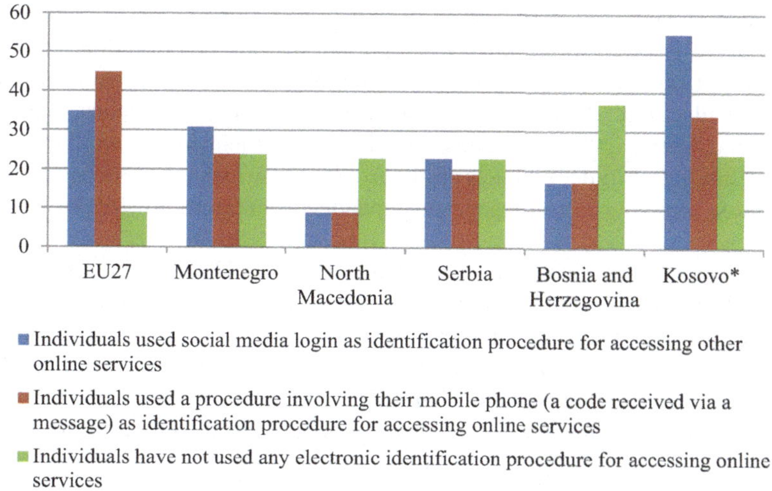

Fig. 8 Percentage (%) of individuals using identification procedures in 2020. *Source* Author's compilation of data from the Eurostat (2021)

Table 5 Security on smartphones in 2020 compared to 2018

	Individuals use a smartphone for private purposes		Smartphone has some security system, installed automatically or provided with the operating system		Smartphone has some security system, installed by somebody or subscribed to it	
	2018	2020	2018	2020	2018	2020
EU27	73	81	32	39	12	11
Montenegro	67	70	33	53	8	13
North Macedonia	61	71	35	42	11	5
Albania	54	n/a	28	n/a	11	n/a
Serbia	58	69	23	29	12	11
Bosnia and Herzegovina	55	68	20	22	5	8
Kosovo*	80	87	32	42	9	12

Source Author's compilation of data from the Eurostat (2021)

6 Elderly and Digital Technology

The most vulnerable end-users of digital transformation and health records who may need the most help, are the elderly. They face many challenges in accessing relevant services due to lower levels of literacy, reduced mobility, and higher levels of disabilities (Gorman 2020). They are at risk of being excluded from access to digital technologies and digital services. Since age comes with a wide range of health-related issues (motor skills, eyesight and hearing deterioration, etc.), older people might not have the knowledge nor the ability to use expensive computers or portable electronic devices, such as smartphones, laptops, notepads, and similar (Seifert and Cotten 2021). It is also less likely for them to be familiar with the newer technology as older people's ability to adopt new technology depends on their willingness, computer self-efficacy, and dependence on prior knowledge (Georgieva 2019).

Protecting patients' data is only one issue in the digital health systems of Western Balkans. The other one is the relationship between the elderly and digital transformation in health services. Compared to the average of all age groups, people who are over 55 in the Western Balkans are less likely to have a smartphone (Table 6) and there is also a considerably smaller share of people in the age group of 55 to 74 who have a smartphone with some sort of security system installed on it (Table 6).

Moreover, it is less likely that the elderly have the knowledge on how to restrict or refuse access to personal data when using or installing an application from a website (Table 7).

There has not been much research about security and privacy with respect to the elderly in the Western Balkans. The research has so far mostly focused on the public/regulatory aspects of privacy, personal data, and COVID-19 (European Data Journalism Network 2022).

In the Western Balkans, for example in Serbia, people had an option to receive COVID-19 certificate online, via regular mail, or in person. If they chose to get the certificate online, they first had to register at the relevant e-government's website.

Table 6 Percentage (%) of people with some security on their phones in 2020

	Individuals use a smartphone for private purposes		Smartphone has some security system, installed automatically or provided with the operating system		Smartphone has some security system, installed by somebody or subscribed to it	
	All individuals	55 to 74 years old	All individuals	55 to 74 years old	All individuals	55 to 74 years old
EU27	81	62	39	28	11	9
Montenegro	70	43	53	28	13	6
North Macedonia	71	44	42	19	5	1
Albania	n/a	n/a	n/a	n/a	n/a	n/a
Serbia	69	41	29	14	11	6
Bosnia and Herzegovina	68	42	22	10	8	4
Kosovo*	80	77	42	35	12	10

Source Author's compilation of data from the Eurostat (2022)

Table 7 Privacy and loss of information in 2020

	Percentage (%) of individuals who use a smartphone for private purposes		Percentage (%) of individuals who already lost information, documents, pictures, or other kind of data on their smartphone as a result of a virus or other hostile type of programs		Percentage (%) of individuals who at least once restricted or refused access to personal data, when using or installing an app on the smartphone	
	All individuals	55 to 74 years old	All individuals	55 to 74 years old	All individuals	55 to 74 years old
EU27	81	62	4	2	52	31
Montenegro	70	43	8	4	39	16
North Macedonia	71	44	10	4	34	16
Albania	n/a	n/a	n/a	n/a	n/a	n/a
Serbia	69	41	4	3	17	6
Bosnia and Herzegovina	68	42	5	2	34	16
Kosovo*	80	77	9	6	37	26

Source Author's compilation of data from the Eurostat (2022)

Only then, people could apply for a certificate to be delivered online. It is not very likely that older people have the skills and the means to register at the relevant e-government's website and hence, they may have opted for a paper-printed COVID-19 certificate provided in person.

However, if a person needed this certificate on multiple occasions, for instance, to enter various public places in EU countries when visiting relatives or others (considering a large diaspora from the Western Balkans in the EU) a smartphone was a necessity. COVID certificates were not needed only to enter shops, markets and similar, in some EU member states these certificates were also needed to enter a bank, a pharmacy and to pay bills at various service providers.

The digital EU COVID certificate that was delivered via internet had to be downloaded on a smartphone. A QR code of this certificate was then read from the phone when entering various public places in the EU.

However, it was not only less likely that an older person had a smartphone (Table 6), but it was also less likely that an older person would understand all its functionalities, including how to download the digital certificate by themselves or how to refuse access to personal data, when using or installing an app on the smartphone (Table 7).

7 Conclusion

This research provides an insight into some social information indicators in the Western Balkans that relate to digital technologies in health, particularly, including COVID-19 digital certificates delivered online. The finding of this research is that extreme situations such as the COVID-19 pandemic show that there is a need to build adequate national health systems. If a country does not have a fully digitized system of health records and does not have a fully operational system that enables patients to receive their health records or other information online, patients cannot do much about it. The Western Balkans is still at early stages of digitalization in healthcare.

This research has found that most people in the Western Balkans, although being online more than ever before, don't seem aware of the dangers of exposing their health and other personal data when browsing the internet. Even as they don't use eHealth to the extent an average person in the EU does, people in the Western Balkans can still unintentionally reveal some sensitive personal data. The percentage of individuals who already lost information, documents, pictures, or other kind of data on their smartphone as a result of a virus or other hostile type of programs was generally higher in the Western Balkans compared to the EU average. Further, the percentage of individuals in the Western Balkans who restricted or refused access to personal data at least once when using or installing an app on the smartphone in 2020 was generally lower than the average of the EU.

It could be argued that these findings can partly be explained by the fact that people in the Western Balkans are less digitally savvy and that they do not know how to install various security applications nor are aware of certain safety, security, and privacy issues when they surf on the internet on their phones.

However, the finding of this research is that there are two layers of concern with respect to digital health and privacy and safety of health records online in the Western Balkans. The first one is people, users of health systems, and users of internet and other technology. There has been a rise in the use of portable devices to access internet in the Western Balkans, despite that data for 2020, the first year of the Covid-19 pandemic show, that many are still unaware or are ignorant of the dangers and the possibilities of protecting health-related and other personal data when browsing the internet and downloading applications on their smartphones. The other layer of concern is the public level and governments' policy decisions to provide better digital health services and to provide them in a safe, reliable, and secure way so as to ensure privacy of digital health records of patients. Governments in the Western Balkans still have a lot to do in this respect.

The main limitation of this research is that the data provided by Eurostat's surveys is limited to social information indicators about the access to technology, digital skills, and how people apply digital technology. However, to understand the motivation of people's behavior on the internet with respect to digital health, security, and privacy, additional and specific questions should be asked. Answers to those questions could clarify people's attitudes to digital health and security and privacy online. For example, is it that people in Western Balkans are less careful on the internet because of the level of their digital skills or because they are not aware of the dangers on the internet? Or perhaps they don't care about their privacy, that possibly being the cultural residual of the past socialist, i.e. collective mindset?

Future research could therefore benefit from focusing on behavioral questions with respect to the security and privacy of digital health processes, patients' medical records, and other relevant data delivered online in the Western Balkans.

References

Albania Report (2021). Albania Report 2021. https://neighbourhood-enlargement.ec.europa.eu/albania-report-2021_en. Accessed 28 Nov 2021

AmCham Montenegro (2021) Position paper on digital transformation of healthcare system of Montenegro. https://digital.net.me/storage/aKG9seSQzyckEABZS2RGEF4qqNf1UI2166oyzXDO.pdf. Accessed 2 Dec 2021

Amnesty International (2021) Amnesty international position on the proposals for a digital services act and a digital markets act. https://www.amnesty.eu/news/amnesty-international-position-on-the-proposals-for-a-digital-services-act-and-a-digital-markets-act/. Accessed 8 Jan 2022

Bhavnani SP et al (2016) Mobile technology and the digitization of healthcare. Eur Heart J 37(18):1428–1438

Baudier P, et al (2023) Digital transformation of healthcare during the COVID-19 pandemic: patients' teleconsultation acceptance and trusting beliefs. Technovation 120.https://doi.org/10.1016/j.technovation.2022.102547. Accessed 25 Apr 2023

BBC (2021) Facebook sued for 'losing control' of users' data. https://www.bbc.com/news/technology-55998588. Accessed 10 Feb 2022

Bosnia and Herzegovina Report (2021) Bosnia and Herzegovina Report 2021. https://neighbourhood-enlargement.ec.europa.eu/bosnia-and-herzegovina-report-2021_en Accessed 28 Nov 2021

Buul AR, et al (2020) eHealth only interventions and blended interventions to support self-management in adolescents with asthma: a systematic review. Clin Ehealth 3:49–62. https://doi.org/10.1016/j.ceh.2020.06.001

Budak J, et al (2014) Privacy concern in western balkan countries: developing a typology of citizens. EIZ working papers EIZ-WP-1402, Ekonomski institut Zagreb, Croatia. EIZ Working Papers EIZ-WP-1402, pp 1–26

Council of Europe (2020) Digital solutions to fight COVID-19. 2020 data protection report. October 2020. https://www.coe.int/en/web/data-protection/-/digital-solutions-to-fight-covid-19-council-of-europe-report-on-data-protection-2020. Accessed 11 Jan 2022

Dom zdravlja Podgorica (2022) Facebook page. https://www.facebook.com/pages/Dom%20Zdravlja%20Podgorica/207541826026643/. Accessed 25 Mar 2022

Elbert NJ et al (2014) Effectiveness and cost-effectiveness of ehealth interventions in somatic diseases: a systematic review of systematic reviews and meta-analyses. J Med Internet Res 16(4):e110. https://doi.org/10.2196/jmir.2790

European Data Journalism Network (2022) Not just apps: privacy, personal data and COVID-19 in the Western Balkans. https://www.europeandatajournalism.eu/por/Noticias/Noticias-de-dados/Not-just-apps-privacy-personal-data-and-COVID-19-in-the-western-Balkans. Accessed 12 Apr 2022

European Commission (2019a) Assessing the impact of digital transformation of health services. Report of the Expert Panel on effective ways of investing in Health (EXPH). https://health.ec.europa.eu/system/files/2019-11/022_digitaltransformation_en_0.pdf. Accessed 10 Apr 2022

European Commission (2019b) Albania and North Macedonia prepare to transpose the EU legislative framework on digital health. https://digital-strategy.ec.europa.eu/en/news/albania-and-north-macedonia-prepare-transpose-eu-legislative-framework-digital-health. Accessed 16 Mar 2022

European Commission (2021a) EU Digital COVID Certificate: Commission adopts equivalence decisions for Georgia, Moldova, New Zealand and Serbia Available at https://ec.europa.eu/neighbourhood-enlargement/news/eu-digital-covid-certificate-adopts-equivalence-decisions-georgia-moldova-new-zealand-and-2021-11-15_en. Accessed 12 Feb 2022

European Commission (2021b) EU Digital COVID Certificate. https://ec.europa.eu/info/live-work-travel-eu/coronavirus-response/safe-covid-19-vaccines-europeans/eu-digital-covid-certificate_en. Accessed 16 Jan 2022

European Commission Reports (2021) Strategy and Reports. [Online]. https://ec.europa.eu/neighbourhood-enlargement/enlargement-policy/strategy-and-reports_en. Accessed 11 Feb 2022

European Commission (2022). European Health Data Space. https://ec.europa.eu/health/ehealth-digital-health-and-care/european-health-data-space_en. Accessed 10 Jan 2022

European Commission (2022a) Cookies policies. https://ec.europa.eu/info/cookies_en. Accessed 11 Jan 2022

European Observatory on Health Systems and Policies (2021) Innovation. https://eurohealthobservatory.who.int/themes/observatory-programmes/innovation. Accessed 18 Apr 2022

European Observatory on Health Systems and Policies (2021a) Use of digital health tools in Europe: before, during and after COVID-19. Policy Brief. https://eurohealthobservatory.who.int/publications/i/use-of-digital-health-tools-in-europe-before-during-and-after-covid-19. Accessed 27 Mar 2022

Eurostat (2021) Eurostat. Data. Database. https://ec.europa.eu/eurostat/data/database. Accessed 11 Mar 2022

Eysenbach G (2002) What is e-health? J Med Internet Res 3(2). https://doi.org/10.2196/jmir.3.2.e20

FTC (2022). Federal Trade Commission. Consumer advice. How to protect your phone from hackers. https://consumer.ftc.gov/articles/how-protect-your-phone-hackers?fbclid=IwAR2HsOEMk8U8xSEPBltK8cp5CxF5COreeM3tdNthlwgEIyuE0TVo02HAMhE Accessed 3 Jan 2023

Georgieva L (2019) Digital inclusion and the elderly: the case of online banking. https://www.semanticscholar.org/paper/Digital-Inclusion-and-the-Elderly-%3A-The-Case-of-Georgieva/171180884ee08e9cc953690cbfaa58b3f809e9a6. Accessed 21 Dec 2022

Gorman M (2020) Reaching older people in a crisis: learning from experience? The Oxford Institute of Population Ageing. Blog. https://www.ageing.ox.ac.uk/blog/reaching-older-people-in-a-crisis

Harst L, et al (2019) Theories Predicting end-user acceptance of telemedicine use: systematic review. J Med Internet Res 21(5). https://doi.org/10.2196/13117

Heinsch M, et al (2021) Theories informing ehealth implementation: systematic review and typology classification. J Med Internet Res 23(5). https://doi.org/10.2196/18500

Hesse BW, Shneiderman B (2007) eHealth research from the user's perspective. Am J Prev Med. 32(5Suppl):S97–S103. https://doi.org/10.1016/j.amepre.2007.01.019

Javaid M and Khan I H (2021) Internet of Things (IoT) enabled healthcare helps to take the challenges of COVID-19 Pandemic. National Library of Medicine. https://pubmed.ncbi.nlm.nih.gov/33665069

Jusob FR et al (2022) A new privacy framework for the management of chronic diseases via mHealth in a post-Covid-19 world. J Public Health (Berl.) 30:37–47. https://doi.org/10.1007/s10389-021-01608-9

Keynes JM (1937) The general theory of employment. Q J Econ 51(2):209–223

Krivokapic, et al (2020) State of pandemonium: digital rights in the Western Balkans and COVID-19. Global Campus Open Knowledge Repository. https://repository.gchumanrights.org/handle/20.500.11825/1622. Accessed 11 Dec 2021

Microsoft (2023) Encrypting your Android device. https://learn.microsoft.com/en-us/mem/intune/user-help/encrypt-your-device-android Accessed 15 Mar 2023
Mulder T (2019) Health apps, their privacy policies and GDPR. Eur J Law Technol 10(1):1–20
NALED (2021) Coordination Body for the digitalization of the healthcare system has been formed. https://naled.rs/en/vest-formirano-koordinaciono-telo-za-digitalizaciju-zdravstvenog-sistema-4699. Accessed 9 Jan 2022
North Macedonia Report (2021) The National ICT Strategy 2021–2025 will put the Republic of North Macedonia at the top in the field of digitalization in the region. The digital future of the country is indisputable. https://www.mioa.gov.mk/?q=en/node/3490. Accessed 7 Feb 2022
Ossebaard HC, Van Gemert-Pijnen L (2016) EHealth and quality in health care: implementation time. Int J Qual Health Care 28(3):415–419. https://doi.org/10.1093/intqhc/mzw032
Petracca F et al (2020) (2020) Harnessing digital technologies during and after the COVID-19 pandemic: context matters. J Med Internet Res 22(12):1–7
Pila J (2020) Covid-19 and contact tracing: a study in regulation by technology. Eur J Law Technol. 12(2):1–21
Report Kosovo (2021). Kosovo report 2021. https://neighbourhood-enlargement.ec.europa.eu/kosovo-report-2021_en. Accessed 28 Nov 2021
Report Montenegro (2021) Montenegro report 2021 https://ec.europa.eu/neighbourhood-enlargement/montenegro-report-2021_en. Accessed 17 Feb 2022
Report Serbia (2021) Serbia report 2021. https://neighbourhood-enlargement.ec.europa.eu/serbia-report-2021_en. Accessed 28 Nov 2021
Seh et al (2020) Healthcare data breaches: insights and Implications. US National Library of Medicine, National Institutes of Health. https://ncbi.nlm.nih.gov/pmc/articles/PMC7349636. Accessed 3 Mar 2022
Seifert A, Cotten SR (2021) Use of information and communication technologies among older adults: usage differences, health-related impacts, and future needs. https://www.oxfordhandbooks.com/view, https://doi.org/10.1093/oxfordhb/9780197510636.001.0001/oxfordhb-9780197510636-e-12. Accessed 5 Mar 2022
Sahama T, et al (2013) Security and privacy in eHealth: is it possible? Paper presented at the 2013 IEEE 15th international conference on e-Health networking, applications and services (Healthcom 2013). https://doi.org/10.1109/HealthCom.2013.6720676
Shamsabadi A, et al (2021) Internet of things in the management of chronic diseases during the COVID-19 pandemic: a systematic review. Health Sci Rep 5(2). https://doi.org/10.1002/hsr2.557
Svendsen MT et al (2021) Pros and cons of eHealth: a systematic review of the literature and observations in Denmark. SAGE Open Med. https://doi.org/10.1177/20503121211016179
UN Resolution (1999) Resolution 1244 (1999)/adopted by the Security Council at its 4011th meeting, on 10 June 1999. https://digitallibrary.un.org/record/274488. Accessed 9 Nov 2022
UNDP (2020) Digital Transformation in the Public Sector in Bosnia and Herzegovina Project (2020–2024). https://info.undp.org/docs/pdc/Documents/BIH/Digital_transformation_prodoc.docx.pdf. Accessed 6 Oct 2021
World Health Organization (2022) European observatory on health systems and policies, COVID-19 and the use of digital health tools: opportunity amid crisis that could transform health care delivery. Eurohealth 28(1):29–34
WHO (2021) WHO/Europe launches Western Balkans Digital Health Network. https://www.euro.who.int/en/health-topics/Health-systems/digital-health/news/news/2021/10/whoeurope-launches-western-balkans-digital-health-network. Accessed 5 Feb 2022
Zivanovic M (2019) Journalists Chief Victims of Digital Rights Violations in Serbia. BalkanInsight. https://balkaninsight.com//2019/11/14/journalists-chief-victims-of-digital-rights-violations-in-serbia/. Accessed 14 Dec 2021

The manufacturer's authorised representative in the EU is Springer Nature Customer Service Centre GmbH, Europaplatz 3, 69115 Heidelberg, Germany. If you have any concerns regarding our products, please contact ProductSafety@springernature.com

Printed and bound by CPI Group (UK) Ltd, Croydon, CR0 4YY
28/09/2026
02224075-0008